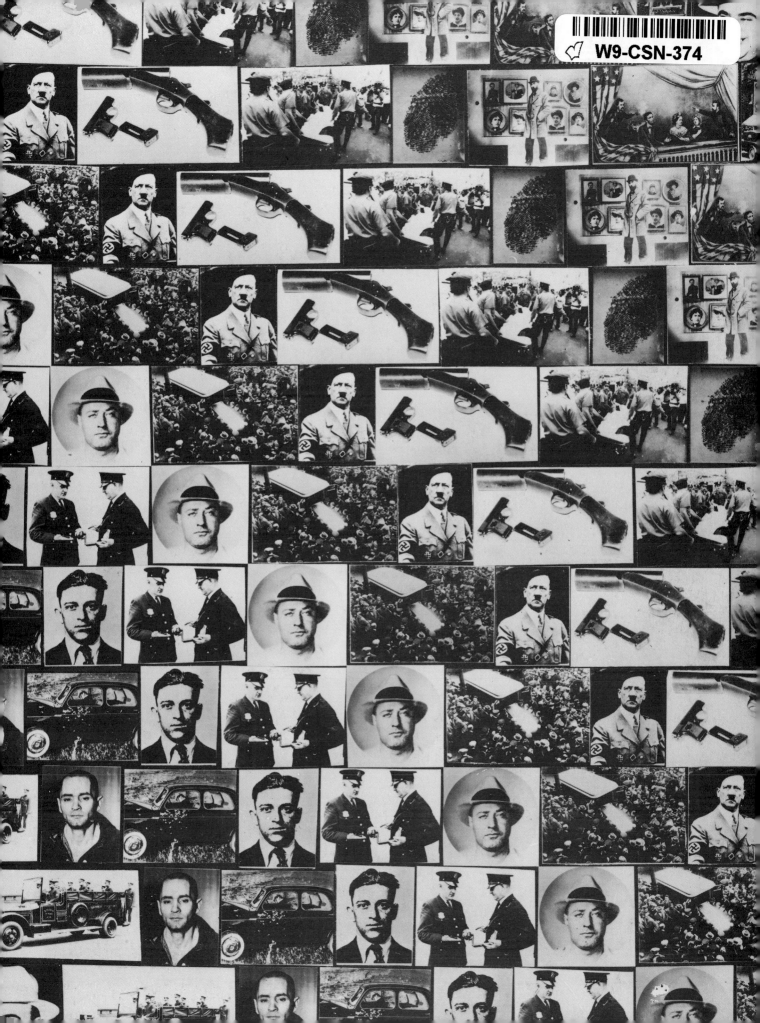

CRIMES AND PUNISHMENT

VOLUME 1

THE SYMPHONETTE PRESS
(A Service of Longines-Wittnauer, Inc.)
Robert G. Bartner   President

PRODUCTION SUPERVISION
Stonehouse Press

PHOEBUS PUBLISHING COMPANY

John Paton	Managing Editor
Angus Hall	Editor
Robin Willcox	Deputy Editor
Don Mason	Production Director

EDITORIAL PRESENTATION
Jackson Morley

ADVISORY EDITORIAL BOARD
H. Montgomery Hyde
Colin Wilson
C. H. Rolph
J. H. H. Gaute
Nigel Morland

© BPC Publishing Limited
And Credit Services Inc. 1973
Filmsetting by Purnell & Sons, Paulton, England
Printed in the United States of America

CONTENTS

For the first time this century here is the story of crime — full, dramatic and uncensored. CRIMES AND PUNISHMENT is a new series of 20 volumes reflecting and investigating the violence with which we live.

Taking a hard and objective look at crime and criminals — their ways and methods and the means by which they are caught and punished — CRIMES AND PUNISHMENT shows how law-breakers live, think, talk, and strike. It also goes behind the scenes with the lawkeepers, the men and women who fight a daily battle against crime in all its many forms.

Each volume of CRIMES AND PUNISHMENT spotlights five different aspects of wrongdoing and aberrant behavior (anything from, say, murder, to forgery, to blackmail, to highjacking, to prostitution), breaking down the offences into their history, motives and methods; ultimately, their detection and punishment. A comprehensive index at the end of the work offers quick reference and cross-reference.

The writers are experts in their various fields, using the full range of their knowledge and talent as they explore the minds of psychopathic killers . . . enter the bars, clubs and hideouts where the 'big jobs' are planned . . . witness the moment and scene of the criminal act . . . tread among the withering court-room crossfire of prosecuting and defending lawyers.

CRIMES AND PUNISHMENT casts a shrewd and penetrating eye upon the sickness of society. It is a contemporary work, created today, and highlighting the problems that, without doubt, will still be with us tomorrow.

THE EDITOR

ARE YOU A DOMINANT PERSON?

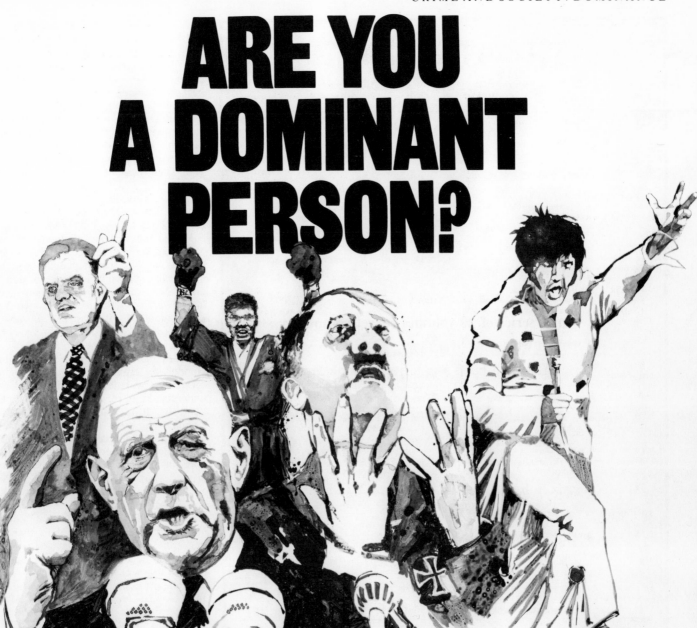

THE LAW OF NATURE demands that human beings, just like any other animal species, have a "pecking order". The way in which one human being may dominate others is less clear-cut than the way in which, say, a wild dog can lead a pack. In a civilized society, it can be argued that dominance (or power) is a dangerous force. It can be said that men were intended to be brothers, not masters and slaves. But it is increasingly being accepted by experts on human and animal behaviour that, however civilized we may be, our way of life is deeply affected by the fact that some of us are much more dominant than others.

The dominant people are *not* a tiny minority. There are lots of them. Your boss may (or may not) be a dominant personality. Your neighbour may be dominant, or your wife, or yourself . . .

Indeed, experts know just how many people in a street or an office or a factory have dominant personalities . . . the answer is quite simply one in every 20, and that is close to being exact.

On page 2 we explain how this figure was arrived at. And we give you the chance to test your own level of dominance.

It is a stimulating idea—and one which has its serious side. For experts have found that dominance has a definite bearing on crime. The new understanding of dominance has brought with it a new understanding of the criminal mind, a New Criminology. This could revolutionize crime fighting and the treatment of criminals.

TEST YOUR DOMINANCE

How dominant are you? These questions, set by
psychologist Dr. Christine Pickard, may tell you something about yourself.

1/Do people gravitate towards you at a party?

(a) Often (b) Sometimes (c) Rarely

2/How much effort do you make to form friendships or business contacts?

(a) A great deal (b) Some effort (c) Very little

3/Do your work and social life turn out the way you want without much effort on your part?

(a) Often (b) Occasionally (c) Never

4/Do people tend to do the things you ask them?

(a) Often (b) Occasionally (c) Rarely

5/Do you expect other members of your family to do what you tell them?

(a) Always (b) Sometimes (c) Never

6/Does your boss frequently act on your suggestions?

(a) Yes (b) Only occasionally (c) Never

7/Do you frequently find yourself facing argument and opposition?

(a) Yes (b) Only occasionally (c) Very rarely

8/Are you easily disliked?

(a) Yes (b) Don't know (c) Definitely not

9/Would you say that you are a lucky person?

(a) Very (b) Sometimes (c) Definitely not

10/Which of the following descriptions fits your attitude to life?

(a) Optimistic (b) Average (c) Pessimistic

11/Would you go to a party or social event on your own?

(a) Any time (b) Depending on circumstances (c) Never

12/Do you think honesty in personal relationships is important?

(a) Very (b) To some extent (c) Hardly at all

13/Do you take the initiative in sexual relationships?

Men: (a) Always (b) Often (c) Occasionally

Women: (a) Often (b) Seldom (c) Never

14/Do you ever allow your views to be changed by your "inferiors" (people who work under you, or your children)?

(a) Often (b) Occasionally (c) Never

15/Do you feel that you must keep your wife/husband in check?

(a) Often (b) Occasionally (c) Never

16/Whom do you secretly envy?

(a) Lots of people (b) Some people (c) Hardly anyone

17/Do you think discipline is important in the family and at work?

(a) Often (b) Occasionally (c) Never

18/Do you think people should automatically respect their elders and "superiors"?

(a) No (b) Only sometimes (c) Yes

19/Do you have any phobias that you know of?

(a) Several (b) A few (c) None

20/Are you in awe of anyone at work?

(a) Quite a few people (b) Only two or three people (c) No one

21/Do you wonder about what might have been?

(a) Often (b) Occasionally (c) Never

22/Do you worry?

(a) Often (b) Occasionally (c) Never

23/Are you prepared to ride roughshod over people to get your own way?

(a) Whenever necessary (b) Sometimes (c) Never

24/Do you think you are an obstinate person?

(a) Very (b) Sometimes (c) Not at all

25/Do you think you are aggressive?

(a) Very (b) Sometimes (c) Not at all

26/Do you lose your temper?

(a) Often (b) Occasionally (c) Never

27/Are you happy to be on your own?

(a) Often (b) Occasionally (c) Never

28/Do you care whether people think highly of you?

(a) Very much (b) To some extent (c) Not at all

29/You and your husband/wife/boyfriend/girlfriend are going out. Do you decide where?

(a) Always (b) Sometimes (c) Never

Check your rating as follows: On questions **1, 2, 3, 4, 6, 8, 10, 11, 13, 23, 24, 25, 26, 27, 29,** score three points for (a), two for (b) and one for (c); on questions **7, 16, 17, 19, 20, 21, 22, 28,** score three points for (c), two for (b), and one for (a); on questions **5, 9, 12, 14, 15, 18,** score two points for (b) and one point for (a) or (c).

How did you rate? This quiz can only give a rule-of-thumb assessment, but if you scored over 70, you are likely to be very dominant indeed; 70-65 indicates a clearly dominant character; 65-45 a moderate personality; below 45, a definitely dominated person.

THE SCENE is your local barroom any night after work. You and some of the boys have got together for a few quick ones before going home. There are four or five of you sitting at a table sipping beer, exchanging anecdotes, telling jokes. Suddenly someone you all know—let's call him Dennis—walks in from the street and strides up to the counter. He orders his drink and stands eyeing your party as if he were thinking of making a bid for you. Then, without being told to or being able to stop yourselves, you all find yourselves on your feet. You hurry over to Dennis, ask him how he's keeping, what sort of a day he's had, what his drink is.

He did not come and sit down with you. You stood up and went collectively to join him. What has just happened, whether you realize it or not, is a case of dominance. Dennis the Dominator has asserted his power, his influence upon you. You don't know why it happened, or how it happened—it just did. That is what dominance is all about.

The human animal has reacted as though compelled, brainwashed, or, in some mysterious way, hypnotized. In order to understand and recognize this social phenomenon, it is first of all necessary to examine the way in which dominance operates among birds and animals. Everyone who has ever kept chickens has noticed the existence of the "pecking order." It is as if each chicken carried a number around its neck. Number ten is allowed to peck number eleven—or any higher number—but has to submit quietly if number nine chooses to deliver an admonishing peck. And the "pecking order" appears to be a law of nature that applies to most tribes of wild animals.

A television film made by the naturalist Jane Goodall on the wild dogs of Africa showed that the leader need not necessarily be a male. The pack was led by a female who exercised complete authority over dogs of both sexes.

Will to succeed

But what is perhaps the most important "discovery" about dominance was not made by any single naturalist; it has simply emerged quietly until it is now generally recognized. It is this: that among *all* animal groups, the number of highly dominant ones seems to be the same—an average of 5 per cent.

The explorer Sir Henry Stanley knew about it at the turn of the century. For when Bernard Shaw asked him how many men could lead his party, if he himself became ill, Stanley replied promptly: "One in twenty." When Shaw asked if this was exact or approximate, Stanley replied: "Exact." He was referring to the will to power, to dominate, to succeed—which tallied with Shaw's own frequently expressed theory of the Life Force; the

A dominant personality can make you a success in your job, in business or politics, in showbiz or sport, in the forces or the church . . . or, for that matter, in crime.

Boxer Ali

General Westmoreland

Preacher Graham

Beatle Lennon

Martin Luther King

Millionaire Ari

Elvis Presley

Mafioso Vito

Leonard Bernstein

Gangster Capone

THE DOMINANT 5 per cent of the population includes a wide range of people. Some dominant men may be bosses in their work, or chairmen of associations, or they may assert themselves at their favourite bar. Women may dominate their husbands, or make careers for themselves. Dominance features strongly among people who reach the top in any activity. Consider the characters above. All they have in common is their dominance. (From top left): Muhammad Ali, General Westmoreland, Billy Graham, John Lennon, Martin Luther King, Aristotle Onassis, Elvis Presley, Vito Genovese, Leonard Bernstein, Al Capone.

inner drive which leads us (or the more dominant among us) to success in our jobs and professions.

It was Robert Ardrey, the American author of *African Genesis,* who first gave publicity to the "one in twenty" theory. Ardrey's research showed him that one of the most closely guarded secrets of the Korean War was that no escapes were made by American prisoners. This was because their Chinese captors had discovered an infallible method of preventing breakouts. They observed the prisoners carefully for a while, then removed the "dominant" ones—the 5 per cent who were leader figures—and put them in a separate compound under heavy guard. Once the leaders were removed, the other prisoners became far easier to handle—in fact, they could be left with almost no guard at all. The Chinese observed that the number of dominant prisoners was always exactly one in twenty.

The Nazis recognized the significance of this when, during World War II, they placed all the most incorrigible escapers together in "escape-proof" prisons like Colditz. More recently, in Britain, the 1966 commission into prison reform headed by Lord Louis Mountbatten recommended that the more dangerous convicts were not split up among a large number of prisons—but were kept together.

Frustration factor

So far, however, no zoologist has conducted careful research to establish why the dominant minority appears to be 5 per cent. A study should be made of leading surgeons, ministers, politicians, sportsmen, and pop stars to ascertain whether or not they form 5 per cent of their profession, or, indeed, separate 5 per cents of the population. Obviously it is not only criminals who are dominant, and Ardrey defines dominance as occurring when "two or more animals (or humans) pursue the same activity." The view is also held that crooks only become crooks because their will power is frustrated or denied in some way—thus rechannelling their efforts to succeed into antisocial areas. One of the few countries where official figures are available is Russia, where the Communist Party of the Soviet Union contains approximately 5 per cent of all the people—14½ million members out of a population of 242 million. *continued*

An overcrowded environment can turn a dominant character to crime. It was "the only way to get somewhere" for London's gangland czars the Kray twins, pictured at brother Reggie's wedding

In the U.S. scientific probes have been made into the whole question of dominance, and the researches of John B. Calhoun—at the National Institute of Mental Health at Bethseda, Maryland—threw up one of the most disturbing observations on the subject of power over others. Calhoun wanted to observe the behaviour of rats under conditions of overcrowding.

A large number of rats were placed in three interconnecting cages. The "king rat" took over the central cage for himself and his harem; the other rats were forced into the other two cages, so they were now grossly overcrowded. *And the dominant 5 per cent quickly became a criminal 5 per cent.* These "criminal rats" did things that are never seen among rats in nature. Rats have an elaborate and self-protecting courting ritual; but these rodents wandered around in gangs, raping any spare females they chanced upon. They also became cannibals, eating the baby rats.

Here, then, it seems, we have an immediate explanation of the high crime rate in the slum areas of our great cities. Overcrowding produces a kind of violent opportunism among the dominant 5 per cent. One of the Kray twins—the brothers who, in the 1960's, ruled over the crime kingdom of London's East End—said that in their environment crime was the only way to "get somewhere".

Pointless brutality

The state of mind produced by overcrowding leads to an attitude of desperation, which, in turn, leads the weaker members of the society to become even weaker and so disappear or go under (female rats, for example, tend to abort), while the dominant ones became more violent, grabbing at whatever food or sex they wanted. Under these conditions all sense of leisure vanishes. Crimes become brutal, and pointless. The dominant children may also become criminals.

An item in the world press for November 1972 stated briefly that two boys, aged 11 and 12, had been arrested in New York for raping a seven-year-old girl and then throwing her to her death from the roof of the tenement in which they lived. It was the overcrowded-rat syndrome seen in human terms.

From the point of view of the emerging "new criminology" it makes no difference whether the dominant minority is 5 per cent or 4 per cent or 6 per cent. All that is important is to recognize that, in any society, there is a small group whose dominance is definitely higher than that of the others. And that, under conditions of stress, this dominance may express itself in crime.

A graphic example of this occurred on a warm June evening in 1956, when the chief forester of Büderich, a village near Düsseldorf, was out patrolling some woods in which a number of courting couples had recently been attacked and murdered. Suddenly he came across a man crouching in the bushes, holding a revolver. In a clearing a few yards away, two lovers were kissing in a parked car. The forester, who was armed, succeeded in arresting the Peeping Tom and then took him to Büderich Police Station.

There the prisoner identified himself as Werner Boost, a 28-year-old mechanic from Düsseldorf. It was while Criminal Commissioner Eynck was interviewing Boost that his secretary rang to say that a man named Franz Lorbach wanted to see him. Lorbach was a small, pale man with a weak chin. And what he wanted to report was that Werner Boost was a mass murderer. Eynck quotes him as saying: "He's a monster, an ogre. I'm in his power—hypnotized by him. He forces me to do things I don't want to . . ."

He told Eynck that for more than three years, Boost had been preying on courting couples in the woods. At first, he only robbed them, while Lorbach looked on. Then he began forcing the couples to take drugs that would stupefy them, and he and Lorbach would rape the women. One car they approached in January 1953, contained two men—although Boost did not realize this until he had wrenched open the driver's door, and shot the driver, a Dr. Servé, through the head. He ordered Lorbach to kill the other man, but Lorbach couldn't do it; he whispered to the man to lie down and sham dead, and then struck him with the butt of his gun.

In November 1955 and February 1966, there were two more murders of courting couples in the Düsseldorf area. Friedhelm Behre and Thea Kurmann were battered unconscious; the girl was raped; then the car was pushed into a disused quarry filled with water, where they drowned. Peter Falkenberg and Hildegard Klassing were killed more elaborately; he was shot, and she was given an injection of cyanide; then their car was driven into a haystack and burned.

Boost denied everything; but ballistic evidence proved that he was the killer of Dr. Servé, and he was sentenced to life imprisonment. If Lorbach's account of Boost's crimes is even half true, then Werner Boost is Germany's most spectacular criminal since Peter Kürten, the Düsseldorf sadist and mass murderer who was executed in 1931.

Strange relationship

In retrospect, this relationship with Lorbach is the strangest aspect of the case. Boost was a loner—a man, according to Lorbach, possessed by feelings of malevolence towards the human race. "To him, killing a human being is no different to slaughtering an animal." He didn't need an accomplice, and even if he did, Lorbach was the worst choice he could have made. Lorbach was a coward and an incompetent; once, when he'd failed to kill a female cashier on Boost's orders, he paid Boost about 600 marks "as compensation".

Eynck describes Lorbach as having a face like a rabbit. Boost bound Lorbach to him by giving him drugs, which may help to explain Lorbach's unwilling slavery. But it does not explain why Boost wanted such a companion. The evidence seems to indicate that, in some odd way, Boost needed Lorbach as much as Lorbach needed Boost; more, perhaps, since Lorbach hated his servitude and wanted to escape.

It was this kind of strange and seemingly inexplicable relationship that, in 1936, fascinated a young Jewish psychologist called Abraham Maslow. Maslow spent hours watching the monkeys in the Bronx Zoo, New York. Their behaviour puzzled him. To begin with, they seemed to think of nothing but sex—"the screw-

Britain's gangster Kray twins were hardly the world's only infamous partners in crime. There were many, many others, often even more menacing. The deadly partnerships of the dominator and the dominated. People who were quite harmless until they met . . . but their meetings were fatal. Alone, they hurt no one . . . together, they meant murder . . .

Not just two people, but a whole murderous band committed the Sharon Tate murders. They called themselves "The family". They were dominated by Charles Manson: "Man's Son". They treated him as their Messiah.

The jeering, nagging, self-styled "Superman" Richard Loeb (above, left) dominated his less prepossessing fellow student Nathan Leopold. Their friendship cost the life of Bobbie Franks.

Lonely moment for the "Lonely Hearts Killers". Fat, oversexed Martha Beck dominated Raymond Fernandez, a con man. He swindled love-hungry widows. She decided his victims should die.

ing went on all the time" said Maslow. But that was more-or-less explainable to a Freudian. After all, Freud had asserted that sex is the basic impulse in all animals. What baffled Maslow in this simian Sodom and Gomorrah was that male apes mounted other males, females mounted other females, and on occasion, females even mounted males. Were they all "wantons"? And then, one day, the answer struck him. It was always the highly dominant apes that mounted the less dominant ones, and it made no difference whether they were male or female. He was witnessing the ape equivalent of "pecking order".

This made Maslow interested in the whole phenomenon of dominance. Maybe Freud was wrong about the importance of sex. The logical thing, Maslow decided, was to study dominance in women — the naturally undominant sex. Between 1937 and the early 40's, he made careful case studies of nearly 200 women. The results, when he published them, were so startling that psychologists did not know what to make of them.

Sexual experiments

What was so remarkable was that the women seemed to fall quite clearly into *three* groups, which Maslow labelled High Dominance. Medium Dominance, and Low Dominance. High dominance women tended to be highly sexed. Most of them masturbated without feeling guilt; they enjoyed sexual experimentation; they were promiscuous. Many had had lesbian experience. In order to achieve full sexual satisfaction, these women needed a highly dominant male. One highly dominant woman was a nymphomaniac who could have an orgasm just by looking at a man; yet with one male, she had not been able to achieve a climax because "I just couldn't respect him."

Medium dominance women tended to be gentle souls, altogether less experimental. They wanted to marry "Mr. Right", and they looked for a kind, thoughtful man who would be a good home-builder. In courtship, they liked soft music and soft lights and romance; highly dominant males frightened them, and struck them as brutal.

Low dominance women did not really like sex at all; they thought it was dirty, to be indulged in only for the purpose of producing children. They considered the male sex organ to be crude and ugly. (High dominance women found it beautiful.) They wanted the kind of man who would admire them from a distance.

One interesting point to emerge was that *all* women preferred a man of slightly higher dominance than themselves — not *too* domineering or he frightened them. In keeping with this, high dominance males tended to find medium dominant females sentimental and sloppy; as to low domin-

ance woman, they might take them to bed, given the chance, but they would never experience much personal involvement.

A couple in history who appeared to have shared the right and mutually satisfying "domination relationship" were the Duke and Duchess of Marlborough. The Duke was a professional soldier renowned for his brilliant use of mobility and firepower. He gained a number of famous victories, the most notable being his defeat of the French and Bavarians at the Bavarian village of Blenheim in 1704. On returning home from these triumphs, he found that dominance and sex went together as naturally as powder and shot. And his wife the Duchess contentedly recorded in her diary: "My lord returned from the war today and pleasured me twice in his top boots."

In the sphere of crime, dominance-based partnerships are usually of a lethal and destructive nature. When a high dominance personality, with criminal tendencies, decides to form an alliance with a medium dominance personality — simply for the pleasure of having a slave and disciple — the result can be highly explosive. For crime *is* a way of asserting dominance, and the submissiveness of the slave leads the Master to seek out new ways of expressing his power. The history of crime is full of these relationships between high and medium dominance personalities.

Apart from the two cases dealt with in this book, "Granite Woman" Ruth Snyder and her corset salesman lover, Judd Gray; and Ian Brady and Myra Hindley, the British Moors murderers — there are many examples of a warped relationship between a highly dominant criminal and a mainly undominant accomplice. The partnership of Martha Beck and Raymond Fernandez — a petty confidence swindler who specialized in swindling love-hungry American widows out of their savings — became internationally known as "The Lonely Hearts Killers". Martha, a fat and oversexed nurse, was also a dominant and unpleasant personality — she had been deprived of the custody of her children for ill-treating them — but not a criminal. And it was Martha who decided to join Fernandez in his swindling activities — and who also decided that the victims should die so they couldn't complain.

But the Manson case is certainly the most bizarre example of dominance-murder. When Charles Manson came to San Francisco in 1967, he was 33 years old, and had spent most of his adult life in jail for petty crimes. Later publicity portrayed him as a demonic, Svengali-like figure with smouldering eyes; in fact, he attracted followers by his gentleness, charm, and intelligence. There was something of the Charlie Chaplin tramp about him, the slightly comic man-of-sorrows, permanently bullied by the world.

Like Brady and Loeb, he preached a superman philosophy, derived mainly from a science fiction novel by the American author Robert Heinlein, *Stranger in a Strange Land*. The disciples gathered round, and Manson (whose name, as one of his girls pointed out, meant Man's Son) led them around California like a new messiah, preaching universal love and the innocence of the senses.

As he became accustomed to this new role, Manson began to dream of fame; he wanted to "be somebody", an influence like Bob Dylan or the Maharishi, the Indian mystic who, for a time, influenced and guided the Beatles. But all his efforts to become a singing star and launch long-playing records came to nothing.

He began to preach revolution, the overthrow of society, the destruction of the "pigs" and capitalists. He was the "leader"; his "family" accepted him almost as a kind of god; he had to *do* something to prove himself worthy of their devotion. And so he ordered his followers to commit murder — of the pop musician Gary Hinman, of the film star Sharon Tate and her house guests, of the supermarket owner Leno Labianca and his wife.

Desire for thrills

In the second half of the twentieth century, the pattern of murder seems to be changing. The Leopold and Loeb "superman" murder — in which the two young Chicago students went out and killed 14-year-old Bobbie Franks for "kicks" — was labelled "the crime of the century" by journalists of the 1920's. They found the case unique and without apparent motive. The killers came from wealthy families and had no obvious reasons for frustration.

But, seen in the light of Loeb's dominance over his more intellectual but less prepossessing partner, the crime — and its motive — becomes comparatively easy to comprehend. Curiosity, the desire for "thrills", the need to prove themselves "better" and less "bourgeois" than their friends and relatives drove them to murder. Without Loeb's nagging, jeering and ever-present "superiority" over him — it is doubtful if Leopold would ever have been anything more dangerous than a scholar too bright and insufficiently creative for his own — and other people's — good. The yearning to act in a criminal way would have been there; but he would never have acted alone.

Our problem today, then, is to ensure, as far as possible, that the dominant one and the one who wishes to be dominated are kept apart. Until that is done, partnerships as deadly as those of Leopold and Loeb, Snyder and Gray, Brady and Hindley, will be a menace in our midst — a menace that could strike at any of us, anywhere and at any time.

THE GRANITE WOMAN AND THE PUTTY MAN

It had been a passionate affair. "You are my Queen, my Momsie, my Mommie," he told her. "And you are my Baby, my 'Bud,' my Lover Boy." Ruth Snyder was a powerful woman, and she dominated the weak Judd Grey. They loved together and died together . . . when Ruth Snyder finally got the meanness off her ample chest.

HOUSE OF DEATH:
The three-storey clapboard home in Queens, New York State, where Ruth Snyder tried half a dozen times to arrange fatal "accidents" for her husband. Cheerful Albert Snyder, a "good, solid, silent man", apparently suspected nothing, even when she gave him poisoned whiskey (below)

DOUBLE INDEMNITY: "Mommie" Ruth Snyder used daughter Lorraine to ensure respectability when she had hotel assignations with her lover. She was keen on insurance . . . and took out a policy worth the best part of $100,000 (left) on her husband's precarious life.

She wanted a slave, he wanted a mother ... and they met on a blind date

HE WAS nothing to look at as he entered the little Swedish restaurant, peered myopically around, and went nervously up to a booth at the back of the room. With his cleft chin, round wire-rimmed glasses, slight build, and eyes that were constantly blinking, he resembled nothing more than what he was—a drummer (or commercial traveller) who would never earn more than his current salary of some $5000 a year. But to his blind date in the booth —gum-chewing Mrs. Ruth May Snyder— he represented everything she had looked for in life and marriage and so far failed to find: an adoring, full-time slave.

It was in June 1925—the fifth year of Prohibition in the United States, the year in which Charlie Chaplin appeared in *The Gold Rush,* and the year when Anita Loos published her "gold-diggers" novel, *Gentlemen Prefer Blondes*—that Judd Gray and Ruth Snyder formed a liaison that was to bring about the murder of Mrs. Snyder's husband, Albert, and eventually take her and Gray to the electric chair in Sing Sing prison. But on that hot summer's afternoon in Henry's restaurant in New York City they were too busy sizing each other up, eating *smörgasbord* and drinking bootleg gin to sense that fate—and mutual friends—had done them a tragic disservice in bringing them together.

Ignoring the couple with them in the booth, they took turns to relate the sad and hopeless stories of their marriages; the fact that neither of them had the spouse that he or she had yearned for; the atmosphere of bitterness and tension that pervades a home with no love, respect or understanding in it. It was Ruth —her thick blonde hair set-off by a grey fox fur draped over her shoulders, her wrists clanking with the cheap copper trinkets she habitually wore, her firm thrusting jaw aimed at Judd like a pistol —who, first of all, as she put it, "got the meanness" off her ample chest. What she had to say was not novel, but it made Gray—whose job was selling ladies' corsets—lean sympathetically forward.

According to herself, Ruth Snyder— then aged 30 and of Swedish-Norwegian stock—had been the victim of a man, Albert Snyder, who ten years earlier had taken advantage of her youth, innocence and naïvety and manoeuvred her into a marriage she did not really want. "He was so mean, that guy," she told Judd, taking his hand in hers beneath the table.

"He took me out dining and dancing, then got real angry when I wouldn't come across and get into the sack with him. I was a self-respecting girl then and so he changed his line. He bought me a box of chocolates with a diamond solitaire in them. Picture that! I was all of 19 then— 13 years younger than him. He had this good job as art editor of *Motor Boating*— that's a Hearst magazine, you know—and the day we got married I was too weak and faint to go to bed with him. He had to wait till I was better before he got his way. But to him I was never any better than the ex-switchboard operator who worked in the typing pool."

A quiet, honest man

As he listened to this lament—which could have come straight from one of the silent picture melodramas of the time— Judd Gray felt nothing wrong, nothing false about her words. Even at 19 Ruth must have been a strapping, full-figured girl, and the thought of anyone pushing her around—let alone pushing her into marriage—was more than somewhat absurd. Albert Snyder—curly-haired, cheerful, and wind- and suntanned from long solitary hours of boating and fishing—was just not the sort of man to bully anyone, and certainly not an inexperienced girl who claimed to be religious, God-fearing, and a virgin. Later, after Albert's death, his editor and publisher, C. F. Chapman, was to say of him: "He was a man's man . . . a quiet, honest, upright man, ready to play his part in the drama of life without seeking the spotlight or trying to fill the leading role. Our world is made up of good, solid, silent men like this."

Gray, however, knew and cared nothing for this as the lunch-hour wore on and three and then four o'clock passed. In comparison with Ruth's marriage—a relationship that alternated between blazing rows and frozen silences—his own domestic background was of peace, tranquility and eternal boredom. His wife, Isabel, was so seldom seen or heard by anyone that she had taken on the aspect of an "invisible woman". Few of Gray's colleagues at the Bien Jolie Corset Company had ever met or spoken to her, and some of them did not even know that the 32-year-old salesman had a wife at all. In his autobiography written in the Death House, Gray said frankly:

"Isabel, I suppose, one would call a home girl; she had never trained for a career of any kind, she was learning to cook and was a careful and exceptionally exact housekeeper. As I think it over searchingly I am not sure, and we were married these many years, of her ambitions, hopes, her fears or her ideals— we made our home, drove our car, played bridge with our friends, danced, raised our child—ostensibly together—married.

Never could I seem to attain with her the comradeship that formed the bond between my mother and myself . . ."

It took nearly four hours for Snyder and Gray to exchange marital and emotional histories. They said goodbye to their mutual friends in the booth at Henry's and arranged to meet again in August—after Ruth, Albert, and their seven-year-old daughter Lorraine had returned from a boating holiday on Shelter Island. Although Judd Gray did not then know it, he was the latest in a string of "men friends" with whom Ruth had gone dancing, beer-drinking, and who had helped her to devour plates of her favourite pretzels. On the evening of August 4, Gray rang the Snyder residence—a three-story clapboard house in Queens Village, New York City—and asked Ruth to have dinner with him at "their place"—Henry's Swedish restaurant.

After the meal and drinks Gray— with a daring that came more from the rye than any personal quality—invited Ruth to come back to his office on 34th Street and Fifth Avenue. "I have to collect a case of samples," he said lamely. "The latest thing in 'corselets'." Ruth smiled at his modesty—the word "corset" never crossed his lips—and agreed to his suggestion. Once inside the office she took off her scarf, ostensibly because she was suffering from holiday sunburn. "I've some camphor oil in my desk," said Gray solicitously. "Let me get it for you." He did so and proceeded to dab the oil over Ruth's blistered neck and shoulders. "Oh, that's so good!" she exclaimed. "No one is ever kind to me like this!" Gray flushed at her words. "I've something else for you," he murmured. "A new corselet. Please let me fit it on for you." Ruth shrugged. "Okay," she said, "you can do that. And from now you can call me 'Momsie'."

Lust and indiscretion

So in the deserted offices of the Bien Jolie Corset Company Ruth Snyder and Judd Gray began their affair—which was to burn with increasing ardour until March 1927, when they were trapped, arrested, and then turned on each other like warring rats. In the meantime, however, their lust and their indiscretion knew few limits. As often as they could they spent the night—or part of the night —in Manhattan hotel bedrooms, when Gray would sink to his knees and caress Ruth's feet and ankles. "You are my queen, my Momsie, my Mommie!" he declared, looking up at her imperious face. "And you are my baby, my 'Bud', my Lover Boy," she replied. Sometimes, by way of "respectability", little Lorraine Snyder would be taken along and left in the lobby while her "parents" retired upstairs. It was at this stage that Mrs.

Snyder first told Gray of the strange series of "accidents" that had befallen her husband in the summer of 1925 — shortly after she and Gray had first met.

The first incident occurred when Albert Snyder was jacking up the family Buick in order to change a tire. Suddenly, as he lay by the hub, the jack slipped, the car toppled sideways, and he only just missed being badly injured. A few evenings later he had a mishap with the crank, struck himself on the forehead and fell down unconscious. Some men might have felt that two such near escapes were enough, and that it might be a case of third time unlucky. But not Snyder. Later that August he again entered the garage of his salmon-painted house at 9327, 222nd Street, Queens, and stretched beneath the car with the engine running. Like a dutiful wife Ruth brought him a glass of whiskey to keep out the cold and praised his skill as a mechanic. She went back into the house and within a few minutes of drinking the whiskey Albert felt strangely sleepy. Just in time he noticed that the garage doors had somehow swung shut and that he was inhaling carbon monoxide fumes. He just managed to wriggle from under the car and reach the fresh air before being poisoned.

Ruth was desperate

If Snyder saw nothing ominous or significant in these happenings, then Judd Gray certainly did. "What are you trying to do?" he gasped, as Ruth ended her story. "Kill the poor guy?" She hesitated. "Momsie can't do it alone," she answered. "She needs help. Lover Boy will have to help her." At the time it is doubtful if Gray took her seriously. After all, they had both been drinking more than they should and had spouted more "big talk" than was wise. He only realized she was in earnest when she next met him and said triumphantly: "We'll be okay for money. I've just tricked Albert into taking out some hefty life insurance. He thinks it's only for 1000 dollars, but it's really for 96 thousand — if he dies by accident. I put three different policies in front of him, only let him see the space where you sign, and told him it was the thousand buck policy in triplicate. He's covered for 1000, 5000, and 45 thousand with a double indemnity accident clause!"

After this Snyder had three more close shaves with death — in July 1926 when he fell asleep on the living room couch and was almost gassed; in January 1927 when he was taken violently ill after Ruth had given him bichloride of mercury to "cure" an attack of hiccoughs; and in February when Ruth "unwittingly" turned on the gas tap in the living room. More by good luck than caution or commonsense Snyder survived all these attempts on his life. Ruth was now desperate and was determined there would be no "miraculous escape" from her seventh attempt.

"My husband's turned into a brute — a killer!" she claimed. "He's even bought a gun and says he'll shoot me with it!" This time, she continued sternly, there would be no slip-up — Albert would die and she and Judd would live richly ever after. One night in February 1927 they booked into the Waldorf-Astoria Hotel and there Ruth gave Judd his instructions. He was to buy some chloroform on his next trip out of town — to Kingston, New York — and also purchase a sash weight and some picture wire. "That way," she explained, "we have three means of killing him. One of them must surely work!" For a moment Gray raised objections to her plan, but he became obediently silent when she threatened: "If you don't do as I say then that's the end of us in the bed. You can find yourself another 'Momsie' to sleep with — only nobody else would have you but me!"

To prepare him for his coming role, she invited him round to Queens one night when Albert and Lorraine were away. She got drunk with him and then — as Gray later testified — "We went upstairs to her daughter's room, where we had intercourse." After that — encouraged by erotic love-play and fearful that it would abruptly end — Gray agreed to everything Ruth said as, stage by stage, she masterminded the "accidental" death of her still unsuspecting husband. One such "planning meeting" took place over lunch at Henry's, with Lorraine as an inquisitive witness as slips of paper outlining the imminent death of her father were handed back and forth across the table. She overheard some of the guarded conversation, but not enough for her to warn her father about what to expect in the early hours of Sunday, March 20.

At a bridge party

It was then that Gray — reinforcing his resolution with sips of whiskey from a flask — took a bus from downtown Manhattan to Queens Village and let himself into the Snyder house through an unlocked side door. The time was just after midnight and Ruth, Albert, and Lorraine were out at a bridge party in the home of one of their neighbours, Mrs. Milton Fidgeon. They returned tired but as happy as they ever were at about two o'clock — with Gray then hidden in the upstairs spare bedroom. The chloroform, sash weight, and picture wire were already concealed under the pillow of the bed, and he sat steadily drinking and staring at the blue "immigrants's" handkerchief and Italian newspaper which he had brought with him as false "clues".

Gray was not the only person who had been drinking that night. Albert Snyder had consumed more alcohol than he was used to, and after putting the car away he lurched upstairs, seconds after a snatched conversation between his wife, in the corridor, and Gray in the middle bedroom. With Lorraine put to bed and Albert lying in their room in a drunken haze, Ruth slipped along the hall and rejoined her lover. She was wearing slippers, a nightgown and negligee, and after kissing Gray she hissed: "Have you found the sash weight?" "Sure," he nodded. "Keep quiet, then. I'll be back as quick as I can."

Whispered consultation

Half-an-hour later Ruth left the master bedroom and held another whispered consultation with Gray. Together they finished the last of the whiskey and at three o'clock they were ready to act. There was no sound in the house, nor in the street outside, and apart from being tight Albert Snyder was also deaf in one ear. It is debatable if he would have heard the conspirators had they resorted to shouting at each other. "Okay," breathed Ruth. "This is it." Taking Gray by the hand she led him out of the spare bedroom and along the darkened corridor. He was wearing long rubber gloves so as to leave no fingerprints on the sash weight. It was she who carried the chloroform, wire, handkerchief, and some cotton waste.

They entered the front bedroom quietly, furtively. There, for the first and last time, Gray saw Albert Snyder — the man he had been ordered to kill. He paused for a moment, as if appalled by the reason for his being there. Then as Ruth opened her mouth to say something, he raised the weight with both hands and brought it crashing down on Snyder's exposed head. The blow was a strong one — but not strong enough to kill the sleeping man. Snyder awoke, sat up, and began to fight for his life. He clenched his hands and struck out at the half-seen intruder. Again Gray smashed the weight against Snyder's skull — this time drawing blood. The injured man caught hold of Gray's necktie and as he did so the weight fell to the floor. "Help, Momsie!" cried Albert pitifully. "For God's sake help me!" Whether or not he saw his wife in the room was never established. But Ruth answered him by retrieving the weight, lifting it with her strong and muscular arms and battering him on the top of the head with it.

Incredibly, Albert was still alive. He remained so until Grey clambered over his twitching body . . . until Ruth stuffed the chloroform-soaked cotton waste into his mouth and nostrils . . . until finally she tied his hands and feet and then methodically strangled him with the picture wire. There was blood everywhere — but mostly

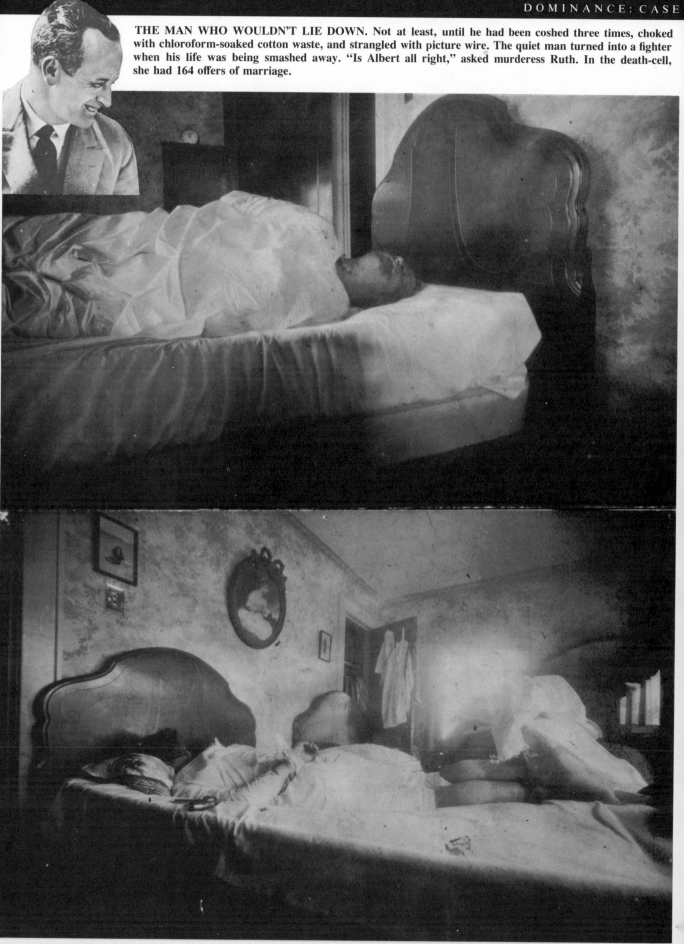

THE MAN WHO WOULDN'T LIE DOWN. Not at least, until he had been coshed three times, choked with chloroform-soaked cotton waste, and strangled with picture wire. The quiet man turned into a fighter when his life was being smashed away. "Is Albert all right," asked murderess Ruth. In the death-cell, she had 164 offers of marriage.

on Ruth's nightgown and the buckskin gloves she had borrowed from Gray, and on the salesman's freshly laundered shirt. For the next hour they washed themselves, sponged or changed their clothes (Gray put on a clean blue shirt of Albert's), hid the sash weight in the cellar, removed her jewellery and furs, and disarranged the ground floor furniture and cushions to make it seem as if a burglary had taken place. Only then did Gray tie his mistress up, fasten cheesecloth over her mouth and leave her lying in the spare bedroom, together with the Italian newspaper. He was ready to travel to the Onondaga Hotel in Syracuse, Kansas, and resume his corset selling activities first thing on Monday morning. As he left he looked back at Ruth Snyder—possibly for the first time with disgust and loathing—and said: "It may be two months, it may be a year, and it may be never before you'll see me again." One thing was sure: he and Snyder were never to drink, dance, make love, or even speak to each other again.

Curious tapping

Dawn broke gently in Queens Village on the morning of March 20. Young Lorraine Snyder was tired after her late night at the grown-ups' party and would have slept in had it not been for the curious tapping she heard at her bedroom door. Puzzled, she called out to her father and then her mother. Getting no reply she jumped out of bed and ran bare-footed to open the door—from where she saw her mother lying gagged and bound in the corridor. Lorraine bent and untied the cheesecloth and her mother told her to run and get help. The girl did so and a few minutes later Ruth was babbling out her story to her neighbours, Harriet and Louis Mulhauser. "It was dreadful, just dreadful!" she cried hysterically. "I was attacked by a prowler . . . He tied me up . . . He must have been after my jewels . . . Is Albert all right?" Mr. Mulhauser went to the main bedroom and came back white-faced with the news that Albert had two gaping head wounds and was dead.

Twice more that morning Mrs. Snyder repeated her thin and preposterous story of being attacked by "a big, rough-looking guy of about 35 with a black moustache. He was a foreigner, I guess. Some kind of Eyetalian." She gasped this out to Dr. Harry Hansen of Queens, who was called to the house to examine the body and check Ruth for any sign of assault. He found none and was convinced that her account was "a fabrication of lies". This opinion was shared by Police Commissioner George McLaughlin, who headed the 60 policemen who converged on the Snyder house before breakfast. Ruth—pale and trembling and far from being

"The Granite Woman" she was to be dubbed by the press—was grilled for 12 hours by McLaughlin and Inspector Arthur Carey.

Their suspicions had first been aroused by the frantic disorder of the downstairs rooms. "This doesn't look like a professional burglary to me," growled Carey. Ruth looked resentfully at him. "What do you mean?" He indicated to the turned over chairs and cushions. "It just doesn't look right." "How do you mean?" "I've seen lots of burglaries," he replied. "And they are not done this way. Not with killing." A search of the house soon revealed Ruth's rings and necklaces stuffed beneath a mattress, and a fur coat hanging in a closet. No one then had any doubts about it being an "inside" job.

After examining an address book containing the names of 28 men—including that of Judd Gray—and on discovering a cancelled check made out to Gray for $200, Ruth Snyder was taken to the Jamaica precinct police station, where she was tricked into making a partial confession. Told that Gray had already been arrested and had "told all", she admitted that she and the corset salesman had plotted to kill her husband and then fake a break in. "But I didn't aim a single blow at Albert," she protested. "That was all Judd's doing. At the last moment I tried to stop him—but it was too late!"

Terrified, snivelling

By then detectives had found the blood-stained sash weight in the basement and had come across the insurance policies which made Albert Snyder a rich man—once he was dead. The next move—acting on information provided by Ruth—was to arrest the terrified and snivelling Judd Gray at his Syracuse hotel. The officers who brought him to New York City intimated that Snyder had not, in fact, died of his head wounds. He had been doped with chloroform and then strangled while unconscious. By the time the train pulled into 125th Street station, and Gray was taken from the private compartment to a waiting police car, he, too, had given his version of the night's deed. Faced with a murder charge he unexpectedly showed more courage than his "Granite Woman" lover and freely admitted to his part in the slaying of Snyder. He did not, however, cover up for Ruth and recounted everything she had said and done in the house in Queens. "I would never have killed Snyder but for her," he wept when he had completed his statement. "She had this power over me. She told me what to do and I just did it."

From then on the case against Gray and Snyder proceeded with all the implacability of the law. On April 18, 1927, their trial opened in Queens County

Courthouse and continued there for the next 18 days. Ruth appeared dressed in a black coat and hat, with a black rosary and crucifix conspicuously dangling at her throat—while Gray wore a double-breasted blue pinstripe suit with knife-edged creases in the trousers. Among the many star reporters and sob sisters who packed the press box was Peggy Hopkins Joyce, who gushed in the New York *Daily Mirror*: "Poor Judd Gray! He hasn't IT, he hasn't anything. He is just a sap who kissed and was told on! . . ."

Passionate vampire

"This putty man was wonderful modeling material for the Swedish-Norwegian vampire . . . She was passionate and she was cold-blooded, if anybody can imagine such a combination. Her passion was for Gray; her cold-bloodedness for her husband . . . You know women can do things to men that make men crazy. I mean, they can exert their influence over them in such a way that men will do almost anything for them. And I guess that is what Ruth did to Judd."

On May 9 Snyder and Gray were duly found guilty as charged. Both their subsequent appeals were refused and they were sentenced to die in the electric chair in Sing Sing at 11 o'clock on the night of January 12, 1928. While in the Death House they both wrote their autobiographies, and Ruth received 164 offers of marriage from men who—in the event of her being reprieved—were eager to exist humbly beneath her dominance. But there was no reprieve, and "Momsie" and "Lover Boy" perished within four minutes of each other. They kept their last rendezvous when they were laid out in the prison's autopsy room on a pair of stone slabs. However, if Ruth's religious convictions were anything to go by, it was not quite the end of their relationship—or of their triangle with Albert. In a poem published shortly before her death, and apparently addressed to all those of the police, press, and public who had "sullied" her name as a loving wife and mother, she said:

"You've blackened and besmeared a
    mother,
Once a man's plaything—A Toy—
What have you gained by all you've
    said,
And has it—brought you Joy?

And the hours when 'Babe' needed my
    love,
You've seen fit to send me away—
I'm going to God's home in heaven,
Ne'er more my feet to stray.

Someday—we'll all meet together,
Happy and smiling again,
Far above this earthly span
Everlastingly—in His reign."

IN THE CHAIR:
The last seconds
of Ruth Snyder's
life . . . a unique
last picture, shot
by a newsman
with a hidden
camera.
In court, her
lover said he
would never have
killed but for
her. "She had
this power
over me."

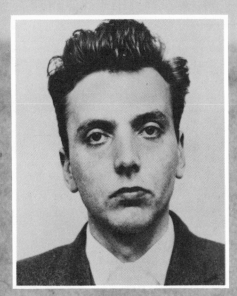

BRADY AND HINDLEY
THE MURDERERS OF THE MOORS

"All over the place . . . we have been practically all over the place," said Myra Hindley. With Ian Brady, she had haunted the bleak Pennine moorlands of Northern England. Their ghoulish journeys ended when shallow graves were discovered on the moors. For the dominant Brady and his worshipping mistress, the next journey was to the courtroom. Some called it, "The Trial of the Century".

Brady and Hindley ...
"I love him," she croaked
"And I still ... I love him"

THE DOCK, surrounded on three sides by four-inch thick bulletproof glass, dominated the courtroom. It had been specially altered and strengthened at the request of the British police, who, weeks before the trial began, feared that an attempt might be made to assassinate the prisoners — 28-year-old Ian Brady and his worshipping mistress, Myra Hindley. As they sat behind the glass — safe from any guns there might be in court, but exposed to the public's hostility — they sucked mints, passed copious notes to their counsels, and occasionally nudged one another — especially if an adjournment was due. Once, losing her composure for a moment, Hindley stuck her tongue out at a reporter who stared too nakedly at her. But Brady's impassiveness never faltered; he appeared to regard the proceedings as a tiresome formality, a charade to be enacted before he was found guilty and sent to prison for life. "They smell blood," he told a policeman stoically. "I'll be convicted whatever happens out there."

The trial of Brady and Hindley — an event which the judge, Mr. Justice Fenton Atkinson, said had been called "the trial of the century" — opened at Chester Assizes on Tuesday, April 19, 1966. In its own perverse and macabre way, it was just as impressive an occasion as a theatrical first night or a fashionable film première. Hundreds of journalists and television reporters from every part of the world descended on Chester Castle, and the Post Office installed a special cable and rows of telephones to handle their calls. Although only 60 seats were available to the public, scores of spectators — mainly middle-aged women in floral hats or silk headscarves — scrambled to get a place in the gallery of No. 2 Court. A corps of

VICTIM: Homosexual Edward Evans (far left). He was picked up at a railroad station snack bar by Ian Brady, and taken home. At the house Brady shared with Myra Hindley, Evans was battered to death with an axe. Brady asked brother-in-law David Smith to help in the killing, but Smith was frozen by the horror of what he saw. He reported Brady to the police, and is pictured (right) going to court with his wife. Evidence given by Mr. and Mrs. David Smith helped send their brother-in-law to jail for life. Accomplice Myra Hindley also received a life sentence ... a deadly partnership was finally broken by prison walls.

MURDERER'S HOME: Myra Hindley grew up in a city slum ... a child of World War II, daughter of a paratrooper. Her lover's hero was Hitler

five well-known authors was present, hoping to concoct bestsellers from the affair, and in the distinguished visitors' gallery another 23 people looked down on the crowded courtroom, or arena.

There were few citizens in Chester — or indeed in Britain — who did not know why Brady, a £12-a-week stock clerk, and Hindley, her hair dyed a startling shade of lilac, were in the reinforced dock. They were accused of murdering three young people — Edward Evans, a 17-year-old homosexual, Lesley Ann Downey, a child of 10, and John Kilbride, aged 12. It was common knowledge that the sexually-assaulted bodies of John and Lesley

had been discovered by the Lancashire police in shallow graves on Saddleworth Moor, near Manchester, and that Evans had been found in a bedroom of Hindley's council house home with his head smashed in by an axe. There appeared to be no rational explanation for the crimes, and in the 14 days that followed those in the court listened to a twentieth-century horror story as Sir Elwyn Jones, the Attorney-General, submitted that, "In association with all these killings there was present not only a sexual element but an abnormal sexual element, a perverted sexual element."

Hushed courtroom

The main prosecution witness was Hindley's brother-in-law, David Smith, 18, a delinquent with an unenviable police record of violence and brutality. Despite his conduct in the past, it was Smith who had informed the police the morning after he had seen Brady beat Edward Evans to death. The murder took place on the evening of October 6, 1965, after Brady had picked up the youth outside the buffet of Manchester Central Station and brought him to 16 Wardle Brook Avenue, Hattersley — the box-like house in which he shared a bedroom with Myra Hindley and living quarters with her grandmother. Wearing tight-fitting blue jeans, and with his dark brown hair falling over his forehead in the manner of the late James Dean, Smith told a hushed court how he had been summoned round to Hindley's house ostensibly to drink some miniature bottles of wine. A minute or so later he heard "a hell of a scream", followed by Hindley shouting "Dave, help him!" Clutching a stick he had brought with him, he ran from the kitchen and into the living room where he saw a scene that made him "freeze".

"My first thoughts were that Ian had hold of a life-sized rag doll and was just

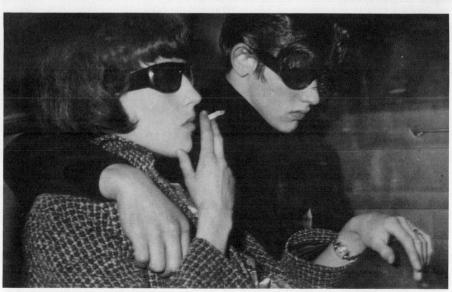

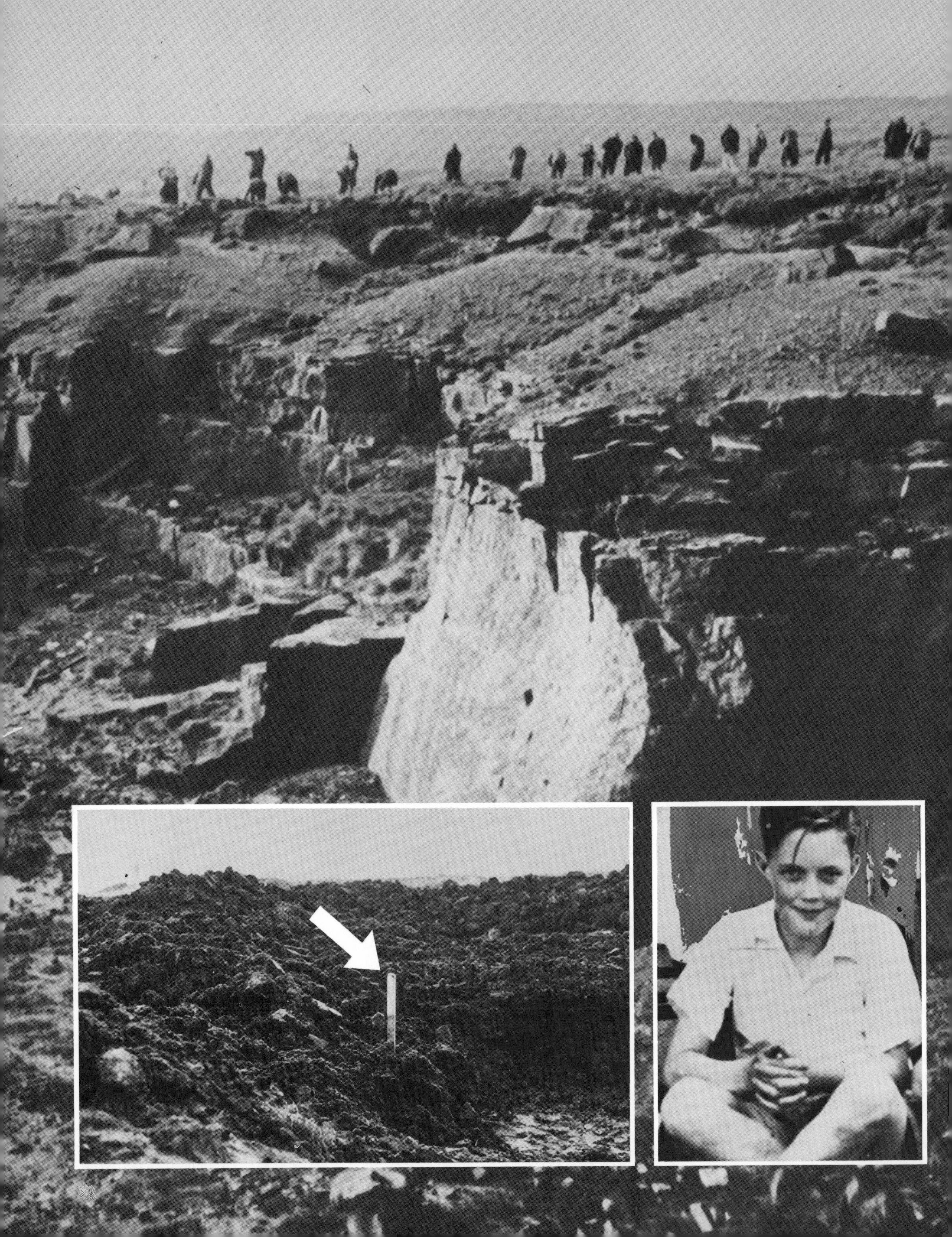

waving it about," he said tightly. "The arms were going all over. Then it dawned on me that it was not a rag doll. It fell against the couch not more than two feet away from me. My stomach turned over. It was half screaming and groaning. The lad was laid out on his front and Ian stood over him with his legs apart with an axe in his right hand. The lad groaned and Ian just lifted the axe over his head and brought it down upon the lad's head. There were a couple of seconds of silence and the lad groaned again, only very much lower. Ian lifted the axe way above his head again and brought it down. The lad stopped groaning then. He was making a gurgling noise like when you brush your teeth and gargle with water. Ian placed a cover over his head. He had a piece of electric wire, and he wrapped it round the lad's neck and began to pull it; and he was saying: 'You f . . . ing dirty bastard', over and over again. The lad just stopped making this noise, and Ian looked up and said to Myra: 'That's it. It is the messiest yet!' "

Supreme pleasure

As Smith left the witness stand—after admitting to Brady's counsel, Mr. Emlyn Hooson, Q.C., M.P. that he had written in a notebook that, "People are like maggots, small, blind, worthless, fish bait. Rape is not a crime. It is a state of mind. Murder is a hobby and a supreme pleasure"—the spectators in the court relaxed. Surely, they told themselves, they had heard the cruellest, the bloodiest, the most chilling details. But, unbelievably enough, there was worse, far worse, to come. Turning to the killing of Lesley Downey—who had disappeared after visiting a fairground at Hattersley on December 26, 1964—the judge had to decide whether or not to allow a tape recording to be played, a recording made by Brady and Hindley in which the terrified youngster pleaded for safety, for her mother, for her life.

Leaning gravely forward, Mr. Justice Atkinson said: "There is a question whether this piece of evidence should be heard in camera or not. There has been so much talk, that in my opinion we have no right to exclude the public. Anyone who wishes not to listen should leave now. During it I request complete silence. The Attorney-General will beforehand read out the transcript, at dictation speed."

It was at this stage, as the transcript

VICTIM: John Kilbride, aged 12 (left) was sexually assaulted. His body was found in a shallow grave (arrowed) by police searchers on the moors. Brady denied all knowledge of his death, but the Attorney-General said that Kilbride was "killed by the same hands" as the other Moors victims

POLICE CHIEF Joe Mounsey discovered the bodies. After arresting Brady and Hindley, police became their protectors against any assassination bid

was read out and the tape played, that the assassination attempt—if there was to be one—would be made. Police closed in and formed a protective semicircle in front of the dock, their eyes roving from face to face as they scanned those in the press box, the well of the court, and the galleries. As the spool began to revolve—and the words and then the screams were heard—a number of women in the public gallery shuddered and closed their eyes. The all-male jurors (half of whom appeared to be under 30) lowered their heads, a man in the distinguished visitors' gallery put his hand over his face, and a policeman attended to another man who slumped forward in distress.

It was the screams punctuating the tape which turned most people's stomachs—and then there was Lesley's voice, shrill with panic and fear, as she begged, whispered, and sobbed. "Please God, help me!" she cried. " . . . Can I just tell you summat? I must tell you summat. Please take your hands off me a minute, please . . . I can't breathe . . . What are you going to do with me? . . . Don't undress me, will you? . . . It hurts me. I want to see mummy, honest to God . . . I have to get home before eight o'clock . . . Or I'll get killed if I don't. Honest to God . . . It hurts me neck . . ."

In a way the most appalling section of the tape came towards the end when a radio was turned on, bells rang out, and two Christmas-style songs were heard: *Jolly St. Nicholas*, and *The Little Drummer Boy*. Later, opening Brady's defence, Mr. Hooson was to say: "It is terribly, terribly important that you dispose from your minds all the natural revulsion one has in reading or hearing evidence connected with the death of children." But as, after 16 minutes and 21 seconds, the tape whirred to a close there was no one in the court—with the possible exception of the two accused—who did not sit stun-

ned and sickened, and who found it hard not to allow their "feelings to be aroused to the exclusion of dispassionate justice."

The evidence of the recording was more monstrous even than the photographs Brady had taken of Lesley, showing her naked and with a scarf over her mouth, posing obscenely in the shoddily furnished bedroom. It was not until the ninth day of the trial that Brady was escorted by two prison officers from the dock to the witness stand. People craned forward to look at him as, sallow-faced and lanky, he affirmed rather than take the oath on the *Bible*. In appearance he seemed neither better nor worse than any of the young men who lived in Hattersley—a drab estate which acted as an overspill for Manchester. He wore an ordinary grey suit, plain white shirt and had a neatly-folded handkerchief in his breast pocket. He might boast of worshipping Hitler, agree with the French writer the Marquis de Sade that inflicting pain upon others was the ultimate thrill, and believe in the Germanic philosophy of the superman who was "beyond good and evil". But none of this was apparent until the illegitimate son of a Glasgow waitress arrogantly answered questions put to him by Hooson.

Despite an accent that veered between a thick Scottish brogue and a Lancashire drawl, he spoke out firmly and loudly. Yes, he had spent the autumn of 1964 discussing a "perfect payroll robbery" with his disciple David Smith. As he spoke, his cold, pale eyes were as blank and lifeless as stones seen under water, and a ray of animosity seemed to stretch between him and the public. It was a two-way band of hatred and it broadened and intensified when he admitted to offering Lesley Downey ten shillings to pose for him and Hindley in the nude, and to unintentionally killing Evans as part of "a bit of practice".

Insolent contempt

During this stage, and throughout the cross-examination that followed, he showed his wholesale contempt for the trial and all its trappings, and displayed his insolence towards the judge and the Attorney-General (he never addressed them as "My Lord", or "Sir"). In contrast to this, Sir Elwyn Jones spoke to him in polite, restrained tones, as if interviewing a somewhat sullen and disinterested job applicant. "You never intended Evans to leave that room alive?"—"Yes," came the answer. "The right side of his skull was smashed to pieces and some of his brains were on the floor?" Brady nodded. "Yes—in fact Smith made a joke about it. He said, 'He was a brainy swine, wasn't he!' " And—how did he feel when he had heard Lesley Downey's screams filling the courtroom?

The answer was he found it "embarrassing".

Later on Brady demonstrated some of the reasoning power and misplaced "brilliance" which had dominated Smith and made Hindley his eager slave. The exchange came when Elwyn Jones asked him about his library: "This was the diet you were consuming. Pornographic books, books on violence and murder?" – "Not pornographic books. You can buy them at any bookstall . . ." "they are dirty books, Brady" – "It depends on the dirty mind. It depends on your mind . . . Let me give you the names of just two." (Here the judge intervened saying: "*Uses of the Torture Chamber, Sexual Anomalies and Perversions*.") Brady shrugged. "These are written by doctors. They are supposed to be social . . ." "Was your interest in them on a high social plane?" – "No, for erotic reasons . . ." "Of course. This is the atmosphere of your mind. A sink of pornography, was it not?" – "No. There are better collections than that in lords' manors all over the country."

Warped philosophy

Although Brady admitted that he had murdered Evans, he denied any knowledge as to how Lesley Downey had died, and said he knew nothing of the disappearance and death of young John Kilbride. Both the children were found in graves on the moors only 400 yards apart. Lesley had been stripped of her tartan skirt and pink cardigan, and John's trousers and underpants had been rolled down to the thighs, indicating sexual interference. After spending $8\frac{3}{4}$ hours in the box Brady was allowed to return to the dock, to sit next to Hindley – the typist who had worked for the same chemical distributing firm as himself, and who had adored him for a year before he spoke to her, writing in her red-bound diary:

MOTHERS: Mrs. Kilbride (left) and Mrs. Downey. Their children were victims. Friend Linda Clark (inset) was with Lesley Downey the day she vanished

"Ian looked at me today . . . He smiled at me today . . . The pig . . . he didn't look at me . . . He ignored me today . . . I wonder if he'll ever take me out . . . I almost got a smile out of him today . . . Ian wore a black shirt and looked smashing . . . He is a loud-mouthed pig . . . I love him." Then, shortly before Christmas 1961, she was able to record: "Eureka! Today we have our first date. We are going to the cinema."

The movie Brady took her to see was *Trial at Nuremburg*, which dealt with Nazi war criminals and atrocities, and he chose this as an introduction to his warped and secondhand philosophy of "power over others". They were both children of the slums (she was a war baby, the daughter of a paratrooper), but there their early resemblance ended. Brady had been a boy who enjoyed torturing cats, flashing the flick-knife he habitually carried, and viewing as many horror movies as he could get into. His boyhood nickname in the Glasgow Gorbals had been "Dracula", whereas Hindley had been of slightly above average I.Q. as a schoolgirl, had always had religious tendencies and was later to return to the Roman Catholic church in which she had been raised.

Expressionless voice

Interrupted from her note-taking and the scowls she delivered across the court, she was led to the witness stand, leaving Brady to resume sketching the brutal looking thugs with fierce black eyes and low foreheads – which was his way of killing time during the long and repetitive hours of the trial. By then, the 11th day of the proceedings, Hindley's lilac hair

had undergone a bizarre change. It was now dyed a banana-yellow with tell-tale black zigzags at the roots. It looked as if she was wearing a grotesque raffia wig – a squat figure in a speckled tweed suit, pale blue blouse, a pair of white high-heeled shoes belonging to her mother, and giving every indication as to why she was called "square-arse" by the local youths.

Like Brady, she affirmed instead of taking the oath. With her hooked, parrot nose and thick lips there was nothing outwardly attractive about her, and this impression was heightened when she spoke. Her expressionless voice was low-pitched and hoarse as she answered her counsel, Mr. Godfrey Heilpern, as to her feelings towards Brady. "I loved him," she croaked, "and I still . . . I love him." She then explained that she was suffering from a sore throat, and told how she had passed her driving test in November 1963 – when she was aged 21 – and had driven Brady around the moors and countryside of Lancashire in an Austin Mini Traveller. "All over the place . . . we have been practically all over the place," she said.

Frightened, upset

Although she lacked Brady's surly self-confidence, she maintained her poise until Mr. Heilpern brought up the subject of the tape recording. She frowned and clenched her hands as he said: "You have heard that recording played and you have had a copy of the transcript? – Yes . . . What are your feelings about that?" – "I am ashamed." The lawyer nodded and went on to the night when Lesley Downey had been taken to the house in Wardle Brook Avenue. "What was the child like at the beginning?" he asked. "Willing or reluctant or what?" There was a pause, then Hindley replied that the little girl had been quiet at first, and then frightened and upset when she was taken upstairs.

She added: "As soon as she started crying I started to panic because I was worried. That is why I was so brusque and cruel in my attitude, because I wanted her to be quiet. I didn't expect her to start making such a noise . . . The front door was wide open. The bedroom door was open and the bedroom window was open. I was frightened that anyone would hear. I just wanted her to be quiet and I said, 'Be quiet until we get things sorted out.' The girl sat on the bed. I switched on the radio then because I was hoping she would remain quiet and that the radio would help to alleviate her fears."

After that, claimed Hindley, Lesley left the house with Smith and she and Brady did not see the child again. In answer to Mr. Heilpern she also said she had nothing at all to do with the

VICTIM: Lesley Ann Downey, aged 10 (top). She went to a Christmas fair . . . and vanished. Brady and Hindley taped her screams for mercy before murdering her. Lesley's body was also found in a shallow grave on the moors by police. At the trial, the horrifying tape was played back to a stunned court, and obscene photographs of Lesley taken by Brady and Hindley were shown. "Dispose from your minds all natural revulsion," said the defence Queen's Counsel

29

killing and burying of John Kilbride, and it was not until she was cross-examined by the Attorney-General that her role in the two other murders became more apparent. Hardening his voice, Sir Elwyn asked her how she had reacted to the scream made by Edward Evans as he was attacked by Brady: "You could not stand the scream?" "The noise was so loud I put my hands over my ears." "This Court has heard of another scream, more than one, in a room where you were?" "Yes." "The screams of a little child of ten, of your sex, madam?" "Yes." "Did you put your hands over your ears when you heard the screams of Lesley Ann Downey?" "No." "Why not?" "I wanted her to be quiet." "Or get the child out and see that she was treated as a woman should treat a female child, or any child?" "I should have done and I didn't. I have no defence for that. No defence. It was indefensible. I was cruel." "Cruel and pitiless?" "I was cruel." "And pitiless?" "I was cruel."

Depraved killers

Finally, after 5 hours and 46 minutes, she came to the end of her evidence and rejoined Brady—who pointedly looked away from her—in the dock. The trial of

A MOTHER'S FAREWELL to a child whose last cries for help had been in vain. "I was cruel," Myra Hindley told the court. "I am ashamed."

the century was now in its closing stages and in winding-up his final address the Attorney-General said dramatically: "My submission is that the same hands killed all three of these victims, Evans, Downey, and Kilbride—and these are the hands of the two accused in the dock." The two defence counsel followed by asserting that—although Brady was patently guilty of murdering Evans—there was no evidence to show that he, or Hindley, had been responsible for the deaths of the other two victims. And, although nothing had been openly stated, there was a feeling in the court that the accused were not normal, not balanced, not sane. Aware of this, Mr. Justice Atkinson warned the jury: "I suppose that hearing and reading about these allegations, the first reaction of kindly, charitable people is to say this is so terrible that anyone doing anything like that might be mentally afflicted. You must put that aside at once . . . It is a presumption of our law that anyone who comes into the dock is sane. There has not been the smallest suggestion that either of these two are mentally abnormal or not fully and completely responsible for their actions. If, and I underline it, the prosecution is right, you are dealing with two sadistic killers of the utmost depravity . . ."

The jurors listened attentively to the careful summing-up. Then, at 2.40 p.m. on Friday, May 6, they retired to consider their verdict. They were out until

five o'clock, when they returned and pronounced Brady guilty of all three murders, and Hindley guilty of the murders of Edward Evans and Lesley Ann Downey; she was found not guilty of the murder of John Kilbride, but guilty of harbouring Brady knowing that he had committed the crime.

Equally horrible

Once the judge heard that the trial came to an abrupt, almost anticlimactic end. "Ian Brady," he said coldly, "these were three calculated, cruel, cold-blooded murders. I pass the only sentence which the law now allows, which is three concurrent sentences of life imprisonment." Brady did not flinch and the judge said dismissively to the prison officer in the dock, "Put him down." Hindley now stood alone as Brady left her without a glance. She nervously thrust another mint into her mouth and chewed on it as the judge said: "In your case, Hindley, you have been found guilty of two equally horrible murders and in the third as an accessory after the fact. On the two murders the sentence is two concurrent sentences of life imprisonment. On the accessory charge a concurrent sentence of seven years' imprisonment."

She paled, swayed as if to fall and was supported by a woman jailer who helped her down the steep flight of steps to the cells below.

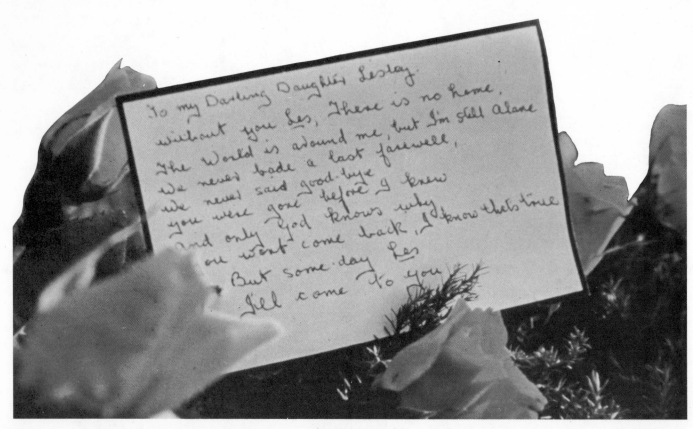

THE CRIME BUSTERS...
HOW IT ALL STARTED

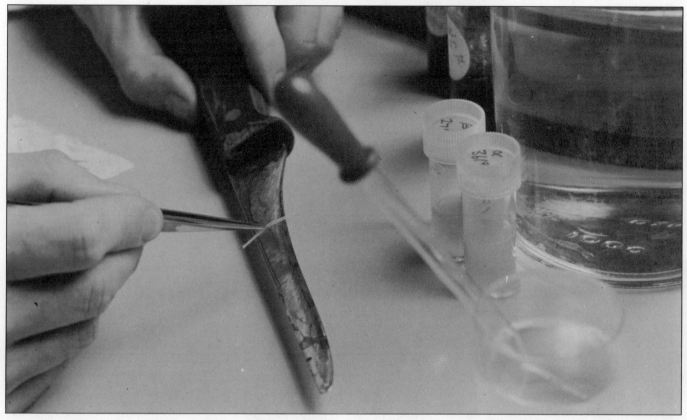

A criminal may be caught red-handed, or simply give himself up. He may be ratted on by an informer, or spotted by a witness. Or he might be trapped by the resourcefulness of those whose mission is to beat crime. The battle against crime is as old as criminal activity . . . as old as man. But its weapons are ever-changing.

One of the most effective weapons in society's battle against crime is science. With the pace of advance in modern science, the battle becomes increasingly sophisticated, but the idea is hardly a new one. Indeed, it goes back to the days of the Old Testament. It was in 930 B.C., when Solomon, the third king of Israel, was confronted with the two women who had just had babies. One baby had died, its mother had secretly changed it for the live one (while the second mother slept), and Solomon had to decide which of the two shouting women was the live one's mother. "Bring me a sword!" he said. "Cut the living child in two; give half to one, half to the other." The women's demeanour instantly decided which was the true mother and the surviving baby was spared. There is reason to believe that the basis

of the story is much older than Solomon or Israel, but it can be taken as marking the arrival in the courts, whenever it was, of forensic science in the form of experimental psychology. Today it would be called forensic psychiatry and it would all be done by doctors.

At a more practical level, the early development of forensic science was less dramatic. It was many centuries before this method of crime-fighting gained pace.

In 1786 a Scottish crofter and his wife came home to their cottage after a day in the fields and found their teenage daughter murdered. Suspicion fell upon a young man named Richardson; but for some time there was no evidence on which he could be arrested. Even when there was judged to be enough, he promptly pro-

BLOOD-TESTING is becoming an increasingly important area of forensic science. A key advance was the development of methods to test blood that has been dry for some time.

duced what seemed to be a perfect alibi. Then, rather belatedly it must seem today, the police took plaster-casts of some footprints near the cottage, and found that the pattern of the hobnails was exactly the same as that on Richardson's boots. Then further and similar "forensic" evidence began to accumulate. Stains on the stockings he had worn on the day of the murder were found to be bloodstains (though they could not, in those days, be identified as belonging to any particular blood-group). Mud and sand on the stockings *could,* however, be

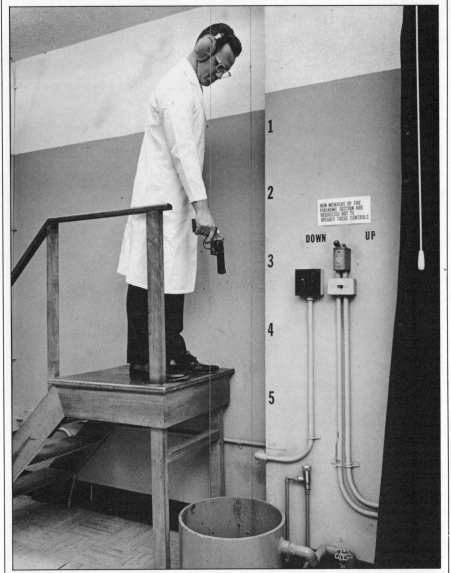

BALLISTICS is one of the most sophisticated areas of forensic science. "Whose gun fired the bullet?" may be solved by microscopically matching sections from a bullet found at the scene of the crime with a test-fired specimen.

proved to be mud and sand from the cottage garden. It was largely on this evidence that Richardson was convicted at Dumfries in 1787.

The Richardson case thus offers all the classic features of a prosecution founded on forensic science: identification of the suspect (by footprints), identification of the clues (the blood and, more exactly, the sand and the mud), and association of all the clues with the man Richardson.

But that, in 1787, was about the extent of what could be called forensic science, and so it officially remained for the next 100 years — though outstanding members of the "Bow Street Runners" and the original "Peelers" — so called after Sir Robert Peel, the Home Secretary, who, in the 1820's, created the London police — who were given extraordinary personal licence and developed some ingenious stratagems of their own, were perhaps serving the interests of science without knowing it.

Man-measurement

In 1879 Alphonse Bertillon, of the French Department of Criminal Police, began to develop a system of classified "anthropometry" — which simply means man-measurement. It was not Bertillon's invention, but he was the first to persevere with it, in the face of universal ridicule, and finally gain reluctant official approval. No two people have the same measurements *in combination*: the circumference of the head and chest, the length of the ears, nose, fingers, arms, legs, feet and so on. List all these against one criminal's name, argued Bertillon, and you can always identify him whatever he does about his name, his beard, his hair, his walk, his clothing.

And Bertillon was right. His system was slow and laborious but it was just about infallible. If you recorded the measurements of 14 parts of a man's body, the odds against any other man's having the same combination of measurements were 286,435,456 to one. Nevertheless for six years he was derided as a crank (which in some ways he was), rebuked for wasting his time, and ordered by successive Prefects of Police under whom he served to stop romancing and get on with his clerical duties.

Meanwhile, however, the science of identification by fingerprinting — which was probably of great antiquity — had been revived, developed and applied to criminology by an official in the Indian Civil Service named William Herschel. Both in Bengal and in England he had to meet exactly the same kind of ridicule, fight the same kind of battles, as Bertillon was doing. It was soon established, of course, that the odds against two men having identical fingerprints ran into meaningless billions; that, in fact, there existed no such possibility. But unlike Bertillon, Herschel allowed himself to be discouraged by official hostility or stupidity, and fell back on the use of fingerprints for his own administrative purposes—for example, getting the thumbprint "signatures" of Indian labourers unable to write when drawing their pay. He had been doing it for 20 years before he made his futile attempt to interest the authorities.

These two systems, anthropometry and fingerprinting, became almost battle slogans. Anthropometry had reached the United States, which had (and still has) about 40,000 separate police forces. Between them they spent so much money installing the measuring apparatus, the filing systems and the clerks that the usual "vested interest" barrier to further progress was quickly established. It is worth remembering that one of the most scornful critics of fingerprint identification was Bertillon himself; and that he allowed himself to believe, at the time of the Dreyfus case in France, that he was a handwriting expert as well as an anthropometrist. (He "identified" Dreyfus's handwriting, quite wrongly, and stuck to his confident and stupid opinion even when it was proved, five years later—while Dreyfus was on Devil's island—that he was wrong and Dreyfus innocent.) From 1880 onwards a Scottish medical missionary in Japan, Henry Faulds, was urging the infallibility of fingerprints for identifying the absent criminal who had left his prints at the scene of his crime. And Sir Thomas Galton, the illustrious founder of the science of eugenics, or 'fine' breeding, began to urge upon the Home Office in 1894 that fingerprinting was an exact science of identification: even in 1892 he had calculated that the chances against error were 64,000,000,000 to one.

Sherlock Holmes

It was a Buenos Aires police officer, Juan Vucetich (born in what we now call Yugoslavia) who finally convinced world criminologists of every school—and they are a mutually critical lot—about the great superiority of fingerprints, in convenience and simplicity and above all in speed of operation. And it was Vucetich whose initiative and energy hastened the inevitable change, expensive as it was for everyone. Anthropometry had been used in England only from 1894 until 1900.

And it was in the 20th century that other forms of forensic science came into their own—encouraged, to an appreciable extent, by the ingenuity of the Sherlock Holmes stories and by Conan Doyle's friendly contacts with senior police officers. Not enough acknowledgment has ever been accorded to the effect of the imaginative detective fiction of that period on the climate of public opinion, and the

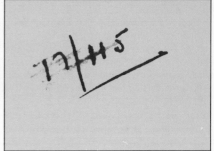

FINGERPRINTING was pioneered in the 19th century. A barely-visible print can be "developed" with the use of a powder, a brush and a trained hand (above). Just as no fingerprints are alike, so no two typewriters ever produce quite the same result when challenged by the microscope (right). When the written word has been obscured, defacing marks may sometimes be removed by infra-red photography (below).

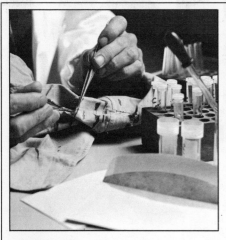

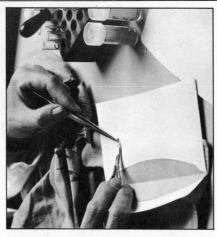

BLOOD-GROUPING techniques are becoming more and more sophisticated. Today, the tiniest bloodstain, can be virtually conclusive. Such a sample

can be submitted to 15 different tests. This way, the odds against an incorrect identification are reduced to one in a hundred, or even less.

THE TESTS all use varying systems by which blood can be grouped. Anyone's blood can be examined in this way, and rarely would the same combination of

results be produced. The tests are carried out by activating the blood with a re-agent substance. The reaction which takes place helps to establish its characteristics.

creation of an ideal sleuth beside whom the real-life policeman could be made to seem ineffectual—sometimes even in his own eyes. The Bordet blood test could already distinguish animal from human blood: today we can prove that human blood belongs to a group of individuals, though not (yet) that it is the blood of anyone in particular.

Spectacular advances

In America the famous Crime Detection Laboratory in the Northwestern University at Chicago has advanced the boundaries of forensic science at a speed that is almost spectacular. It is still the model for most police and university crime laboratories, and the man who put it on the map was Dr. Calvin H. Goddard, universally known for his work on the linking of firearms and bullets. But of almost equal importance in that story is the name of Charles E. Waite of the New York State Prosecutor's Office—a

man who "solved crimes as a hobby" and became involved, in 1916, in the investigation of a gun murder in Orleans County, New York. It was the case of Charles E. Stielow, a farm labourer accused of shooting the farmer and his housekeeper. It was one of those American cliff-hangers in which the convicted man is actually strapped in the electric chair when the reprieve comes through. Stielow's case is known to criminologists throughout the world as the one which established the new science of forensic ballistics, by which any bullet, so long as it is not seriously distorted by impact, can be proved to have come from a particular gun. Waite proved by microphotography that the murder bullets could never have been fired from Stielow's revolver. In doing so he established not only forensic ballistics but also the probability that many a man, in that gun-ridden land, had been executed for a crime he did not commit. It wasn't long before ballistic experts were able to

prove, not merely that a bullet could *not* have been fired from gun No. 1, but that a bullet could *only* have been fired from gun No. 2.

So are the peculiarities of individual typewriters—faults in spacing, type alignments, changes in type face through wear and tear. No two machines are alike. Similarly it has long been common knowledge and experience that no two people have identical *handwriting*. This leaves us a long way from being able to prove that one man must have written two separate documents or signatures; and yet this is what handwriting experts are sometimes expected (and will sometimes even profess) to be able to "prove". Handwriting experts, in their capacity to establish the falsity or even the genuineness of "questioned documents", are often witnesses of great value; but they have limitations which the genuine experts willingly recognise, while the quacks and charlatans (e.g. those who read "character" and fortunes) recognise none.

Contradictory evidence

The trouble about expert witnesses, even scientific ones, is that they have so often been able to discredit the name of "science" by giving evidence in total opposition to each other. This gave juries —and the general public—the feeling that the best forensic science was available to the highest bidder, whether prosecution or defence; and because the prosecutor is usually the State, it has the most money. The truth is that evidence which is genuinely scientific, *exactly* provable, cannot be refuted by science itself. In Britain, before the passing of the Road Safety Act 1967 and the introduction of breathalysers and blood-alcohol tests, eminent physicians often gave evidence flatly contradicting each other about a motorist's fitness to drive. Not any more. They can't argue with a blood-alcohol reading unless they can prove (or believe they can) that it was rigged.

Thus the many forms which murder takes, the many motives behind it, have generally nourished the development of forensic science: jealousy, greed, sexual excitement, fear, misery, compassion, superstition, political idealism, bravado. Each of them is likely to involve methods of aggression, and of concealment, which the scientific investigator is now more and more likely to discover or defeat. From 1910, when Hawley Harvey Crippen was arrested in mid-Atlantic as a result of a police radio message—the very first use of wireless telegraphy in a criminal case— until the modern use of microscopy, tape-recorded "voice-prints", the analysis of poisons, etc., the swift progress of modern technology has gone on increasing the greatest of all deterrents to murder: the growing certainty of detection.

JEALOUSY

IT CAN be stronger than the love it so often accompanies. Jealousy is the most potent of human emotions . . . and often the most potently poisonous. The green-eyed monster, as Shakespeare called it, is something of a mass-murderer . . . with a spectacular style in killing. But is a passion-crazed person insane?

Popperfoto

IN THE annals of homicide, there are few truly unique crimes. Most types of murder have been committed before, and will be committed again. Yet there is a bizarre and ghastly originality about the murder committed by a middle-aged Victorian lady named Christiana Edmunds in 1871. In the second part of the nineteenth century, Brighton, in southern England, was a highly respectable seaside town, much favoured by the retired middle classes. Christiana Edmunds was a bad-tempered, sharp-tongued virgin who lived there

with her aged mother. Her exact age is not known, but descriptions of her bring to mind lyricist W. S. Gilbert's lady who could "very well pass for forty-three in the dusk with the light behind her".

Life for the waspish Miss Edmunds was unexciting, and she had few male acquaintances. Predictably, she was subject to attacks of headaches and other neurotic ailments. One day when the headache was exceptionally severe, a new doctor was called in, the charming and popular Dr. Beard. He divined correctly that Miss

THREE'S A CROWD . . . so one man had to die. Caught in an emotional whirlpool, Edith Thompson persuaded her lover (left) to kill her husband (right).

Edmunds needed affection and attention rather than aspirin. He only intended to be kind; but his manner was so captivating that by the time he left the room, Miss Edmunds was wildly infatuated with him. A short while later she began to write to him long and emotional letters. He was too good-natured to rebuff her, and pen-

35

ned kindly replies. At this point, Christiana Edmunds became convinced that Dr. Beard was willing to marry her – or would be, if he hadn't already happened to be married. Mrs. Beard was younger and more attractive than Miss Edmunds; the benevolent Dr. Beard would not abandon her by choice.

One day Christiana Edmunds called on Mrs. Beard for tea, and presented her with a box of chocolates. In the Victorian era, chocolates were not sealed in cellophane; the confectioner often provided the box himself, and put the chocolates in by hand. So Mrs. Beard was unsuspicious when her visitor opened the box and insisted that she should eat a chocolate with her tea. She bit into a chocolate cream, which was so bitter that she instantly spat it out. Miss Edmunds was apologetic; she said it must be the fault of the confectioner. Mrs. Beard

pretended to agree; but as soon as her husband returned home, she told him that his "mad female admirer" had tried to poison her. Dr. Beard agreed. He called on Miss Edmunds and told her firmly that their acquaintance must come to an end immediately.

Outrageous story

Miss Edmunds was lucky; she had escaped being arrested as a poisoner. But she was too hysterical to see it that way. She collapsed with nervous prostration. All she could think of for days was that Dr. and Mrs. Beard suspected her of attempted murder, and might well be repeating their "outrageous story" to their acquaintances. Tortured by this conviction, she conceived an extraordinary scheme for vindicating herself. If someone else—someone totally unknown to her—should die of a poisoned chocolate from

the same confectioner, it would prove that the chocolates were to blame. Her next problem was how to insert poison into chocolates that were still in the shop. She overcame this difficulty by accosting a small boy in the street, and asking him to go and buy her half a pound of chocolates. With considerable care, she put strychnine into them. Then she found another small boy to take them back to the shop and explain that they were not the kind she wanted. The unsuspecting assistant changed them. A few days went by, and no one died. Miss Edmunds got impatient, and sent another youngster to buy chocolates. Still nothing happened. She had obtained the strychnine in March 1871, and as April passed, and then the first week of June, she began to despair of her plan. Gradually, however, people started to purchase the poisoned chocolates; some felt sick, and complained to

the confectioner that the sweets were bitter. But it was not until June 12, 1871, that a four-year-old boy accepted a chocolate cream from his uncle, and died within half an hour of strychnine poisoning.

The result was all that Miss Edmunds could wish. The story was picked up by newspapers all over England. The confectioner's chocolates were examined, and some were found to contain strychnine. No one doubted that it was an unfortunate accident; nevertheless, it created panic.

Curiosity aroused

Meanwhile, Dr. Beard failed to call on Miss Edmunds to apologize for doing her an injustice. She wondered how she could best remind him of the "insult" he had paid her. She even went to the local police, and offered to give evidence at the inquest about her own experience of bitter chocolates. But the officers were too busy to bother with her. They were fully occupied with routine enquiries at chemist's shops. All recent purchasers of strychnine were checked; all were able to prove they had a legitimate reason for wanting it. All, that is, except a "Mrs. Woods", of Hill Side, Kingston, Surrey, who could not be traced. But since the coroner had by then recorded a verdict of accidental death on the little

boy, this hardly seemed to matter. Or it didn't until the chemist told the police that his register had been borrowed, ostensibly by the coroner. And that the date on which this had happened was *after* the inquest. Their curiosity aroused, the police examined the register more closely, and found that a page had been torn out — the page before "Mrs. Woods's" entry. A messenger had apparently called at the shop with a letter signed with the coroner's name.

Now "Mrs. Woods" came under suspicion, and it was not difficult to trace her, and to identify her as Christiana Edmunds. The police got hold of a specimen of her handwriting — which was identical with the signature of Mrs. Woods. Officers questioned hundreds of small boys, and found the ones who had bought the chocolates and returned them to the shop. Without further ado Christiana Edmunds was arrested. She was tried in January 1872, and her defence pleaded insanity — a plea which the court refused to accept. Dr. Beard's letters to her were read aloud. They seemed unnecessarily affectionate, and the doctor explained that he was convinced Miss Edmunds would lose her reason if he rebuffed her. Gossips took a less charitable view, and as a result his practice suffered. Miss Edmunds was found guilty and sentenced to death. She was reprieved, however, and

spent the rest of her life in Broadmoor — the State institution for the criminally insane, built in 1863 in Berkshire. There she exercised her bad temper and imperious manners on the other prisoners, and regarded herself as the social leader of the place. If it had not been for her curious mistake in tearing out the wrong page of the poisons book, she might have lived on into old age as a respectable, if discontented, member of Brighton society.

Violent infatuation

On one issue, however, there is no doubt. Christiana Edmunds *was* insane. Dr. Beard was telling the truth when he said she might lose her reason if he rejected her. For her behaviour — offering to testify at the inquest, sending for the poisons book, and tearing out the wrong page — was typical of the attention-seeking lunatic. Another strychnine poisoner, the Glasgow-born Victorian women murderer, Dr. Neil Cream, drew the noose around his own neck by writing letters in which he accused other people of the crimes he had committed in both Chicago and London. Like Miss Edmunds, he also approached the police and offered to testify at a time when no one suspected him. This curious kind of exhibitionism, directed at self-destruction, is also manifested by the great majority of "jealousy-killers".

This suggests an unorthodox conclusion: that most people who kill out of jealousy are insane, and should be treated as such. The French have always recognized the *crime passionel* as a special category, amounting to second-degree murder. But the English and the Americans are inclined to take a moralistic standpoint. They feel that passion is no excuse for murder. Self-control is what counts, and the person who gets carried away by sexual jealousy deserves all he gets. This view is based on logic, but not upon fact. The court that rejected Miss Edmunds's plea of insanity felt that a wicked and selfish woman *could* value her reputation so highly that she would commit murder to make people think well of her. And no doubt such a person could exist. The fact remains that Miss Edmunds was insane rather than wicked. Her mother suspected it before she met Dr. Beard; and her violent infatuation for the doctor suddenly brought it out.

Where English law is concerned, the problem lies in the definition of insanity. In 1843, a young schizophrenic called Daniel M'Naghten, decided to murder Prime Minister Sir Robert Peel — the founder of the British police system — whom he was convinced was persecuting him. He mistook Peel's private secretary, Edward Drummond, for the Prime Minister, and shot him in the back in Whitehall, killing him. At his trial the prosecution presented witness after witness to prove that he was sane, and his chances of acquital looked slim. But a brilliant defence saved him—and also changed the course of legal history, by establishing that a criminal who does not know the nature of his act is not guilty by reason of insanity.

In that sense, however, Christiana Edmunds was not insane. She was not suffering from delusions; she intended to kill. Obviously, there is something wrong with the M'Naghten definition of insanity. It doesn't require delusions; just a strange kind of blindness. Sanity depends on how you *react* to a chal-

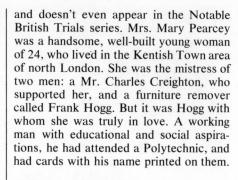

lenge. The twentieth-century French novelist Marcel Proust gives a graphic example of this. Suppose you are standing in a crowded street, talking to someone about how much you hate crowds. Your companion says he quite agrees—and then pulls out a revolver and proceeds to shoot the passers-by. It is not his hatred of crowds that makes him insane: you may hate them just as much yourself. It is his *reaction* to his hatred: what he thinks permissible. Judged by this standard, most of the famous jealousy killers were at least partly insane. This certainly applies to Britain's three most notorious cases: Mrs. Pearcey, Edith Thompson, and Ruth Ellis.

The Pearcey case is now half-forgotten,

and doesn't even appear in the Notable British Trials series. Mrs. Mary Pearcey was a handsome, well-built young woman of 24, who lived in the Kentish Town area of north London. She was the mistress of two men: a Mr. Charles Creighton, who supported her, and a furniture remover called Frank Hogg. But it was Hogg with whom she was truly in love. A working man with educational and social aspirations, he had attended a Polytechnic, and had cards with his name printed on them.

Unlucky creature

He seemed to be above the slum environment in which he lived with his young wife and baby. As to his wife, Phoebe, she was an ailing, unlucky sort of creature. Hogg had married her because she was three months pregnant with his child, and ever since her marriage, Phoebe Hogg had been worried about her husband's interest in the handsome Mrs. Pearcey.

On Friday, October 24, 1890, Mrs. Pearcey invited Phoebe Hogg to her house for tea. Phoebe arrived with her baby in the pram at about half past three. She was never seen alive again. Late that evening, her body was found not far away in Crossfield Road, Hampstead, with the throat cut from ear to ear. The baby carriage, saturated with blood, was found in nearby Hamilton Terrace, St. John's Wood, and the corpse of the 18-month-old girl was discovered later on building land nearby. When reports of the murder appeared in the newspapers the next morning, Phoebe's sister-in-law Clara called on Mrs. Pearcey, and asked her to accompany her to the morgue to see the corpse. Mrs. Pearcey went, but she found the sight upsetting.

A detective Inspector who was in the morgue considered her behaviour "very suspicious", and his men duly went to search Mrs. Pearcey's home. Mrs. Pearcey didn't openly object to this, and while the search progressed, she sat down at the piano and burst into song. The police found bloodstains all over the place; when they asked Mrs. Pearcey what she'd been doing, she went on singing: "Killing mice, killing mice, killing mice."

After that the trial was a straightforward affair. There was no doubt about Mrs. Pearcey's guilt. Neighbours testified to hearing screams coming from the

HISTORIC CASE: The last woman to be hanged in Britain was Ruth Ellis (right). In the London of the 1950's, her lifestyle was judged to be both glamorous and immoral. She shot her lover (top) with a Smith & Wesson .38 revolver outside a bar in fashionable Hampstead, London. Left: the leader of a protest against her execution.

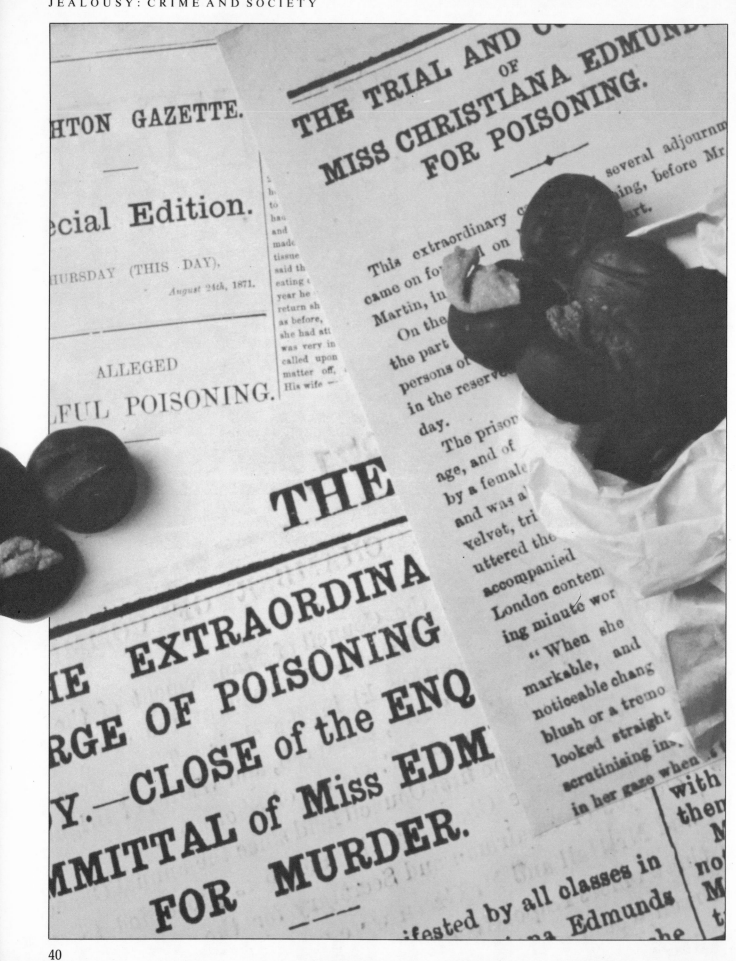

house around teatime on the Friday afternoon. The curtains had been drawn all day, Mrs. Pearcey having told a neighbour that her brother had died. Medical evidence showed that Phoebe Hogg had been knocked unconscious with three violent blows on the head before her throat was cut. Mrs. Pearcey then placed the body in the baby carriage, and put the baby on top of it—by this time, she had probably suffocated the child, although this was not definitely established. She covered both bodies with a black shawl, and then set out pushing the baby carriage past her victim's house, on towards Hampstead. In spite of the dark, several people saw her. It was early, and the streets were crowded with Friday shoppers. She dumped the body of the mother in Crossfield Road, then went on a mile to Finchley Road, where she threw out the baby, then another mile farther on to leave the baby carriage.

Curious conduct

Her curious conduct while the police were searching the house suggests that, at the time, she wanted to be thought insane. In fact, she pleaded innocence, in the face of all the facts, and maintained her innocence to the gallows. Everything about the crime, however, points to insanity. She obviously planned it—hence the story about her dead brother and the drawing of all the curtains—but there wasn't a chance in a thousand of her getting away with it. She could have smothered the unconscious Phoebe; instead she cut her throat, so drenching the house with blood. Then, instead of waiting until midnight, when the streets would be quiet, she walked along the busy Prince of Wales Road, where she was immediately recognized by several acquaintances. Mrs. Pearcey, however, was not insane within the meaning of the M'Naghten rules; there were no delusions. Yet she was so obsessed by the thought of Frank Hogg that she couldn't think straight. Under the circumstances, to describe her as sane is merely a quibble.

Emotional fantasy

Neither Edith Thompson nor Ruth Ellis was quite so obviously obsessional. Both lived in a strange, twilight world of emotional fantasy. The defenders of Edith Thompson say that the whole scheme for killing her husband was pure make-believe, and that even the great pathologist, Sir Bernard Spilsbury, agreed that her story of administering powdered glass ("big pieces, too") was absurd.

CHOCOLATES, tea and strychnine were served to begin an extraordinary chapter of crime for Christiana Edmunds, a waspish virgin insane with jealous love. Her bizarre murder-plan was unique.

THE RESPECTABLE seaside resort of Brighton was favoured by the retired middle classes in Victorian times. Here in West Street was the fatal sweetshop. The child victim lodged in the arrowed house.

This is probably true; but her letters reveal that it was she who first thought up the notion that her husband should die, and she who kept urging her lover, Frederick Bywaters, to kill him. On the other hand, her distress when it actually happened was obviously real: the frenzied cry of "Don't, oh don't!", and her sobs as she rushed to find help. It is the completely self-contradictory nature of her impulses that suggests she was caught in the same emotional whirlpool as Christiana Edmunds and Mrs. Pearcey. As to Bywaters, he was half-insane with jealousy when he stabbed Percy Thompson—convinced that the woman he loved was being virtually raped by her sex-hungry husband. Like Thompson himself, he was a victim of Edith's strange fantasies.

On the surface of it, the Ruth Ellis case seems a classic *crime passionel*. Ellis, a 28-year-old, shot her ex-lover

David Blakely outside the Magdala public house in Hampstead, North London, in April 1955. She was incensed, so she claimed, by the fact that he was having an affair with another woman. On closer examination her "motive" ceases to make sense. Although Ruth Ellis and David Blakely had been passionate, if quarrelsome lovers for two years, both had slept with other people. At the time she killed Blakely, Ruth Ellis was living with one man, sleeping with another, and married to a third. Clive Gunnell of England's Westward Television, who was with Blakely when he was shot, has stated that Ruth Ellis—who had had a miscarriage two weeks before committing the murder—was basically a kind of exhibitionist: "She wanted to be famous." Or notorious. It begins to sound altogether more like the "exhibitionism" of Neill Cream and Christiana Edmunds.

A British jury found Ruth Ellis guilty, and, despite a widespread public outcry, she was hanged—the last woman to die on the gallows in England. The 1951 case of Pauline Dubuisson, which has many similar features, reveals the altogether more flexible attitude of the French. In France, the penalty for a *crime passionel* may be as little as a few months in prison; the penalty for capital murder is death. When 24-year-old Pauline Dubuisson's former lover was found shot through the head in his Paris apartment, it certainly seemed to be a *crime passionel*. Pauline had turned on the gas tap and lay unconscious by the stove. Closer investigation revealed that she had bought the gun weeks before, and had made several threats against medical student Felix Bailly's life. This made it a capital murder charge.

Pauline Dubuisson proved to be a tempestuous character. Her diary revealed such a lurid sex life that the police described it as her "orgy book". During the war she had been the mistress of a German colonel and held nude orgies with soldiers; after the liberation of France indignant neighbours had shaved her head. She was undoubtedly a nymphomaniac, sleeping with as many men as possible and recording their lovemaking techniques. She had an affair with Bailly which ended when he went to study in Paris. In any case, he was tormented by jealousy at her infidelities. In Paris, he became engaged to a less volatile girl. Pauline heard about it, and went to see him in Paris; she later claimed they again became lovers for a while. Then Felix told her their relationship was finally over. This was the point at which she bought the revolver, and announced her intention of shooting him. She found him in his apartment early one morning, and shot him in the back of the neck.

Lasting sentiment

The French jury decided that, whatever the motive was, it was not straightforward jealousy. Pauline was too emotionally mixed up for that. But neither was it an ordinary premeditated murder. The jurors therefore compromised, and found her guilty of non-capital murder, which involved life imprisonment. In France, Ruth Ellis would have received the same benefit of the doubt. For jealousy—described by Shakespeare as the "green-eyed monster"—can sometimes be as strong, if not stronger, than the love it so frequently accompanies. "I can't really love him because I'm not jealous of him," women sometimes say. Pauline Dubuisson took this a stage further when she stated, "I wanted to force myself to love other people, in order to persuade myself I was capable of having lasting sentiment for Felix."

The subject is as complex, dark, and contradictory as the workings of the human mind itself. But to the seventeenth-century French aristocrat and moralist, La Rochefoucauld, there was no mystery about jealousy at all. He summed up and dismissed the emotion in his famous book of *Maxims,* when he wrote: "In jealousy there is more self-love than love."

MURDER HOUSE: A woman's throat was cut, and her baby murdered, behind carefully-drawn curtains in this house. The murderess then placed both bodies in the baby's pram, covered them with a shawl, and wheeled them through the streets before dumping them. Not long after the murders, Priory Street was tactfully re-named Ivor Street. It was later completely redecorated.

THE SOCIALITE AND THE PLAYBOY

Thaw and White . . . and the champagne murder at Madison Square Gardens

New York socialites had packed into Madison Square Garden for the opening of a new musical, *Mamzelle Champagne*. The show was not going well. In the informal atmosphere of the roof garden, where everyone sat at tables instead of in conventional theatre seats, people moved about, chatting with friends. Suddenly there was a gunshot, followed by two more. Every eye turned to Stanford White, at 52 America's most distinguished architect. Slowly his elbow slipped from the table at which he had been sitting alone. The table overturned with a tinkle of breaking glass, and White slumped to the floor with a bullet in his brain and two more in his left shoulder.

Over him, unmoved, a smoking pistol in his hand, stood Harry Kendall Thaw, 34-year-old playboy and wastrel son of a Pittsburgh railroad and coke magnate. There was silence for a moment. Then Thaw, the pistol held above his head, made his way out of the roof garden to join his wife, Evelyn, and two guests in the elevator lobby.

They had all got up to leave a few moments earlier at Evelyn's instigation

SENSATIONAL SHOOTING: The gunman was the son of a railroad magnate . . . the victim was the most famous architect in all America.

because the show was so boring. She had reached the lobby with the guests before realizing that her husband was not with them. Then came the shots. "Good God, Harry, what have you done?" she asked in bewilderment as he joined them with the pistol still clutched over his head.

Meantime, back in the roof garden, screaming women fought their way to the

43

HER BEAUTY was as vague and intangible as that of a lily, or any other frail or delicate thing. It lay over her face like a gossamer veil . . . and she haunted Harry Thaw even in his cell, according to a newspaper cartoonist on the New York "Evening Journal".

Culver

exit. The manager tried to restore order by jumping on a table and shouting: "Go on playing. Bring on the chorus." The shock of having a murder committed before their eyes, however, seemed to have paralyzed both musicians and chorus girls. Then a doctor fought his way through the stampeding audience to White's side. He lay in a pool of blood, his face blackened and unrecognizable from powder burns. He was already dead.

Out in the elevator lobby, a fireman disarmed Thaw, who did not offer any resistance. A few moments later a policeman arrived and arrested him. Together they walked to the nearest police station in the Tenderloin—a district notorious for its prostitution, lawlessness, and graft. There Thaw identified himself as "John Smith", a student, of 18 Lafayette Square, Philadelphia. A visiting card found on him when he was searched, however, revealed his real name.

Great party-goer

Thaw made no comment. "Why did you do this?" the sergeant in charge asked him. "I can't say," Thaw answered laconically. Several reporters had tracked him down by this time, but Thaw—at least until he had consulted his lawyer— refused to make any further statement.

The shooting took place on the night of June 25, 1906. The next day it dominated the front pages of newspapers across

the United States. Even the New York *Times,* not given to sensationalism, ran the heading:

THAW MURDERS STANFORD
WHITE
Shoots Him on the Madison
Square Garden Roof
ABOUT EVELYN NESBIT
"You've Ruined My Life," He
Cries and Fires
AUDIENCE IN A PANIC
Chairs and Tables Are Overturned
in a Wild Scramble
For the Exits

Stanford White, a big man with a thatch of red hair and a moustache to match, was a national figure. He has been credited with being the greatest single influence in beautifying the rather drab, brownstone New York City of the nineteenth century. Madison Square Garden itself, with its amphitheatre for horse shows and prize fights, and its theatre, roof garden, restaurant, and arcade of fashionable shops, was his creation. So were the memorial arch at Washington Square and the Hall of Fame at New York university.

But there was another side to the dignified architect. He enjoyed mixing in theatrical and Bohemian circles, was a great party-goer, and, although married, had a quick eye for a pretty girl. In fact, it was only the stage manager's promise to introduce him to a chorus girl who

had taken his fancy, that kept him sitting through the dull *Mamzelle Champagne.*

For his part, Thaw's life had consisted of one notorious escapade after another. During a brief spell at Harvard, he had devoted himself almost exclusively to studying the finer points of poker. Later, he tried to ride a horse into one of several exclusive New York clubs which had barred him. He had also driven a car through a display window, lost $40,000 in a single poker game, and thrown a party in Paris at which his guests were the French capital's leading whores.

Unspecified services

The bill for the Paris party, including jewellery and trinkets handed out to his guests for unspecified services rendered, was said to be $50,000. It was hardly surprising, therefore, that on the death of his father, Thaw found himself cut off with an allowance of $200 a month until such time as he showed himself responsible enough to handle his $5 million share of the $40 million estate. However, his doting mother, Mrs. William Thaw, enabled him to resume the wastrel's life he enjoyed by upping his allowance again to $80,000 a year.

As might be expected, it was sex that led to the tragic crossing of the paths of White and Thaw. Thaw's wife was the former Evelyn Nesbit, a photographer's model who graduated to the chorus of

HE MISSED his love in jail, but he did not forgo all his pleasures. Prison breakfast was lavish for Harry Thaw, a man of notorious and costly escapades.

the famous musical *Floradora*. She was one of the beauties asked nightly: "Tell me, pretty maiden, are there any more at home like you?"

She had an oval face, copper curls, hazel eyes, a voluptuous mouth, and a splendid figure. When Thaw eventually came to trial, and his wife was called to give evidence, columnist Dorothy Dix, wrote: "Her beauty consists in something as vague and intangible as that of a lily or any other frail or delicate thing. It is something that lies over her face like a gossamer veil, infinitely appealing . . ."

Despite, or possibly because of, her apparent frailty, White had seduced her when she was just 16. Thaw had married her on April 4, 1905—14 months before the shooting—when she was 20. In the interval, he had twice lived with her as man and wife on trips to Europe, and had caused a major New York scandal when the two of them were evicted from a hotel where they were again cohabiting.

In the events which followed the shooting, the principals fell into roles as clearly defined as those in an old-fashioned melodrama. White was the aging roué, seducer of young girls . . . Thaw the chivalrous avenger, who dwelt so long on his wife's dishonouring that he eventually had a "brainstorm" and killed the man who had wronged her . . . Evelyn, the young innocent, brought to a life of shame by a man she looked upon almost as a father, now standing loyally by the man she loved, the man who had made an honest woman of her.

Mrs. Thaw, Senr., who was in England visiting her daughter, the Countess of Yarmouth, also announced that she was returning to the United States to stand by her son. "I am prepared to pay a million dollars to save his life," she said.

Thaw's trial did not begin until January 21, 1907. In the intervening seven months, White underwent a character assassination in the newspapers that was unprecedented for an American of distinction moving in respectable society. There were so many tales about his amorous activities that, for even half to be true, he would have had to have slept with a large proportion of the women and teenage girls in New York.

A typical story concerned a 15-year-old model, Susie Johnson, who had been the highlight of a Bohemian party which White attended. She had risen out of a giant pie and exhibited her charms—"lilliputian, tender, rose-coloured breasts, and evasive hips, proclaiming precocious puberty"—clad only in a wisp of chiffon.

White was so taken with her, the story in the New York *Evening Journal* went on, that he plied her with champagne and, when she was in a stupefied condition, took her back to his apartment—"furnished with Oriental splendour"—and seduced her. Later, he turned her out penniless. "Girls, if you are poor, stay in the safe factory or kitchen," were the last words of the story which, it was said, Susie had told to a friend before dying at the age of 23 and being buried in a pauper's grave.

The campaign of slander and vilification against White was masterminded by Ben Atwell, a press agent hired by Thaw's mother. Mrs. Thaw Senr. also backed a play based loosely on the construction which the yellow press put on the known events.

Gave girls swings

It featured three characters named Harold Daw, Emeline Hudspeth Daw, and Stanford Black. On his first appearance, Black brutally assaulted a blind man who was asking for news of his beautiful young daughter. The Girl in the Pie incident was featured in another lurid scene. The play ended with Daw shooting Black during a performance in a roof garden theatre, then declaring from his cell at The Tombs (where Thaw was being held awaiting trial):

"No jury on earth will send me to the

chair, no matter what I have done or what I have been, for killing the man who defamed my wife. That is the unwritten law made by men themselves, and upon its virtue I will stake my life."

There is evidence that the episode with Susie Johnson did take place at a party, given by an artist friend, which White attended. It seems probable, however, that the seduction part of the tale was inspired by what happened to Evelyn Nesbit before she became Mrs. Harry Thaw, and was seen as a useful overture to the story she would tell in court.

Evelyn first met Thaw in the summer of 1901 when she was 16 and a girlfriend took her to lunch at the architect's apartment on West 24th Street. A second man was there but left after the meal. White then took the two girls upstairs to a room where there was a red velvet swing. He gave the girls swings in turn. "Right up to the ceiling," Evelyn recalled. "They had a big Japanese umbrella on the ceiling, so when we were swung up very high our feet passed through it."

White did not lose touch with his new discovery. He met her mother by arrangement and suggested that Evelyn should have some dental treatment. He sent her a hat, a feather boa, and a long red cape.

Throughout, he always behaved with the utmost correctness. "At supper," said Evelyn, "he wouldn't let me have but one glass of champagne, and he said

45

I mustn't stay up late. He took me home himself to the Arlington Hotel, where we were staying, and knocked at my mother's door."

Then came the day when Evelyn's mother decided to visit friends in Pittsburgh, but did not like to leave her daughter alone in New York. When he heard of this, White immediately offered his services. "You may leave her with me in perfect safety," he said. "I will take care of her." He also made Evelyn promise that she would not go out with anyone but him while her mother was away.

Mirrors round bed

White paid for her mother's trip and, the second night after her departure, sent a note to the theatre – Evelyn by this time was appearing in *Floradora* – asking her to a party at the West 24th Street apartment. When she got there, however, there were just the two of them. "The others have turned us down," White explained somewhat lamely.

He suggested they should have something to eat nevertheless, and afterwards offered to show her the rooms she hadn't seen on her previous visit. He took her up some tiny back stairs to a bedroom. "He poured me a glass of champagne," said Evelyn. "I don't know whether it was a minute after or two minutes after, but a pounding began in my ears, then the whole room seemed to go round."

When she came to, she said, she was in bed. All her clothes had been torn off. White, naked, lay beside her. There were mirrors all round the bed. "I started to scream," she said. "Mr. White tried to quieten me. I don't remember how I got my clothes on or how I went home, but he took me home. Then he went away and left me, and I sat up all night."

White called the next day and found her still sitting in a chair, staring out of the window. "Why don't you look at me, child?" he asked. "Because I can't," she replied. Then he told her not to worry because "Everyone does those things" She asked if the *Floradora* sextet, and various people she had met with White, made love. "They all do," he said, adding that the most important thing was not to be found out, and making her promise not to say a word to her mother about what had happened.

Amid all the subsequent mudslinging, Thaw, the "chivalrous avenger", did not escape. Before the trial one enterprising reporter unearthed details of a suit brought against him by a girl named Ethel Thomas in 1902. She told how, at the start of their relationship, Thaw had lavished affection upon her and bought her flowers and jewellery.

"But one day," she went on, "I met him by appointment, and, while we were walking towards his apartment at the Bedford, 304 Fifth Avenue, he stopped at a store and bought a dog whip. I asked him what that was for and he replied laughingly: 'That's for you, dear.' I thought he was joking, but no sooner were we in his apartment and the door locked than his entire demeanour changed. A wild expression came into his eyes, and he seized me and with his whip beat me until my clothes hung in tatters.'"

Evelyn, too, it was said, had undergone a similar experience during the first of her two European holidays with Thaw. She had suffered so much at his hands, in fact, that, on her return, she had gone to Abe Hummel, a celebrated shyster lawyer, and sworn an affidavit about the way Thaw had treated her.

The trouble had begun while they were staying at Schloss Katzenstein, a castle Thaw had rented in the Austrian Tyrol. One morning she had come down to breakfast wearing only a bathrobe. After the meal Thaw accompanied her to her bedroom where, "without any provocation", he grasped me by the throat and tore the bathrobe from my body, leaving me entirely nude except for my slippers.

". . . His eyes were glaring and he had in his right hand a cowhide whip. He seized hold of me and threw me on the bed. I was powerless and attempted to scream, but Thaw placed his fingers in my mouth and tried to choke me. He then, without any provocation, and without the slightest reason, began to inflict on me several severe and violent blows with the cowhide whip.

Besought him to desist

"So brutally did he assault me that my skin was cut and bruised. I besought him to desist, but he refused. I was so exhausted that I shouted and cried. He stopped every minute or so to rest, and then renewed his attack upon me, which he continued for about seven minutes. He acted like a demented man. I was absolutely in fear of my life . . . It was nearly three weeks before I was sufficiently recovered to be able to get out of my bed and walk.

"During all the time I travelled with Thaw, he would make the slightest pretext an excuse for a terrific assault on me . . . He also entered my bed and, without any consent, repeatedly wronged me. I reproved him for his conduct, but he compelled me to submit, threatening to beat and kill me if I did not do so . . ." It was on this trip, she also claimed, that she had discovered Thaw was a cocaine addict.

Why, people wondered, had she married a man who treated her so badly? Evelyn's motives seem clear – the desire for wealth and position. Thaw, it appears, was "persuaded" to marry her by White at her family's instigation. The alternative to this was a charge – backed up by the affidavit – of corrupting a minor (Evelyn had been only 18 at the time of her first European holiday with Thaw).

The trial, which began on January 21, 1907, did not end until April 11. Then, after being out for more than 24 hours while an inquisitive crowd of 10,000 milled around under the courtroom windows, the jury announced that they had been unable to reach a verdict. On the final ballot, it was later learned, seven had voted Thaw guilty of first-degree murder, five had voted him not guilty by reason of insanity.

Thaw was kept in custody until his second trial started early in January 1908. This time his "ordeal" was shorter. On February 1 the jury – after again being out for more than 24 hours – found him not guilty by reason of insanity, and he was committed to the New York state asylum for the criminal insane.

Escape by limousine

Attempts by his lawyers to get him released were protracted and unsuccessful, and, on the morning of August 17, 1913, Thaw escaped from the asylum. With the aid of a limousine waiting outside the gates, he then sought refuge in Canada. The next month, under heavy pressure from the U.S. government, the Canadian Minister of Justice agreed to return him to the United States.

Put in jail in Concord, New Hampshire, Thaw fought a long legal battle against being returned to New York. It was not until December 1914 – over a year later – that the U.S. Supreme Court decided that this should happen. Back in New York, Thaw faced another long trial at which most of the evidence given at the two previous hearings was repeated. Finally, on July 16, 1915, he was declared sane and not guilty of all charges.

It was a victory of money over justice, and over commonsense for, only 18 months later, he was indicted for kidnapping and brutally whipping Frederick Gump Junr., a 19-year-old Kansas City youth. Once again Thaw was declared insane, but a week-long court hearing reversed the decision.

His bizarre behaviour periodically made the headlines until his death in February 1947, at the age of 76, after a heart attack. A photograph at the time showed him bespectacled and shrunken, looking more like a retired business executive than the sadistic paranoiac that he was.

FINAL TRIANGLE: Was the appealing Evelyn really a young innocent? Was White a father-figure turned seducer? Was young Thaw a chivalrous avenger? It was melodrama in the old-fashioned style.

DO SOMETHING DESPERATE, DARLING

She died for her vanity . . . and a nation's morals. But did she really persuade her masterful lover to kill her "cad" of a husband? The fatal passion of Edith Thompson and Frederick Bywaters was writ large in love letters. They caused a sensation in court . . . a story of love and murder in the suburbs.

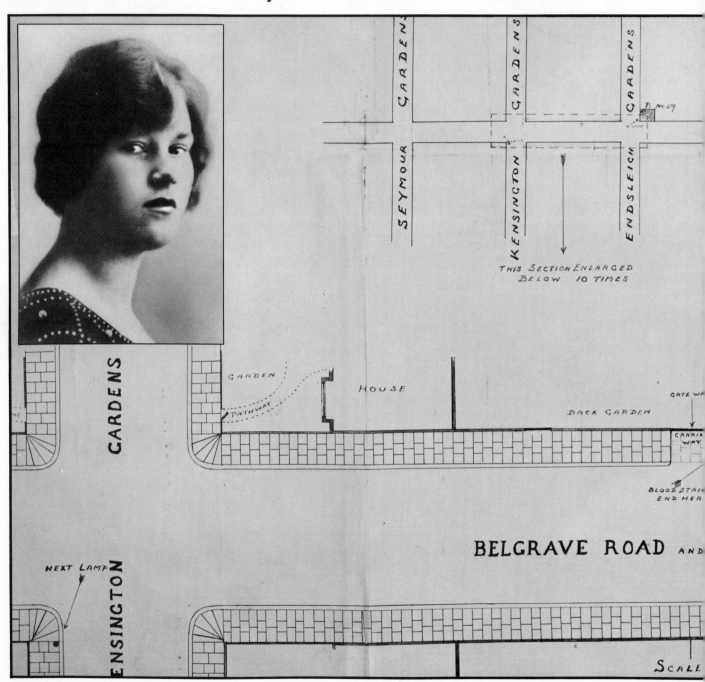

THE TRIAL which began in No. 1 Court at the Old Bailey in London on the morning of December 6, 1922, before a jury of eleven men and one woman was unquestionably the most sensational one of the year in England if not for the whole period between the two World Wars. It aroused nationwide interest, so much so that when the court doors were opened there was a line outside of more than 50 people which had formed during the previous afternoon and throughout the night for the few seats available in the public gallery.

The accused were Frederick ("Freddy") Bywaters, a 20-year-old laundry steward on an ocean liner, and his mistress Edith ("Edie") Thompson, a married woman, who worked as manageress-bookkeeper in a firm of wholesale milliners in the City of London and was eight years older than her lover. Just over two months previously, Edith's husband Percy Thompson, a 32-year-old shipping clerk, had been killed near his home at Ilford, a small town in London's commuter belt, when returning late one night with his wife. Bywaters was charged with his murder, while Edith Thompson was charged with inciting her lover to carry out the killing after she had unsuccessfully tried to kill him herself by giving him poison and mixing powdered glass with his food.

As soon as the judge, the venerable-looking Mr. Justice Shearman, had taken his place on the Bench in the historic wood-panelled courtroom, the accused were brought up by a policeman and a female wardress from the cells below where they had been anxiously waiting. As they took their places in the dock, Bywaters, a good-looking youth with curly dark hair, gave the impression of being a virile almost animal type, essentially a

MURDERER: Youthful seaman Frederick Bywaters was a man of action. His mistress's life was being "made hell" by her husband. So Bywaters stabbed the husband, while Edith cried, "Oh, don't, oh, don't!" In the death cell, Bywaters insisted: "She never planned it. She's innocent."

man of action, determined and masterful. His companion, however, looked pale, and she trembled slightly as she followed Bywaters and gave her plea to the Clerk of the Court as he had done: "Not guilty".

Edith Thompson's defence was in the hands of Sir Henry Curtis-Bennett, King's Counsel, who was a fashionable leading advocate of the day in criminal cases. As his counsel Bywaters had Mr. Cecil Whiteley, another eminent K.C. and a prominent criminal lawyer. The prosecuting team was led by the Solicitor-General, Sir Thomas Inskip, since it was customary for a Law Officer of the Crown to prosecute in any case involving a poison charge. Sir Thomas was a stern Sabbatarian and no criminal could expect any mercy at his hands.

Enough for an elephant

On the table in front of the Solicitor-General was a large bundle of letters, 62 in all, which Edith Thompson had written to Bywaters in the course of their love affair and which had been recovered by the police, some in the house in London where Bywaters had lived with his mother and others in his locker on his ship. Some of them were to be described by the judge as "gush". Certainly Edith analyzed her feelings and emotions in remarkable detail. Her favourite term of endearment for her lover was "Darlingest", contracted to "Darlint". The letters breathed a curious passion, in which the writer depicted herself as half mother and half slave-mistress. She also described how she had tried to do away with her husband on several occasions.

"You said it was enough for an elephant," she wrote in one letter. "Perhaps it was. But you don't allow for the taste making it possible for only a small quantity to be taken." And again: "I'm going to try the glass again occasionally — when it's safe. I've got an electric light globe this time." In fact, according to her, she used the light bulb three times in his food, "but the third time he found a piece — so I've given it up — until you come home."

Be jealous, darling

They were foolish letters to write and even more foolish to keep. Incidentally Edith Thompson never referred to her husband in them by his Christian name, but always as "he" or "him". In one letter she wrote:

"Yes, darlint, you are jealous of *him* — but I want you to be — he has the right by law to all that you have the right by nature and love — yes, darlint, be jealous, so much that you will do something desperate."

In this letter she enclosed a cutting from a newspaper which described how a

Conway

Syndication International

VICTIM (left and above) with wife. "Is marriage improper because the law acknowledges it? Is illicit love noble?" A "wicked affection" ended in a fatal stabbing. The knife was found in a grate at the side of Belgrave Road. "Right-minded persons will be filled with disgust," said the judge.

woman's death had been caused by taking a bowl of broth made from the carcase of a chicken which had been killed by rat poison. Other cuttings enclosed in Edith's letters contained headings like "Patient Killed by an Overdose", "The Poisoner Curate", "Poisoned Chocolates", "Masterful Men", and "Woman the Consoler".

Compromising passages

Edith Thompson's counsel had been shown these highly compromising letters before the trial opened, since under the rules of criminal procedure the prosecution was bound to disclose them to the defence if it was intended to introduce them as evidence against her. Not only did they contain passages suggesting on the face of them that Edith had tried to kill her husband with poison and powdered glass, but they also plainly indicated that that on at least one occasion she had aborted herself and had a miscarriage after becoming pregnant by her lover.

Thus Sir Henry Curtis-Bennett had to reckon with the prosecution showing that she was not merely an adulteress but also

a self-abortionist as well as a potential murderess. The nature of her relations with her husband were also reflected in certain passages in the letters describing how, after Bywaters first went to sea, she rejected her husband's sexual approaches. Eventually, however, she yielded to him and became "the dutiful wife" which she thought was the best way to allay his suspicions if she and Bywaters had to take what she called "drastic measures".

Realizing that the letters were dynamite, Sir Henry did his best to persuade the judge to rule that they were inadmissible as evidence against his client. Therefore, as soon as the jury had been sworn, Sir Henry jumped to his feet and with a glance in the direction of the bundle of letters informed the judge that he had an objection to make to certain evidence which he understood the Solicitor-General proposed to put before the jury. The jury were then sent out of the court room while Curtis-Bennett and Inskip argued the point with the judge.

Admissible evidence

Briefly Curtis-Bennett's argument was that the letters could not and should not be admitted until the prosecution had shown that Mrs. Thompson took some active part in the murder—if it was murder—of her husband. The Solicitor-General replied by submitting that they were admissible because she was being charged as a principal in the second degree, although she did not strike the

fatal blow. "The crime is one where one hand struck the blow," said Inskip, "and we want to show by these letters that her mind conceived it and incited it—the evidence of that is the letters that Mrs. Thompson wrote to the man who struck the blow."

After listening patiently to the argument, the judge then gave his ruling. "I think these letters are admissible as evidence of intention and motive," he said, "and I shall admit them." Turning towards Edith Thompson's counsel, he added: "I do not think you can contest the letters, showing the affectionate relations between the parties, are not evidence of motive in so far as they show affection."

Sir Henry was overruled. He had done everything he could to exclude the damning letters; now he knew that the task before him was all the more difficult. He glanced at his client in the dock. Her face, almost hidden by the brim of her black velour hat, looked anxious and drawn.

The jury were then brought back to court, and the Solicitor-General proceeded to open the case for the Crown. "May it please your lordship, members of the jury," he began, "on October 4, a little after midnight, Percy Thompson was stabbed to death on his way home from Ilford station. He was in a dark part of the road, not over-well lit at the best of times, when he was struck, first of all, apparently from behind, and then in front, by some assailant. The only person

present was his wife, Mrs. Thompson, who is now in the dock. She is charged with Bywaters, who is said by the prosecution to have been the assailant, with the murder of Percy Thompson."

It was a sombre tale which the Solicitor-General went on to relate. Husband and wife had been to the theatre, and as they were walking along the road from Ilford station to the terraced row of suburban houses in Kensington Gardens where they lived, a man suddenly jumped out of the shadows. Seizing Percy Thompson by the arm, he said, "Why don't you get a divorce from your wife, you cad?"

Thompson, who appeared to recognize the man, replied, "I've got her, I'll keep her, and I'll shoot you."

Strange attacker

The assailant then pulled out a knife from his coat pocket. With it he stabbed Thompson several times, while Edith Thompson shouted, "Oh, don't! Oh, don't!" The attacker turned, ran off, and disappeared into the darkness. Meanwhile Percy Thompson fell to the ground, blood pouring from his mouth. He was dead before a doctor, who had been summoned, arrived on the scene followed by the police.

Edith Thompson was still in too hysterical a condition to tell the police very much except that her husband had been "attacked by a strange man". However, a woman named Mrs. Fanny Lester, who lived in the same house with the Thomp-

Radio Times Hulton Picture Library

NATIONWIDE INTEREST: The result is awaited outside the court. After two hours, the verdict was "guilty". Mrs. Bywaters testified at the appeal.

sons was also questioned, and it was Mrs. Lester who put the police on the track of the killer. She stated that about 18 months previously Frederick Bywaters had lodged in the house for some weeks. He had left due to a row he had had with Percy Thompson caused by the attentions Bywaters had apparently been paying Edith. The police also learned that Bywaters was a steward with the P. & O. line. In turn this led the officers to find the letters Edith had written to him and which he picked up at the various ports at which his ship called.

Stifled sobbing

Bywaters was eventually traced to the home of Edith Thompson's parents who lived at Manor Park, near Ilford. There he was arrested and taken to Ilford police station where he was formally charged with the murder. Later that day Edith Thompson was picked up and taken to the same police station where she was likewise charged on the basis of the letters with being a principal in the murder; or, alternatively, with being an accessory to it.

At this time neither she nor Freddy Bywaters knew that the other had been arrested. As she was being led past a window of the police station, she looked in and saw her lover sitting there obviously in police custody. The sight shook her extremely. "Oh, God, why did he do it?" she cried, the words coming out involuntarily between stifled sobs. "I didn't want him to do it."

Under police interrogation, Bywaters agreed with what his mistress had said. At the same time he did his best to shield her and insisted that she knew nothing of his intention to waylay Percy Thompson on their homeward journey from the theatre. Both prisoners signed statements confirming what they had told the police when they were arrested, and they were put in evidence by the prosecution in

addition to Edith Thompson's letters.

The story of the fatal encounter which Bywaters told in his statement was as follows:

"I waited for Mrs. Thompson and her husband. I pushed her to one side, also pushing him up the street . . . We struggled. I took my knife from my pocket and we fought and he got the worst of it . . .

"The reason I fought with Thompson was because he never acted like a man to his wife. He always seemed several degrees lower than a snake. I loved her and I could not go on seeing her leading that life. I did not intend to kill him. I only meant to injure him. I gave him an opportunity of standing up to me as man but he wouldn't."

Bywaters stuck to this story when he went into the witness-box on the third day of the trial, although he did qualify his admission, "I only meant to injure him," by saying that what he really intended was "to stop him from killing me."

Nor could the Solicitor-General shake him in cross-examination about his mistress's compromising letters, for which the witness had a ready explanation.

"As far as you could tell, reading these letters," Sir Thomas Inskip asked, looking sternly at the man on the witness stand, "did you ever believe in your own mind

that she herself had given any poison to her husband?"

"No," replied Bywaters with an air of self-confidence, "it never entered my mind at all. She had been reading books. She had a vivid way of declaring herself. She would read a book and imagine herself as the character in the book."

He also stated in reply to the Solicitor-General that it was Percy Thompson who attacked him first. The expression on Sir Thomas Inskip's face clearly showed that he did not believe the witness. "Do you mean to suggest that he made the first assault upon you?" he asked incredulously.

"Yes, he did."

"And that you then drew your knife?"

"I did."

"Is it the fact that you never saw any revolver or any gun at that moment?"

"I never saw it, no," Bywaters had to admit.

Mr. Cecil Whiteley, K.C., did something to repair the damage caused by this admission when he re-examined his client about the possibility of Percy Thompson having a gun. "Although I never saw a revolver," said Bywaters, "I believed that he had one, otherwise I would not have drawn my knife. I was in fear of my life."

"At any time have you had any intention to murder Mr. Thompson?" defence counsel asked in conclusion.

Tension mounted

"I have not," replied Bywaters firmly and unhesitatingly. He added that he had met Mrs. Thompson in a teashop near her place of work on the afternoon of the killing, but he strongly repudiated the prosecution's suggestion that the purpose of the meeting was to plot her husband's death.

The atmosphere of tension mounted when the usher called out "Edith Jessie Thompson", and the prisoner left the dock to follow her lover on to the witness stand. There was no need for her to testify. Had she remained silent, the prosecution could not have commented upon the fact. The only evidence against her consisted of the letters, and Curtis-Bennett would have preferred to have dealt with them himself in his speech to the jury, rather than risk his client being cross-examined by the ruthless Solicitor-General and probably convicting herself out of her own mouth.

However, Edith Thompson brushed aside all her counsel's objections, determined as she was on getting the limelight. She realized the enormous public interest in the case, her counsel said afterwards, and decided to play up to it by entering the witness box.

The story of her relations with Freddy Bywaters, which she told in her examination-in-chief, was a curious one. She and her husband had known the Bywaters family for some years, she said, the acquaintance going back to the days when her brother and Bywaters were schoolmates. In June 1921, Bywaters was on extended leave from his ship, and he accompanied her husband and herself on a holiday to the Isle of Wight in the south of England. At that time she and Freddy, she went on, were no more than friends. The friendship continued after Freddy went to live with the Thompsons as a paying guest until his ship was ready to sail.

"How did you become lovers?" her counsel asked her.

"Well," said Edith, "it started on the August Bank Holiday. I had some trouble with my husband on that day—over a pin!"

Kissed on lips

It was a fine sunny afternoon and all three were in the garden at the back of the house. Edith Thompson was sewing. Suddenly she looked up and said, "I want a pin."

"I will go and get you one," said Bywaters.

When he returned with the pin, husband and wife were arguing, Percy Thompson saying she should have got the pin herself. Edith Thompson then went into the house to prepare tea. Her husband followed her and a further argument ensued as she was laying the table in the sitting room. Her sister Avis Graydon was expected, but she was a little late and, unlike his wife, Percy Thompson did not want to wait for her. He went on to make some uncomplimentary remarks about Edith's family and then began to beat her. Finally he threw her across the room and she collided with a chair which overturned. Hearing the noise from the garden, Bywaters rushed in and told Thompson to stop.

"Why don't you come to an amicable agreement?" said Bywaters. "Either you can have a separation or you can get a divorce."

Thompson hesitated before replying. "Yes—No—I don't see it concerns you."

"You are making Edie's life a hell," said Bywaters. "You know she is not happy with you."

"Well, I have got her and I will keep her."

Edith went upstairs and Bywaters returned to his room. After a short while she joined him there, when he comforted her and for the first time kissed her on the lips. When he came back to the sitting room, he extracted a promise from her husband that he would not knock her about or beat her any more. But Thompson flatly refused to take any steps towards obtaining a legal separation or a divorce from his wife. Shortly afterwards, Bywaters left the house and went to stay with his mother.

During the next few weeks—he was due to embark early in September—he and Edith met secretly from time to time. Most of these meetings took place in tea shops or municipal parks such as Wanstead or Epping Forest near Ilford. There

THE DETECTIVES who handled the case. Who made the first assault? Did Percy Thompson have a gun? Was the crime planned over tea that afternoon?

were not many opportunities for more than hand holding at dance teas and an occasional embrace on a bench. It was the age of the *thé dansant,* and at one of these occasions the orchestra played *One Little Hour,* which became "their tune". However, just before Bywaters' ship sailed on September 9 the two became lovers, apparently going to a small hotel for the purpose and registering under assumed names.

Poison letters

Questioned by her counsel about the letters and the news cuttings, she explained that she had deliberately deceived her lover into thinking that she wished to poison her husband, but that she had no intention of acting upon what she had written. She had sent the letters with their suggestive enclosures, so she said, because she was anxious to keep Freddy's love. Occasionally he would go out with other girls, one of whom was Edith's unmarried sister Avis, and Edith thought that he might be tiring of her.

When the Solicitor-General rose to cross-examine, it was not difficult for him to entrap her as Curtis-Bennett had feared he would. Inskip held up one letter in which she had written to her lover:

"Why aren't you sending me something? I wanted you to . . . If I don't

Syndication International

mind the risk, why should you?"

"What was it?" the Solicitor-General asked sternly.

"I've no idea," Edith replied as non-chalantly as she could.

"Have you no idea?"

"Except what he told me."

"What did he lead you to think it was?"

"That it was something for me to give my husband?"

"With a view to poisoning your husband?"

Edith paused before answering, not knowing exactly what to say and looking distinctly uncomfortable. "That was not the idea," she said at last, "that was not what I expected."

"Something to give your husband that would hurt him?" the Solicitor-General went on.

"To make him ill," she blurted out.

Replying to further questions, Edith Thompson admitted that she had urged Bywaters to send the "something to make him ill", instead of bringing it. "I wrote that," she added, "in order to make him think I was willing to do anything he might suggest, to enable me to retain his affections."

Frank explanation

Again the Solicitor-General eyed her severely. "Mrs. Thompson, is that quite a frank explanation of this urging him to send instead of to bring?"

"It is, absolutely," was the unconvincing reply. "I wanted him to think I was eager to help him."

At this point, the judge leaned forward in the direction of the witness. "That does not answer the question, you know," he remarked.

There was little that Curtis-Bennett could do in re-examining his client to repair the damage caused by her replies to the Solicitor-General's questioning. But he did his best. For example, the phrase, "He is still well", which she had used in one letter, he was able to show referred not to her husband but to a bronze monkey that Bywaters had bought in some foreign port and given her as a souvenir. Her defence counsel also made the most of her conduct on the night of the killing.

Extraordinary life

"As far as you could," he asked her, "from the moment you got to your husband, did you do everything you could for him?"

"Everything I possibly could," echoed Edith Thompson.

Curtis-Bennett came back to this point in her favour when he made his closing speech to the jury. "The letters provide the only evidence upon which the charge of murder is framed against Mrs. Thompson," he stressed his words deliberately. "Everything that was done and said by her on that night shows as strongly as it can that not only did she not know the murder was going to be committed, but that she was horrified when she found her husband was killed."

His client was no ordinary woman, he continued. "She reads a book and then imagines herself one of the characters in the book. She is always living an extraordinary life of novels." So far as her relations with Freddy Bywaters went, Sir Henry made it clear that for his part he did not care whether they were described as "an amazing passion" or "an adulterous intercourse" or whatever. "Thank God, this is not a court of morals," he told the eleven men and one woman in the jury box. "because if everybody immoral was brought here I should never be out of it, nor would you. Whatever name you give it, it was certainly a great love that existed between these two people."

Mr. Justice Shearman began his summing-up of the evidence to the jury with the ominous words: "You should not forget you are trying a vulgar, common crime!" Edith Thompson's letters to her lover the judge proceeded to describe as "full of the outpourings of a silly but at the same time a wicked affection".

"Members of the jury, if that nonsense means anything," he went on to say, "it means that the love of a husband for his wife is something improper because marriage is acknowledged by the law, and that the love of a woman for her lover — illicit and clandestine — is something great and noble. I am certain that you, like any other right-minded persons, will be filled with disgust at such a notion. Let us get rid of all that atmosphere and try this case in an ordinary common sense way."

Strongly hostile

The summing-up was strongly hostile to both prisoners. The red-robed and bewigged figure on the judicial bench left little doubt in the jury's minds that "these two by arrangement between each other agreed to murder this man Thompson, and the murder was effected by the man Bywaters". The impression was heightened by the sense of moral indignation expressed by the judge at the prisoners' sexual morals. In the event it took the jury just over two hours to find both prisoners guilty of murder.

"I say the verdict of the jury is wrong," exclaimed Bywaters when he heard it. "Edith Thompson is not guilty. I am no murderer. I am no assassin." These words were echoed by the woman who stood beside him in the dock. "I am not guilty," she cried. And again, after both had been sentenced to death by hanging, she repeated, "I am not guilty. Oh, God, I am not guilty!"

Both prisoners appealed on the grounds that the verdict was against the weight of the evidence and that the judge had misdirected the jury. Each of the appeals was dismissed by the Court of Criminal Appeal, which saw no grounds for quashing the conviction or ordering a new trial, the President of the Court describing it as a "squalid and rather indecent case of lust and adultery" and one which

Radio Times Hulton Picture Library

MERCY MAIL: Petitions (left) for Edith Thompson's reprieve failed. She was hanged at London's Holloway Prison on January 9, 1923, at 9.00 a.m. (right).

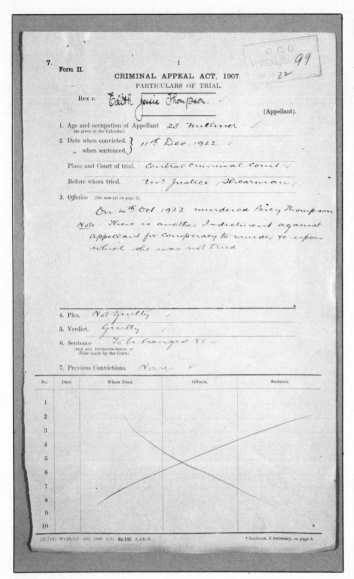

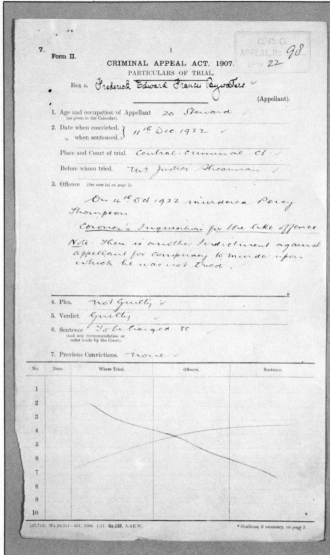

"exhibits from the beginning to the end no redeeming feature"

At the time no woman had been hanged in England for 15 years. Largely for this reason there was considerable public agitation that Edith Thompson should be reprieved, and a petition for reprieve containing many thousands of signatures was sent to the Home Secretary, with whom the final decision rested.

Lawyer's last dash

Three days before the date set for the execution, Bywaters had a meeting with his mother in the condemned cell in Pentonville Prison, where he was being held. He told his mother that he had no grievance against the law so far as he himself was concerned, and that execution had no terrors for him. "I killed him and I must pay for it," he said. "The judge's summing-up was just, if you like, but it was cruel. It never gave me a chance. I did it, though, and I can't complain."

His mistress's case was quite different, he stressed. "I swear she is completely

DEATH DOCUMENTS: They died at the same moment, in places a quarter of a mile apart. Even Bywaters' confession had not swayed the Home Secretary.

innocent. She never knew that I was going to meet them that night . . . For her to be hanged as a criminal is too awful. She didn't commit the murder. I did. She never planned it. She never knew about it. She is innocent, absolutely innocent. I can't believe that they will hang her."

When this was reported to Edith Thompson's solicitor, the lawyer dashed through the night to make a last minute appeal to the Home Secretary who had gone off to spend the weekend at his country house some two hundred miles from London. When he had read Bywater's "confession", the Home Secretary promised to give the solicitor his decision next day, the eve of the execution. He did so, but it was that there could be no reprieve for either prisoner and the law must take its course.

They were both hanged at the same

hour, 9.0 a.m. on January 9, 1923 – she at Holloway and he a quarter of a mile away at Pentonville. Freddy Bywaters met his end "like a gentleman", as he told his mother he would, protesting his mistress's innocence to the last. Edith Thompson, however, had to be carried from the condemned cell to the scaffold by two wardresses as she was in a state of complete collapse during her last moments.

Spoiled her chances

Edith Thompson's leading counsel was greatly upset by the verdict and its outcome, which he felt would have been different if she had taken his advice. "She spoiled her chances by her evidence and demeanour," he said afterwards. "I had a perfect answer to everything, which I am sure would have won an acquittal if she had not been a witness. She was a vain woman and an obstinate one. Also her imagination was highly developed, but it failed to show her the mistake she was making . . . In short, Mrs. Thompson was hanged for immorality."

THE GREAT ESCAPER WHO BECAME A COP

THE residents of the Paris district paid no serious attention to the little old eccentric with the pigtail and three-cornered hat. Wrinkled and bearing a gold-knobbed cane he shuffled through the streets staring into doorways, peering through windows, looking into courtyards. He was regarded as a harmless crank—especially when he knocked on a tailoress's door and told the woman he was looking for his runaway wife. He described the man the wife had supposedly gone off with and asked if such a person had been seen in the vicinity. On learning that he had—and, what was

THE JAILBIRD and galley slave who fled to become a famous crime-buster . . . and the decree appointing Eugène Vidocq head of the famed Paris Sûreté.

more, had only just moved to a new address—the old man started to sob. Taking pity on him, the tailoress helped him to obtain the address and sent him gratefully on his way.

A few days later the "crank"—minus his pigtail and now wearing the garb of a coalman—went to the house and loitered outside until the man he was looking for entered his apartment. The coalman waited until night fell. Then, together with a number of gendarmes, he burst into the upstairs apartment and surprised the man in bed with a woman. While the gendarmes secured and gagged the woman, the coalman grabbed the alleged lover and hurriedly tied him up. Once again François Eugène Vidocq—a master of deception and disguise—had got his man. By posing as an eccentric and then a

coalman, he had captured a notorious thief named Fossard, who had previously frustrated all attempts by the Paris police to arrest him. Not only that, he recovered jewellery and 18,000·francs hidden in the apartment and added to the growing legend of Vidocq—the detective who had been on the wrong side of the law himself, and still strayed across the narrow criminal borderline.

Vidocq believed in the infallibility of setting thieves to catch thieves, and wrote: "During the twenty years I spent at the head of the *Sûreté* I hardly employed any but ex-convicts, often even escaped prisoners. I preferred to choose men whose bad record had given them a certain celebrity. I often gave these men the most delicate missions. They had considerable sums to deliver to the police or prison offices. They took part in operations in which they could easily have laid hands on large amounts. But not one of them, not a single one, betrayed my trust."

But Vidocq was not, as he has so often been called, a reformed crook. He never *was* a crook in the strict sense of the word. Up to his middle thirties he had been a soldier in Napoleon's armies, a show man and puppeteer, a frequent dueller, and admittedly rather a swash-buckler—not to say a womanizer. In 1789 he severely beat up a man who had seduced one of his girl friends, and was sent to prison for breach of the peace. He promptly began a series of spectacular prison escapes, each one leading to recapture and an increased sentence.

This irrepressible man was finally sentenced to eight years in the galleys, and his next escape accordingly took longer to arrange. But in 1799 he was free again, went to Paris and set up shop as a second-hand clothes dealer which he then ran successfully for years. Eventually the

underworld found out who he was, and they mercilessly blackmailed him until at last he went to the police, declared himself, and offered them a bargain.

If they got the threat of recapture and longer imprisonment removed from his life, he would provide them with priceless information from his acquired knowledge of "the criminal scene". They agreed, because crime had broken all bounds and the back streets of Paris had become, since the revolution of 1789-95 inaccessible to any party of less than four or five men armed with swords or pistols. So Vidocq began his job as a "police informer", and in his first year of operation he put more than 800 men behind bars.

SET A THIEF to catch a thief . . . although Britain had its own informer Jonathan Wild (left), Eugène Vidocq was the greatest practitioner . . . he was the inspiration of artists (below, left) and playwrights (below, right).

The following year, 1810, he was made head of the Paris *Sûreté*. To "legalize" his position the authorities arrested him once more and then discharged him with a clean sheet. He set up his new organization on the then revolutionary principle that serious crime can best be fought by criminals. He employed 20 discharged convicts and developed them into the nucleus of a brand-new French Criminal Investigation Department. He planted his men in prisons by having them arrested on sham charges; and got them out again when they had learned enough from the current gossip inside, by pretended escapes or even by bogus deaths and burials. He was the greatest enemy the criminal classes have ever had, and probably the greatest and most methodical of all detectives. His files and archives were colossal and his memory unfailing, and the surviving mystery of his 23 years as head of the *Sûreté* is that he was never assassinated by his underworld rivals.

As it was he lived another 24 years, set up a private detective agency (the first in the world and the inspiration for many a writer of who-dun-its), and himself became a prolific author. He compiled a work of reference on the criminal classes of France, a book about the rehabilitation of criminals, and two immense but undistinguished novels about criminal life. There is a much-quoted book called *The Memoirs of Vidocq,* which he did not write and which he utterly repudiated for its dishonesty. He became friendly with the novelist Honoré de Balzac, and supplied him with the material for countless stories, becoming himself in due course the basis of Balzac's famous detective Vautrin in the *Comédie Humaine.* In his old age he became a counter-espionage agent to the Emperor Napoleon III. Napoleon III's destruction of the Republic and his reckless foreign adventures got the country into its disastrous war with Prussia in 1870.

By then Vidocq, who had shared the general worship of the power-drunk Emperor, had been dead for 13 years: he was perhaps lucky not to see his Emperor's downfall and execration. But in France his name is remembered as vividly as that of the fictitious Sherlock Holmes in Britain or the real life Alan Pinkerton in the United States.

Contempt and hatred

Although he was a colourful character, he was accounted an honest man. And though he was drawn into the "crime war" by an acquired contempt and hatred for the criminals he came to know, he was also the first to recognize that ex-prisoners are better able than anyone to bring about the reform of an ex-prisoner; a belief which has recently been revived both in the United States and in Britain, where ex-prisoners' organizations (such as Recidivists Anonymous, based on Maidstone Prison in Kent) maintain a rehabilitation service with considerable success.

No other country ever had anyone like Vidocq. A century earlier, an English highwayman and truly squalid crook, named Jonathan Wild, secret "organizer" of the London underworld, was induced in 1715 by the available government rewards to turn "thief-taker", and sent many of his old accomplices to prison or the gallows. He was a dandy in his dress, always carried a gold-headed cane, and kept an office in London and an estate in the country, each with a big staff of servants. But the offenders he turned over to the authorities were those who refused to submit to his criminal organiza-

ROYAL COBURG THEATRE,

UNDER THE SOLE MANAGEMENT OF MR. DAVIDGE.

First Night of New and most peculiar Drama, which has been many Weeks in Preparation, giving a comprehensive glance at the Crimes, Police, and Manners of the French Metropolis.

FIFTH WEEK of that Unequalled Display of Splendour, the LORD of the MAELSTROM!!!

MONDAY, JULY 6th, 1829, and During the Week,

At Half-past 6 precisely will be presented, an entirely New Melo-Drama, in Three Acts, of peculiar interest, written by Mr. J. B. Buckstone, founded upon Incidents in the Life of *Eugene François Vidocq,* the Secret Agent of the French Police, and which will be produced, with entirely New Music, Scenery, Machinery, Dresses and Decorations, to be called,

Vidocq, the French Thief-Taker!

Music by Mr. T. Hughes.—Scenery by Mr. Danson & Assistants.—Properties by Mr. Eallett.—Machinery by Mr. Durson.—Dresses by Mr. Saunders & Mrs. Follett.

The above Drama is offered to the Public as combining features of entire Novelty & singular Interest. The manners & peculiarities of our Neighbours & Rivals, the French, have always excited, in an intense degree, the curiosity of our Countrymen, and have, therefore, frequently been exhibited for their amusement on the Stage. The present production, however, penetrates into those remote recesses of Society, those dark, mysterious, and sometimes appalling transactions, which are only impervious to ordinary means of observation, but which possess features of the most thrilling interest, the most harrowing pathos. The Hero of the Piece, is himself one of the most singular and interesting characters, that have, in this eventful age, appeared on the Theatre of public affairs in Europe. After an adventurous career as Convict, Bandit, Soldier, and Citizen, he became the principal and confidential Agent of that formidable body the French Police; at once the Defeater of a Burglary, the Detector of mighty Conspiracies. Such opportunities of diving into the mysteries of Life in a Great Capital have fallen to the lot of few; no rank so elevated as to be beyond his access, none so humble as to be unworthy his notice, none so concealed as to elude his penetrating vigilance. The Memoirs of no Hero that ever lived, are, perhaps, so pregnant with information, interest, and amusement; and it is believed, few Dramas have ever been more remarkable for the same qualities than the present. It has been produced with the most scrupulous anxiety to place before the Public a Living Picture of the Events it Delineates.

Colonel St. Jean, of the French Infantry, Mr. Mortimer. Raymond Delzeve, a young Officer of French Infantry, Mr. Cobham.
De Villers and Julius, Officers, his Friends, Mr. Wood and Mr. Worrell. Monsieur Henry, Chief of the Police, Mr. Jameson.
Coco Lacour and Yvrier, Police Agents, Mr. Saunders and Mr. Craddock. Eugene François Vidocq, an escaped Convict, Mr. H. Williams.
Roman, Captain of Banditti, Mr. King. Bisson de Tretz, his Lieutenant, Mr. Franks. Terrier & Coquelle, Bandits, Mess. H. George & J. George.
Fanfan, a Rogue and ci-devant Pastry Cook's Apprentice, Mr. Davidge. Debenne, a Soldier, and pordoned Galley Slave, Mr. M. Corri.
First Soldier, Mr. Nixon. Second Soldier, Mr. Tulley. Serjeant Belle Rose, Mr. E. L. Lewis. Germain & Boudin, Thieves, Mess. Elsgood & Herbert.
Lachique, a Jailor, Mr. H. George. Robert, his Assistant, Mr. Scarbro. Fossard, a Notorious Thief, Mr. Cooke. Fosse, a Brass-Worker, Mr. Porteus.
Jacquard, his Son, Master Meyers, Commissary of Police, Mr. Worrell. Dubois, Raymond's Servant, Mr. Ireland.
Officers of Gens d'Armes, Bandits, Soldiers, Recruits, Mob, Lemonaders, Currant Wine Sellers, Gamblers, Thieves, Gens d'Armes, Bailiffs, &c.
Rosine, devoted to Raymond, Mrs. Bailey. Annette, Vidocq's Mistress, Miss Watson. Mademoiselle Maria, a Humpbacked Lady, Mrs. Weston.
Cecile & Babet, Fruit & Flower Women, Mesdames Lewis & Morris. Jenny, the Brass-worker's Wife, Mrs. Danson. Louise, a Milk Woman, Mrs. Davidge.

Act 1.—Scene 1.—Mountainous View AND APPEARANCE OF **ROMAN's BAND.** Vidocq a Fugitive Convict,—Attack of a Diligence, Vidocq a Brigand. 2.—EXTERIOR OF A RUDE HUT. Arrival of the Robbers with Booty,—a Rogue's Soliloquy	3.—*Interior of Hut, and Retreat of the Banditti.* Robbers carousing,—a Song,—Vidocq accused of Robbery,—his denial of the Charge and Recital of his past Life,—how to detect a Thief,—generous Bandit, Vidocq's departure. 4.—DISTANT VIEW OF LYONS, with **MILITARY ENCAMPMENT!** Recruiting during the Consulship,—a Rogue enlisted, Vidocq a Soldier.	5.—THE CAMP NEAR LYONS. The Female Duellist,—all for Love,—a Discovery,—Duelling the rage,—a Pupil in the Art of Fencing,—mind your Guard,—a Comic Duel,—Interference of Vidocq,—a Duel in earnest,—Malice of Vidocq's Antagonist,—Arrival of the Gens d'Armes with orders for his Arrest. VIDOCQ DENOUNCED AS AN ESCAPED **GALLEY SLAVE.**
Act 2.—Scene 1.—Interior of a Prison. Vidocq a Prisoner,—the Galley Slave's Complaint, they Plunge into the Scrape, and SECOND ESCAPE OF VIDOCQ. 2.—THE ENVIRONS OF PARIS. Where's my Bounty Money?—Where's Vidocq?—Fortunate Drunkenness,—Narrow Escape of Vidocq, Thoughts of a Rogue,—Song.	3.—AN APARTMENT. The Female Duellist married,—Appearance of a Notorious Thief, **THE ROBBERY!** Escape of the Thief with Papers and valuable Booty, the Suspicion,—the Arrest.	4.—ROOM AT ANNETTE's Vidocq's Mistress,—Vidocq at Home,—Thoughts of a better course of Life,—the Gens d'Armes,—the Disguise, the Stratagem,—the Gens d'Armes secured, and THIRD ESCAPE OF VIDOCQ.
Act 3.—Scene 1.—A SQUARE IN PARIS. REJOICINGS FOR THE *Victory of Marengo!* Vidocq's new line of Business,—the Thieves,—the consequences of bad Connections,—Vidocq a Tailor, the ruin of his Establishment,—again denounced,—the Gens d'Armes in pursuit,—the Garret Window, Escape on the Roof. 2.—THE BRASS-WORKER's GARRET. General search for Vidocq,—his concealment in a Bed, Gens d'Armes in the Garret,—their Departure,—Surprise of the Brass-Worker and his Wife,—a Disguise, a Lame Soldier,—and Fourth Escape of Vidocq.	3.—*PARIS.* Who'll buy an Apple Tart?—no being honest among Rogues,—the Thieves disappointed,—Catching a Tartar. THE BATTLE OF THE WOODEN LEG! Victory of Vidocq,—Flight of the Thieves. 4.—*POLICE OFFICE.* The Police Reprimanded,—Vidocq is not to be taken, his Appearance in the Office,—he devotes himself to the Service of the Police,—Fossard Denounced,—Vidocq undertakes to find him,—a Word of Advice from the Chief Magistrate,—a Batch of Thieves apprehended, Reward of Roguery,—Vidocq appointed *The Secret Agent of the French Police.*	5.—THE RUE THEVENOT. Any new Milk or Cream,—the Hump-backed Divinity, Vidocq a respectable old Gentleman,—the Stratagem. 6.—*The Lodgings of the Thief Fossard.* Apprehension of Fossard,—the Jump from the Window, the Pursuit. 7.—A LANDSCAPE. Condemnation of an Innocent Victim,—Procession of Death,—Pursuit of Fossard. 8.—*EXTENSIVE VIEW of the COUNTRY,* WITH THE Ceremony of a Military Execution! The Hunted Thief,—the Word given to Fire,—the Execution suspended. *Death of the Thief Fossard, & Triumph of Vidocq.*

To conclude with, for the 25th, 26th, 27th, 28th, 29th, and 30th times, the encreasingly attractive and unprecedentedly magnificent Legendary Spectacle, in Three Acts, with entirely New Music, Extensive Scenery, Splendid Dresses, and Decorations and altogether unequalled and unattempted Aquatic and other Scenic Effects, founded upon the celebrated Tales of the *Wild & the Wonderful,* and Called, The

LORD of the MAELSTROM!

Or, The Elfin Sprite of the Norwegian Seas.

Otho, ...(King of Denmark and Norway,) .... Mr. MORTIMER. Fredegond, ... (a Scandinavian Prince,) .... Mr. COOKE.
Valachiolf, Foster-Father of the Princess Urilda,) Mr. KING The Unknown Knight, (*****) High Priest of Odin, Mr. FRANKS.
First Conspirator, ... Mr ELSGOOD. Second Ditto, ... Mr. SCARBRO. Gundulph, ... (Pilot of the Royal Galley,) ...... Mr. E. L. LEWIS.
The Princess Urilda, (Daughter of Otho,) Miss WATSON. Elrica and Elswitha, (her Attendants,) Miss HAMMERSLEY and Mrs. MORRIS.
High Priestess of Freya, ... Miss MEARS. Lok, Sunter, Midgard, ... (Evil Divinities,) ...... Messrs. WILMORE, JONES, EDMONTON.
Knights, Lords, Courtiers, Ladies, Priests, Priestesses, Sprites, Guards, &c. &c.

Asgard, - *the Elfin Sprite of the Norwegian Seas,* - Mynheer Von Klishnig,

The Astonishing Gymnasiast, who is the first Professor of the Art of Posturing of the present day.

The Three Valkyries, Mrs. LEWIS, Miss PHAROAH, and Miss H. BODEN. Brandomann, (the Lord or Monster of the Maelstrom, Mr. COBHAM.

Act 1.—GRAND VESTIBULE OF THE PALACE OF THE KINGS OF NORWAY AT SANDAAL.
Tremendous Ravine in the Rocks by Moonlight, with Falling Stream of Real Water.

Act 2--STUPENDOUS CATARACT of the Maelstrom, formed by REAL WATER!
Rushing and Foaming from the Roof of the Theatre to beneath the Stage, comprising various Torrents falling with terrific force in different Directions, constituting the most Tremendous effect ever produced by a simulative Waterfall, and comprising upwards of 17 Tons, a larger Body of Water than was ever before introduced into a Theatre.

Act 3--The Temple of Fifty Fountains in the Mystic Regions of Valhallah!
The whole of the Magnificent Effects in this Scene produced by Real Water.

Doors open at Half-past Five. Second Price at Half-past Eight. Romney, Printer, Lambeth.

Harlingue-Viollet

tion, and in this respect he was the ancestor of the two London gangs headed by the Richardson brothers and the Kray brothers; the forerunner of the American gangster boss such as Al Capone; and the prototype for the present-day Mafia. In 1725 he was himself convicted and hanged for robbery, and his odious story is satirically told by the eighteenth-century author Henry Fielding in his *History of the Life of the Late Mr. Jonathan Wild*. He had turned his knowledge of crime to good account—the reward for the conviction of a highwayman was £40 (worth about £500 or $1500 today) plus the man's horse, weapons, and property.

Informers available

While there was much about Vidocq that was flamboyant, there was nothing odious—although the *Sûreté* came to disown him, and subsequently played down the comparative lack of success achieved by the recruiting, from 1833 onwards, of none but respectable citizens as its new detectives, all of whom it called "inspectors".

From then onwards, however, in France, Britain, and the United States, the "hidden force" of the police-minded thief was indispensable. Each of those countries relied, and now all countries rely, on the availability of informers by the thousand, and sometimes they act as *agents provocateurs*; not always willing ones, certainly not always paid ones. The "picking up" of ex-prisoners for questioning, moreover, is especially easy in France, where there is a long-established system of subjecting the discharged prisoner to an *interdit de séjour*, a document listing a number of cities and towns in which, for the next five years, he may not "live or appear". To be found in any of them means arrest and imprisonment without trial. But in all countries, an ex-prisoner needs to live a very careful life if he values his freedom, and he will certainly never again live a carefree one. In the growing number of countries operating a parole system—which often involves long post-prison periods under supervision and a freedom which is specially precarious—the supply of potential informers is not diminishing.

"In the United States the F.B.I. relies on informants," states William W. Turner, who was an F.B.I. agent for ten years. "Payments are made from confidential funds, the total being one of the F.B.I.'s best-kept secrets. By purchasing information rather than obtaining it through other investigative techniques, the F.B.I. gains a measure of protection

THE GREATEST ENEMY the criminal classes ever had, perhaps the greatest and most methodical of all detectives . . . a flamboyant and colourful character.

against embarrassment to the Bureau. Should a case backfire, the informant can be piously disowned." In the United States, as in England, journalists have actually gone to prison rather than divulge their sources of information: but police officers, New Scotland Yard Special Branch men, and F.B.I. agents are never pressed about it.

Sometimes the police in all countries will actually use an experienced and cooperative ex-crook in setting up a crime —a robbery, an assault, a break-in—by way of an ambush. He is arrested with his accomplices, "offers" to give evidence for the prosecution, and is therefore himself acquitted. The English High Court Judges will have none of this, and if it comes to their notice the other men are also acquitted, and there is trouble for the police for using an *agent provocateur*.

To catch criminals it is not enough to know what an artful man would do in given circumstances. You must more often know what a stupid man would do. And to do this it is necessary, not so much to be naturally stupid as to be capable of stupidity. In setting a thief to catch a thief, the one you set should be chosen with this in mind. But the system has two built-in dangers, one of them old and recognized, the other new, growing, and sinister.

The first is that the informer may be a liar, concerned either to pay off an old score or to distract police attention from something else; the second is that he can (and does) use bugging devices and phone tapping techniques not always accessible to the police, whom he will then feed with the results—in which event all the statutory safeguards are ignored.

In the long run, however, even this abuse of the law may be preferable to living in a country where the police are hobbled by unrealistic rules and regulations, and where the villain is king.

KIDNAPPERS

THEY TRADE in human anguish ... the highest-priced of all commodities. They are a generation of criminals who belong to modern times ... to the times in which it has become possible for the criminal to infiltrate the habitat of the rich and famous, and take human hostages. And, because their victims are rich and renowned, the list of great cases reads like a "Who's Who" of fame and fortune. There was the Lindbergh baby, the Peugeot child, and Mrs. Muriel McKay ...

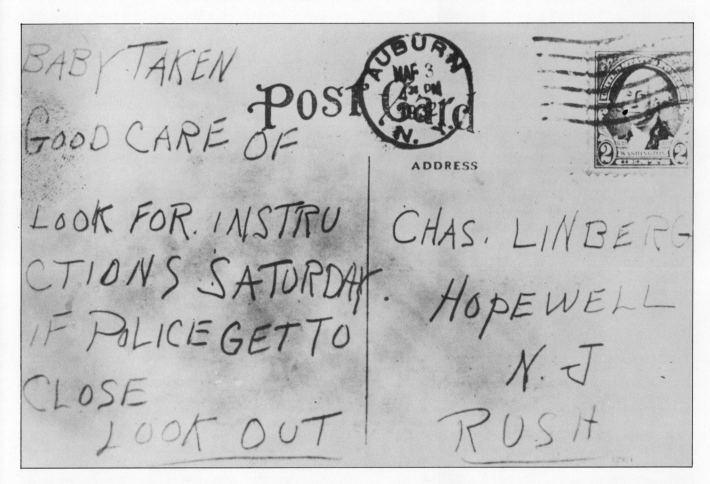

IT WAS not until the second half of the nineteenth century that professional criminals thought of seizing a human hostage and holding him for ransom. In the days when crooks lived in slums, and the rich resided in great houses or country estates, criminals seldom had a chance to encounter the children of the rich. Then came the age of industry and factories. Men acquired fortunes overnight, and many evildoers brooded on how to separate them from their wealth.

It was in the United States, where the rich and the poor rub shoulders, that the first notable modern case of kidnapping occurred. It was conceived in the summer of 1874 when two men made a habit of driving past the home of Christian Ross, a once moderately successful Philadelphia grocer who had recently become bankrupt. The men stopped and spoke to Charley Ross, aged four, and Walter Ross, aged six, as the children played innocently on the sidewalk. On July 1 the children asked their new friends to buy them fireworks for the Fourth of July celebrations.

The men agreed and invited the youngsters to hop into the buggy. A few streets away, they gave Walter 25 cents and sent him to a nearby shop. When the little boy returned, the buggy had vanished, and his brother Charley with it.

The howling Walter was then taken home by a neighbour, and Christian Ross hurried to the police. Everyone was baffled. Why, they asked, should anyone steal a four-year-old baby?

The mystery was solved two days later when the Rosses received a scrawled and badly spelled letter; it said "you wil hav two pay us befor you git him", but did not mention any sum. Such a thing had never been heard of in North America before. Indignation swept the country. Thousands of police joined in the search for "little Charley Ross". No one bothered about search warrants as they burst into any premises that might conceal the missing child. On July 6, Ross received a letter asking for £20,000, and threatening to kill the child if the hunt was not called off. He was told to insert an advertisement in the *Philadelphia Ledger* saying he was ready to negotiate. Instead, he tried to drag out the correspondence, hoping that the kidnappers would provide a clue to their whereabouts.

The men expressed their impatience at his tactics, and he countered by stating publicly that he was "damned if he would compound a felony." His wife, however, was so shattered by the ordeal of waiting that he changed his mind, and agreed to pay $20,000 which he had managed to borrow. Ross went to an appointed rendezvous, but no one appeared to collect the money. So month after month dragged by. There were more appointments, more correspondence, but still no sign of the missing child. The grim story ended six months later, on December 14, 1874, when a burglar alarm sounded in the home of a rich New Yorker, Holmes Van Brunt; it meant that burglars had broken into the summer residence belonging to his brother, next door.

Dying confession

Van Brunt and three other men duly crept up to the house with shotguns, and waited. When, an hour later, the burglars came out, Van Brunt ordered them to halt. Instead, they started shooting. The Van Brunt party fired back with their shotguns, and both burglars fell. One of them gasped out a dying confession: his name was Joseph Douglass, and he and his companion, William Mosher, had kidnapped Charlie Ross. The boy would be returned alive and well within a few days. . . . Then Douglass died.

The confession was undoubtedly genuine, for the police already knew that Douglass and Mosher were the men they wanted: another crook had informed on them. But no sign of flaxen-haired Charley Ross was ever found. A third man named William Westervelt was tried as an accomplice, and sentenced to seven years' imprisonment, although there was no real evidence against him—a sign of how much frustrated anger had been aroused by the kidnapping.

The age of kidnapping had arrived; but fortunately for parents and relatives it got off to a slow start. This was partly due to the death of poor Charley Ross, for in February 1875, the Legislature of

"THE FOX": A manic egoist, with a sadistic desire to make a parent suffer. A grudge drove him to arrange a rendezvous with horror. Edward Hickman was hanged in San Quentin.

Pennsylvania passed a law defining kidnapping, setting the penalty at a maximum of 25 years' solitary confinement and a fine of $100,000. It is a measure of how much horror was excited by the Ross affair. There is also a certain irony in it. The word kidnapping was originally coined in England about two hundred years earlier, and the kids who were "nabbed" were usually sent to America as cheap labour on the tobacco plantations; now America was forced to enact the first law against the crime.

At about the time of the Charley Ross kidnapping, a country on the other side of the globe was being forced to give serious thought to the question of how to stamp it out. In Greece, as in Corsica and Sicily, kidnapping was a long-established custom, and brigandage was looked upon as an almost respectable occupation.

Complete amnesty

In 1870, however, the whole system backfired, and nearly caused the occupation of Greece by England. On April 11, Lord Muncaster, an Irish peer, together with his wife and a distinguished party of tourists, set out to see the ancient battlefield at Marathon—the site of the Athenians' victory over the Persians, around 490 B.C. A group of soldiers warned them about brigands and started to escort them back to Athens; but the soldiers were too slow, and the carriages rushed on ahead. A band of brigands, led by the notorious Arvanitákis brothers, swooped down and seized them, then forced them to run at top speed over rough countryside. Negotiations with the authorities followed, and the females—including a six-year-old girl—were released, together with Lord Muncaster. Four men, including an Italian nobleman,

Count Alberto de Boÿl, remained as hostages. The ransom demanded was £50,000. Alternatively, the brigands sought a complete amnesty. Previous hauls had made them rich; they wanted to be able to return to society.

When he heard of the outrage, King George of Greece was so upset that he offered to hand himself over to the brigands as a hostage. For the next ten days, however, negotiations dragged inconclusively on. The Greek government categorically refused to grant an amnesty. But Takos Arvanitákis, the brigand chief, said there had to be one—otherwise the prisoners would be killed. Troops drew up near the ravine where he held the four prisoners, while negotiators tried to persuade the brigands to take the ransom and withdraw over the Turkish border. Then something went wrong. The troops, unable to resist taking a potshot, opened fire. The brigands fled towards the village of Dilessi, and on the way, the four captives were callously murdered. Seven brigands, including one of the leaders, were killed; six more were captured. Takos and seven others escaped into Turkey.

Invasion threat

The furore that followed was tremendous. England burst into roars of rage. The British said that if Greece couldn't cope with her own brigands, England should invade the country and do it for them. The Russians promptly stated that, in the event of hostilities, they would go to war to help Greece. "Investigating commissions" were set up; dozens of men who had helped the brigands were rounded up. Fifty eventually went on trial, but most were released. The "Dilessi murders", as they were known, became the scandal of Europe, and Greece lost face badly in the eyes of the world. The government was brought down. One of the brigands was extradited from Turkey and beheaded. Takos himself was finally shot two years after the killings. And in Greece, at least, kidnapping ceased to be a more-or-less acceptable custom.

In the United States, on the other hand, its popularity was growing. In June 1907, in the Italian district of New Orleans, seven-year-old Walter Lamana went off trustingly with a man who offered him his hand. His father soon received a demand for $6000, and it gradually became clear that the kidnappers were the Mafia, or "Black Hand". The organization already ran the Italian part of New Orleans as Al Capone was to run Chicago 20 years later. The publicity aroused by the kidnapping led many Italians to admit that they had been paying "protection money" for years. One of the gang was arrested— Frank Gendusa. Under questioning, he admitted to being involved in the kid-

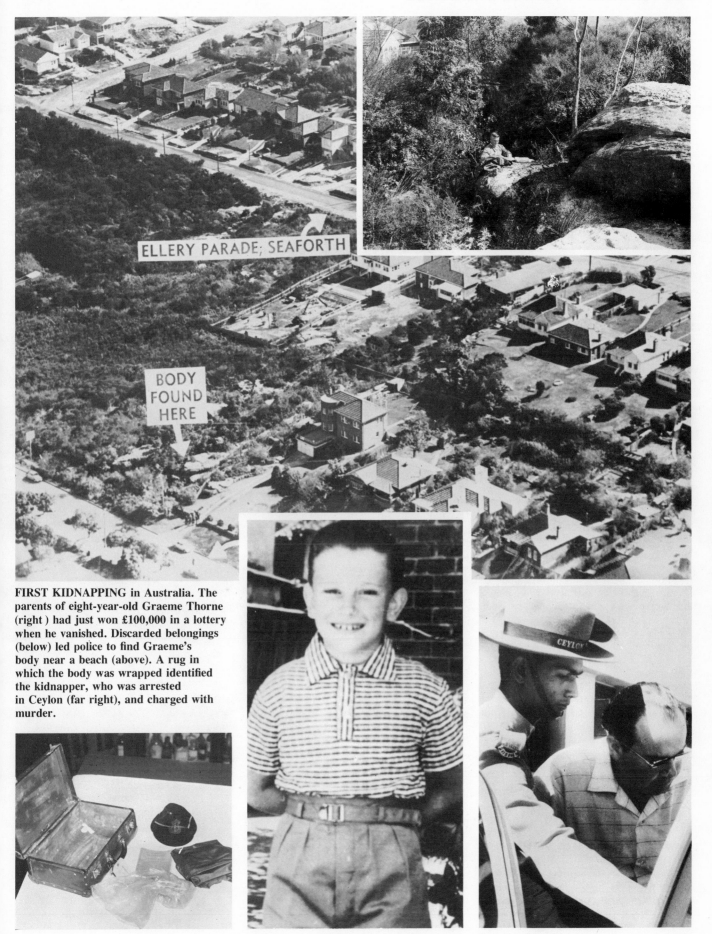

ELLERY PARADE, SEAFORTH

BODY FOUND HERE

FIRST KIDNAPPING in Australia. The parents of eight-year-old Graeme Thorne (right) had just won £100,000 in a lottery when he vanished. Discarded belongings (below) led police to find Graeme's body near a beach (above). A rug in which the body was wrapped identified the kidnapper, who was arrested in Ceylon (far right), and charged with murder.

napping, but said he didn't know where the child was. Other members of the gang were then taken into custody. One of them, Ignazio Campisciano, was captured by a posse, who used a time-honoured method to induce him to talk: they bound his hands, put a noose round his neck, and pulled it tight over the branch of a tree. Campisciano broke down, and led them to a dirty swamp, where wrapped in a blanket, was the body of the missing boy. The child had kept crying for his mother, he said, and one of the men had strangled it. (In fact, Walter had been killed with a hatchet blow.)

Four of the kidnappers went on trial, including Tony Costa, who had actually abducted the youngster. They were found "Guilty without capital punishment", and for a while, it looked as if the angry crowds of New Orleans would take justice into their own hands and lynch them—as they had done in 1890, when nine members of the Mafia were acquitted of the murder of the Chief of Police, and were subsequently dragged from their cells and killed by a mob. But the crowd was persuaded to disperse quietly.

The trial of two other accomplices—Nicolina and Leonardo Gebbia—had to be postponed for another four months because public feeling ran so high. The Gebbias were both found guilty; Leonardo was hanged, and his sister sentenced to life imprisonment. The man who actually killed Walter Lamana was never caught. But at least his crime had one beneficial result: the power of the Black Hand in New Orleans was crushed and broken.

Major undertaking

It was slowly becoming clear, to the police and the general public, that the surest way of dealing with kidnappers—and of lessening the danger to their hostages—was to pay the ransom, then let the police take up the trail. The value of this method was proved in 1909, in Sharon, Pennsylvania. On March 18, a man drove up to the local school and explained that he had been sent to collect Billy Whitla, the eight-year-old son of a wealthy attorney; his father needed him immediately at the office. The boy was allowed to go and that afternoon Mr. Whitla received a ransom note demanding $10,000. No doubt recalling the Ross case, Whitla declined to co-operate with the police. He delivered the ransom according to instructions, and his son was safely returned. Skilful police work, aided by luck, located the room where the boy had been held by a man and a woman. Detailed descriptions of them led to the arrest of James H. Boyle and his wife within six days of the kidnapping. Both were sentenced to life imprisonment.

But it was in the 1920's, the Bootleg era, that kidnapping became a major criminal

undertaking in the United States. Possibly the Sicilian gangsters recalled how lucrative such activities had been in their homeland. For these gang-snatches, children were no longer the automatically chosen victims. The gangsters realized it was just as easy to kidnap a rich business man—and it aroused less public indignation.

Machine-Gun Kelly

Even when it became a crime punishable by death, the crooks didn't seem to be deterred. One of the classic police investigations into such a "snatch" occurred in 1933. The millionaire Charles F. Urschel was sitting on the porch of his home in Oklahoma City, playing cards with his wife and another couple. Suddenly, two men with Tommy guns appeared. When Urschel and his friend refused to say which was Urschel, they were both bundled into a car and driven away. A few hours later, the friend reappeared; he had been released by the kidnappers when they established his identity. Edgar Hoover, Director of the F.B.I., personally took charge of the investigation.

Urschel, so he told the agents, was driven for 12 hours, then taken to a house, where he was blindfolded. He was made to write a ransom note. Then, for the next eight days, he was kept tied up in a dark room. But he kept his wits about him, and noted that aeroplanes flew overhead at 9.45 every morning and 5.45 every afternoon—all except Sunday, when a heavy storm apparently prevented the 5.45 from passing that way. The following day, he was driven a further distance, then put down at a railroad station and released. His ransom of $200,000 had been paid.

The aeroplanes were the only clue the authorities had to go on. Hoover's men studied hundreds of airline schedules. Since the drive had taken about 12 hours, they assumed that the hideaway must be within about three hundred miles of Oklahoma city. Next, after hours of painstaking research, they located an air route that crossed a certain point in Texas at 9.45 each morning and 5.45 each afternoon. They were even able to verify that on the Sunday, a heavy storm had caused the plane to turn off its usual route. The town in question was called Paradise. And in Paradise, they discovered, lived the mother of Kathryn Kelly, wife of a gangster named Machine-Gun George Kelly, who was prominent on their list of suspects for the kidnapping.

Posing as state surveyors, F.B.I. men then called at the house. One of them asked for a drink of water. It tasted bitter with minerals, just as Urschel had described it. A few days later, the F.B.I. swooped at dawn, and found Harvey Bailey—identified as the second kidnapper—with a Tommy gun at his side. Another accomplice, Albert Bates, was

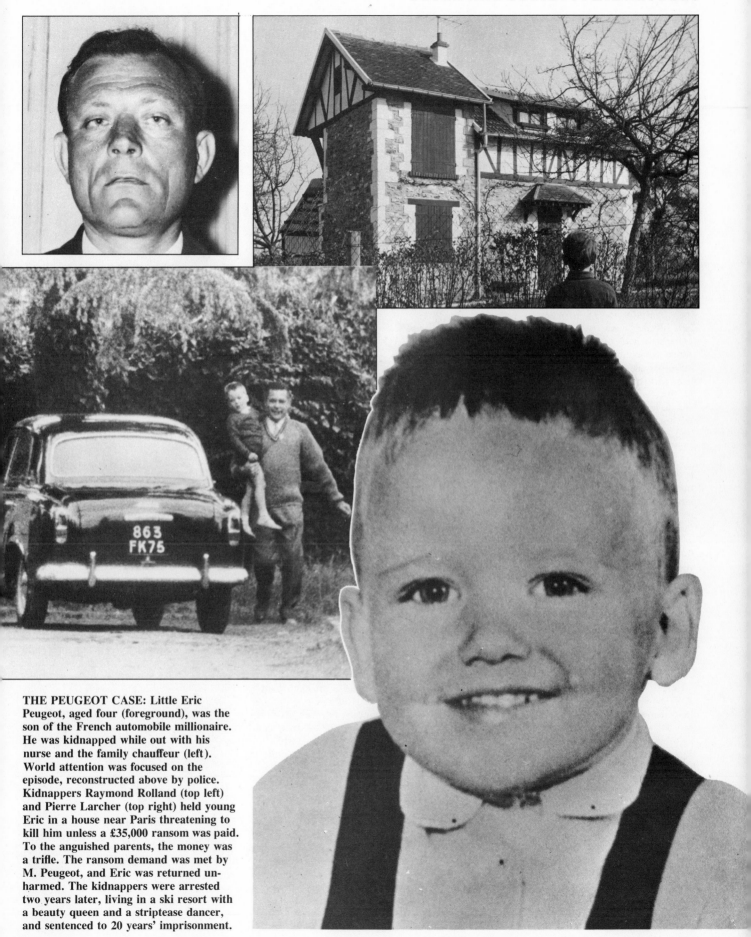

THE PEUGEOT CASE: Little Eric Peugeot, aged four (foreground), was the son of the French automobile millionaire. He was kidnapped while out with his nurse and the family chauffeur (left). World attention was focused on the episode, reconstructed above by police. Kidnappers Raymond Rolland (top left) and Pierre Larcher (top right) held young Eric in a house near Paris threatening to kill him unless a £35,000 ransom was paid. To the anguished parents, the money was a trifle. The ransom demand was met by M. Peugeot, and Eric was returned unharmed. The kidnappers were arrested two years later, living in a ski resort with a beauty queen and a striptease dancer, and sentenced to 20 years' imprisonment.

traced when he got into a fight in Denver, Colorado; the money the police found on him was from the kidnap ransom – the bill numbers of which had all been noted. For a few months, Machine-Gun Kelly became the latest Public Enemy Number One. He even wrote letters threatening to kill Urschel.

Then, in October, a girl in Memphis, Tennessee, confided to a schoolfriend that her "parents" were not actually her parents; they had "borrowed" her. A policeman who heard this story from his child made cautious investigations. There was another dawn raid, and as the armed policemen burst into his bedroom, Machine-Gun Kelly threw up his hands and yelled "Don't shoot, G-men!" It was the first time Hoover's men had been called G-men, meaning Government men, and the name stuck. As for Kelly, he died 21 years later in Leavenworth Penitentiary.

Lindbergh laws

Before the snatching of aviator Charles A. Lindbergh's son in 1932, America's most famous – and horrible – kidnapping case was that of "The Fox". This was the signature on the ransom note sent to Perry Parker, father of 12-year-old Marian Parker. Parker was a Los Angeles banker; and Marian had been abducted from her school one day in December 1928. During the next few days, Parker received more letters, signed "The Fox" or "Fate", and it was clear that the sender had a sadistic desire to make the parents suffer. Finally, Parker kept his rendezvous with the kidnapper; he could see Marian sitting stiffly beside him in the car. He handed over the money, and the man drove off, promising to let Marian out at the end of the street.

MRS. McKAY was the wife of a senior figure in newspaper management. She was abducted by two brothers who lived at Rooks Farm (above).

When Parker reached her, she was dead; her legs had been hacked off, and her eyes propped open with wire. Her legs were found in a nearby park. But the shirt in which they were wrapped gave the police the vital clue; it led them to 20-year-old Edward Hickman, who said he wanted the $1500 ransom money to go to college. He also had a grudge against Parker, whom he considered responsible for a prison sentence he had received for forgery. Hickman proved to be an almost manic egoist, revelling in the publicity. He was hanged in San Quentin jail in 1928.

After carpenter Bruno Hauptmann's execution for the murder of the Lindbergh baby, in 1935, the kidnapping "boom" came to an end. As a result of the case, laws known as the "Little Lindbergh Laws" came into operation in various states. These made it a capital offence to commit kidnapping – even if it did not involve a removal across state lines – if any physical harm came to the victim. In New York State, some time later, a man was convicted of kidnapping for forcing

a young girl – whom he subsequently molested – to accompany him from the street and onto the roof of a nearby building. Even the sending of a ransom note could mean a maximum penalty in a federal court of twenty years' imprisonment, or a fine of $5000, or both.

In 1960 Australia had its first child kidnapping case. Eight-year-old Graeme Thorne was the son of a travelling salesman of Sydney; his parents had recently won £100,000 in a lottery. Graeme's corpse was found near a beach a month after his disappearance, and scientific examination of the rug in which the body was wrapped finally led the police to the house where he had been taken – and eventually to Leslie Stephen Bradley, a married man with three children, who was arrested on board a ship bound for England.

Symbolic damages

England's first kidnapping case occurred in December 1969, when Mrs. Muriel McKay, wife of a senior Fleet Street newspaper executive, disappeared from her home in Wimbledon, South London. Nine years earlier in France, however, another snatch had taken place which gained almost as many world-wide headlines as the McKay story. Little Eric Peugeot, aged four, the son of the Paris automobile millionaire, Raymond Peugeot, was taken from the playground of a fashionable golf club on the outskirts of the city.

His captors – Raymond Rolland and Pierre Larcher – were two small-time crooks who wanted money in order to indulge their taste for nightclubs and blondes. They demanded £35,000 from the Peugeot family – a mere trifle to M. Peugeot, who handed over the ransom himself. Fortunately for him and his wife, the kidnappers kept their word and Eric was returned a short while later unharmed. It was not until October 1962, however, that Rolland and Larcher – who had been captured living it up in a ski resort chalet with a Danish beauty queen and a striptease dancer – were put on trial.

They were each sentenced to the maximum sentence under French law of 20 years' imprisonment. And the Peugeots – who had recovered some £10,000 of the ransom money – were awarded the symbolic sum of one franc damages. A small price, some people thought, for the agony and torment they had suffered. But the truth is that no parent – or lover, or friend, or relative – can ever be adequately compensated for the distress they undergo in such circumstances. One franc or a million, it does not erase the memory of the event. Especially if, as is usually the case, the kidnapping ends in the physical death of the victim, and the mental death of his family.

THE LINDBERGH BABY

Fame followed the pioneer aviator . . .
and the headlines grew when his child was snatched

Anthony Cobb

IT WAS an odd sound, a sharp crack. Colonel Charles A. Lindbergh, the aviator who had made his name a household word around the world by becoming the first man to fly the Atlantic non-stop, paused as he read in the library of his luxurious retreat on Sourland Mountain, a remote, forested peak in New Jersey. The sound was not repeated. The Colonel went back to his book. A few minutes later, Betty Gow, the Lindbergh's nursemaid, decided to look in on Charles, Jr., their golden-haired, 20-month-old baby son. She went into the nursery, turned up the electric heater in his darkened room and went over to the crib. She could hear no sound of breathing. She felt with her hand. The crib was empty.

She dashed out to the landing where she met Mrs. Lindbergh. "Have you got the baby?" she panted anxiously. "No," said Mrs. Lindbergh. The nursemaid rushed downstairs to the library. "Colonel," she gasped, "have *you* got the baby?" "No," he answered. "Isn't he in his crib?"

He didn't wait for her answer. Suddenly he recalled the mysterious sound he had heard. He took the stairs two at a time and switched on the light in the nursery. He was standing in front of the empty crib as his wife joined him in the room. "Anne," he said sorrowfully, "they have stolen our baby."

The possibility of kidnapping had always been in the Lindberghs' minds. They were obvious targets, both rich and famous. The Colonel first hit the headlines with his Transatlantic flight in May 1927, covering the 3600 miles from Long Island to Le Bourget airport outside Paris in 33½ hours.

His next long-distance solo trip was

THE SPIRIT OF ST. LOUIS . . .
Adventurous, romantic, the flying Lindberghs were an ideal match, but their hour of triumph turned to tragedy.

the 2100 mile hop from New York to Mexico City in 27 hours 10 minutes. There he met and fell in love with Anne Morrow, daughter of the U.S. ambassador. It was an ideal match. Mrs. Lindbergh quickly became an accomplished radio operator and joined her husband on a series of flights, pioneering what have developed into America's modern airline routes.

Their first flight as a team was from Los Angeles to New York in 14 hours 45 minutes. To the newspapers of the era

they became "the most romantic and adventurous couple of all time". They seemed to have everything—money, happiness, a satisfying purpose in life. To all those gifts was added in 1930 the joy of the birth of the son they named Charles Augustus Lindbergh, Jr.

Among the precautions they took to avoid a kidnapping was never to reveal in newspaper interviews which bedroom their little son occupied in the Sourland Mountain retreat. Yet now, on this dark night at the beginning of March 1932, someone had found the room and kidnapped him.

Characteristically, in this moment of crisis the Colonel did not lose his calm. "Get the butler to call the police and don't touch anything," he ordered. From a closet he took a Springfield rifle which he had carried with him on many of his flights. He went out into the dark night, but there was nothing to be seen and no sound except the wind whistling through the bare branches of the trees. He went back into the house to console his wife while the first police message flashed out along the whole Eastern seaboard of the United States: "Lindbergh baby kidnapped from his home near Hopewell, New Jersey. Stop and search all cars."

At the house on Sourland Mountain, the police found few clues. Beneath the nursery window were a few footprints, indistinct, as if the kidnapper had either removed his shoes altogether or bound them with sacking. Nearby police found a chisel and a crude ladder in three

THE LINDBERGH BABY (below, left) and the note demanding $50,000 ransom in a mixture of different denominations . . . signed with interlocking circles.

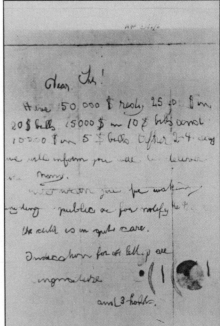

WANTED

INFORMATION AS TO THE WHEREABOUTS OF

CHAS. A. LINDBERGH, Jr.

OF HOPEWELL, N. J.

SON OF COL. CHAS. A. LINDBERGH

World-Famous Aviator

This child was kidnaped from his home in Hopewell, N. J., between 8 and 10 p. m. on Tuesday, March 1, 1932.

DESCRIPTION:

Age, 20 months   Hair, blond, curly
Weight, 27 to 30 lbs.
Height, 29 inches
        Deep dimple in
        Dressed in one-piec

ADDRESS ALL COMMUNICATI
    COL. H. N. SCHWARZK
    COL. CHAS. A. LINDBER

ALL COMMUNICATIONS WILL

March 11, 1932   Supt.

sections. The ladder was broken at the point where the top section joined the middle one. From the start it was believed that it broke as the kidnapper made his escape, and that this was the cracking sound the Colonel heard as he read in the library.

The final clue was the misspelt ransom note, lying on the nursery window sill. It read: *"Dear Sir, Have 50,000 dollars redy, 25,000 in 20-dollar bills, 15,000 in 10-dollar bills and 10,000 in five-dollar bills. After 2-4 days we will inform you were to deliver the mony. We warn you for making anyding public or for notify the police. The child is in gut care. Instruction for the letters are singnature."*

In good care?

The "singnature" referred to, which was kept secret for months to prevent cranks from duplicating it and confusing the trail, consisted of two interlocking circles, one red and one blue. In the centre of each circle was a hole with a third hole equidistant between them. The inference drawn from the note was that it had been written by a German, but that was not much to go on.

The world shared the agony of the Lindberghs as they waited, red-eyed with weeping and fatigue, sustained only by the hope that their son really was "in gut care" and would be restored to them unharmed. Two hundred thousand letters and postcards of sympathy arrived by the sackful at their home. Carloads of police, F.B.I. agents, secret servicemen, reporters and photographers descended on Sourland Mountain, plus some of America's top private detectives, hired by newspapers who hoped they might crack the case before the authorities.

WANTING AND WAITING . . . the world shared the agony of the Lindberghs. Letters of sympathy by the thousand, F.B.I. agents by the carload, but a house which had once been a retreat told the story of the Lindberghs' new emptiness . . . the ladder led from the nursery.

Extra telephone lines were strung to cope with the traffic. From his prison cell, "Scarface" Al Capone, former king of the Chicago underworld, issued a statement promising to recover the missing child if he were granted his freedom. Mrs. Lindbergh made a broadcast to the whole of the United States, Canada, and Mexico, giving instructions on how to mix her baby's feed. "Take care of him," she pleaded. Her poignant words drew a note from the kidnapper, assuring her that her son was well.

The hunt for the kidnapper spread throughout America and from there to Canada, Mexico, Europe, and ships at sea. Yet the first man to make contact with him proved to be Dr. John F. Condon, an elderly educator who had taught and lectured for 50 years in the Bronx district of New York. Moved, like millions more throughout the world, by the Lindberghs' sorrow, he sent a letter to his local newspaper, the *Bronx Home News*, appealing for the return of the baby. The letter, addressed to the kidnapper, said in part:

"For the sake of his own mother, that he may offer restitution for his crime, I offer all that I could scrape together, 1,000 dollars of my own money, so that a loving mother may again have her darling child, so that people will know that the greatest criminal in the world has a bright spot in his heart, and that Colonel Charles A. Lindbergh may know that the American people are grateful for the honor he has bestowed upon the United States by his pluck and daring.

"Let the kidnapper know that I write of my own free will, that no testimony of mine or coming from me will be used against him, and that this is an appeal for the sake of humanity . . ."

The letter was published on March 8,

exactly a week after the disappearance of the baby. By the first post next morning. Dr. Condon received a letter from the kidnapper, identified by the familiar red and blue circles. After contacting the Lindberghs, Dr. Condon made a rendezvous for March 12, late at night on a lonely road bordering Woodlawn Cemetery. He was driven to the spot by a friend, Al Reich, a former heavy-weight boxer. As he went to meet the kidnapper, Dr. Condon said: "Al, if I should never return, remember a child's life is at stake. Forget me. Remember Colonel Lindbergh's baby."

The meeting was a success. The kidnapper, who gave his name as John, accepted that Dr. Condon was acting in

MOMENT OF DESPAIR . . . Mrs Lindbergh arrives at the funeral parlour (top left) to identify the remains of her child (left). The baby's body was found in an area of dense woodland (top, right), not far from the Lindberghs' home. The ransom of $50,000 (above) had proved useless.

other cemetery, St. Raymond's, for the night of April 2. On this occasion, Colonel Lindbergh himself accompanied the Doctor, and, convinced that he was dealing with the genuine kidnapper, took 70,000 dollars with him in a cardboard box. Unknown to the Colonel, the U.S. Treasury had listed the serial numbers of every note—a precaution which was later to prove critical.

The Colonel sat in the car while the Doctor walked towards a voice in the darkness that kept calling: "Here, Dr. Condon, here." It was darker than at the first meeting, but Dr. Condon recognized the kidnapper's voice. He had left the ransom money in the car, hoping to persuade the kidnapper to hand over the missing baby. "John" refused to lead him to the child. "But I will give you full instructions as soon as I have the money," he promised.

Getaway plans

Dr. Condon decided, in the circumstances, that he would at least try to save Colonel Lindbergh the extra 20,000 dollars that had been demanded. "Look, John," he said, "Colonel Lindbergh is not as rich as they say he is. He has been able to raise only 50,000 dollars. Of course, he could have asked his friends for the money but he is not that kind of man. You know that and I know it." The kidnapper was not at first convinced, but ultimately he agreed: "All right, we'll take the 50,000 dollars."

Dr. Condon went back to the car to get the money. As he did so the kidnapper shouted: "Hey, Doctor," as if he feared he was about to be tricked. Colonel Lindbergh heard the call and the man's voice burned itself into his memory, never to be forgotten. Dr. Condon removed the extra 20,000 dollars, then went back to hand the balance over to the kidnapper. Once again he saw "John's" face clearly as he took the money.

The arrangement was that the kidnapper and his accomplices should have eight hours to make their getaway before revealing the whereabouts of the missing baby. The details arrived by post next day. The note said:

"The boy is on the boad (boat) Nelly. It is a small boad 28 feet long. Two persons are on the boad. They are innocent. You will find the boad between Horseneck Beach and Gay Head, near Elizabeth Island."

The Colonel, his personal friend Colonel Henry Breckinridge and Dr. Condon flew to the spot off the coast of Massachusetts. There, however, no one had heard of the *Nelly*. The Colonel flew low over the adjacent waters. There was no sign of the boat or his baby. He realized then that he had been tricked. Embittered, he

good faith. He obligingly took his hat off to let Dr. Condon see his face so that, if they met again, the Doctor would know he was talking to the right person. For his part, Dr. Condon was satisfied that he was speaking with the man who had abducted the Lindbergh child. He showed "John" safety pins of an uncommon design which had been used in the Lindbergh nursery and asked if he knew what they were. "Sure I know," said "John". "They were used to pin the blankets to the crib."

A series of communications now began between "John" and Dr. Condon, "John" sending notes, the Doctor replying through the advertisement columns of newspapers. "John" provided further proof of his authenticity by sending a sleeping suit which was positively identified as the one Charles Lindbergh Jr. had worn on the night of the kidnapping. He also upped his demands from 50,000 to 70,000 dollars, and he threatened to increase it to 100,000 dollars unless the money was paid by April 8.

A second rendezvous was made at an-

returned home and released for the first time details of the negotiations and the serial numbers of the ransom notes.

There could now be little chance that his son was still alive, and what hope there was vanished altogether on May 12. William Allen, a Negro teamster walking in the woods a few miles from the Colonel's home, and only a few yards from the spot where telephone workers had been busy ten weeks earlier rigging emergency lines, stumbled upon a shallow leaf-covered grave. In the grave was the body of a child. There could be no doubt about the identity. The golden curls and the little homemade shirt, stitched together by Betty Gow from one of his long flannel petticoats to keep him warm, told their own story. The Lindbergh baby had been dead since the night of the kidnapping, and he had died from severe head injuries.

The world grieved for the Lindberghs anew and, in the backlash that followed, there was a renewed outburst of earlier charges that the kidnapping must have been "an inside job". Betty Gow, although strongly defended by the Lindberghs, came under suspicion. So did Violet Sharpe, a maid in the Morrow home at Englewood, who went up to her room and committed suicide when police called to requestion her.

Meanwhile there had been several indications that the kidnapper probably lived, like Dr. Condon, in the Bronx. In the first place, there was the prompt reply from the kidnapper to Dr. Condon's appeal, published in the local Bronx newspaper. Then, from time to time, bills from the ransom money had turned up in the area. The issue was settled virtually beyond doubt by a remarkable piece of detection, carried out not by a policeman but by a member of the U.S. Forestry Service, Arthur Koehler. To Koehler fell the task of identifying and tracing the source of the wood used to make the sectional ladder featured in the crime.

Nobody, except Koehler himself, had much faith in the assignment. It was cheap, ordinary lumber of the type sold all over the country. It seemed almost impossible to trace it to the lumber yard that had sold it. But Koehler, who had worked with wood since childhood, was quietly confident. "I can find it," he said. Although it took 18 months, he traced the lumber yard concerned.

They were at the kidnapper's doorstep. But there the trail might easily have ended. Although the company kept a record of purchases, it did not note what sort of

A NEW FIND: Two years had passed since the kidnapping, and again attention was focussed on the Lindbergh case. $13,000 of the ransom money was found at the home (top left) of Bruno Hauptmann. Money was hidden with a gun in a hollowed-out joist (left). Hauptmann was arrested (above) and convicted of murder. He protested his innocence . . .

material it bought. Koehler had traced the lumber from the forest where it had grown, to the mill where it was processed, to the yard that sold it to the kidnapper. That, however, was as far as the telltale marks in the wood could take him.

But "John's" luck was about to run out. What proved his undoing was nothing to do with Koehler, or the police, or the private detectives, or the skilled reporters who had been assigned to track the kidnapper down. He was the victim of an international monetary crisis. On May 1, 1934, more than two years after the kidnapping, President Roosevelt abandoned the gold standard.

At the time, in addition to ordinary currency, the United States had notes known as gold certificates which were freely convertible into bullion. The effect of abandoning the gold standard was that gold certificates were called in and became illegal as currency. For the kidnapper it was about the worst thing that could have happened. Of the 50,000 dollars ransom money, 35,000 had been in gold certificates.

At 10 a.m. one day in mid-September, a Dodge sedan pulled into a Bronx gas station and the driver asked for five gallons of gasoline. He gave the manager, Walter Lyle, a ten-dollar gold certificate in payment. "You don't see many of these any more," said Lyle. "No," replied the motorist, "I've only got a hundred more left." Lyle had forgotten about the Lindbergh case but, as a precaution, took a note of the car's registration number. Then he went to a bank to exchange the certificate for two five-dollar bills. He explained how he came to be in possession of the bill. The teller looked up the serial number. It was part

of the Lindbergh ransom money.

Again the trail was warm. Police checked on the car. It was registered to Bruno Richard Hauptmann, 36, a former German soldier who, inquiries revealed, had entered the United States illegally in 1923.

Hauptmann was arrested outside his Bronx home on September 19. In one pocket he had a 20-dollar bill, also part of the ransom money. Police took him into a rear bedroom to question him. Special agent Thomas Fisk noticed that Hauptmann kept glancing furtively out of the window. "What are you looking at?" he asked.

"Nothing," said Hauptmann.

Gold certificates

Fisk went over to the window. Outside there was a garage. "Is that where you have the money?" he asked.

"I have no money," Hauptmann shouted angrily.

Despite his denial, the police decided to concentrate their search on the garage. In a shellac can, under some old rags and wrapped in newspapers, they found 11,930 dollars in gold certificates, all from the Lindbergh ransom. Police carpenters took the garage to pieces. In a hollowed-out joist they found another 840 dollars of the ransom money. Another 20-dollar certificate was traced to a shoe store where Hauptmann had bought a pair of shoes for his wife, Anna. By the end of the police search, 31,000 dollars were still missing. It never turned up. Nor were any more of the ransom bills passed after Hauptmann's arrest.

His trial for the murder of the Lindbergh baby began at Flemington, New Jersey, on January 2, 1935. Hauptmann pleaded "not guilty" but, although the case dragged on for five weeks, there was never any serious doubt about the outcome. Over and above the ransom money, which he claimed to have been "minding" for someone else, all the evidence pointed to Hauptmann's guilt.

The one thing which did not emerge from the trial was whether the Lindbergh baby had been deliberately killed in his cot, or had died accidentally by falling to the ground when the ladder broke. Hauptmann never talked and still protested his innocence, even after the jury had brought in a unanimous verdict of guilty and New Jersey High Court had rejected every argument in his appeal.

The news that his appeal had failed was brought to Hauptmann in the death house, where he was waiting to pay the penalty for the crime which had shocked the world. It was the eve of his tenth wedding anniversary and his first thought was for his wife. "My God," he exclaimed, "what a fine anniversary present for Anna!"

THE MISSING BODY OF

ROOKS FARM, at Stocking Pelham, in the green English county of Hertfordshire, was the home of two unique kidnappers. But what did the Hosein brothers do with Mrs. Muriel McKay? Where is the body that was never found?

STOCKING PELHAM

On this farm, a woman was imprisoned for more than a month... then she vanished without trace.

Two brothers were charged with her murder. They had planned to seize the wife of a newspaper millionaire, and demand a £1 million ransom. They got the wrong woman...

The Mrs. McKay "missing body" trial ... it was unique in British legal history

NO trial in Britain since the abolition of hanging for murder received more advance publicity than the court room drama which opened in London's Old Bailey on September 14, 1970. The two men who were brought up from the cells below the building to take their places in the dock of the historic No. 1 Court were brothers from Trinidad named Arthur and Nizamodeen Hosein. Although born in the former British colony, they were strictly speaking not West Indians but Indian Moslems whose family had originally come from the sub-continent of India.

Their father Shaffi Hosein was a respectable, hard-working tailor who had settled in Trinidad and owned the house where the family lived near Port of Spain. A deeply religious man, Shaffi also officiated as Imam in the Mosque which served the needs of the local Indian Moslem community in his village. The two boys, Arthur aged 34, and Nizamodeen, 12 years younger, had been brought up according to the teachings of the Koran, the Moslem bible.

The local squire

Together with their sister Hafiza and Arthur's wife Elsa and her two children, they lived at Rooks Farm, Stocking Pelham, near Epping in Hertfordshire. This was a small property of some 12 acres, which Arthur had bought for £14,000 with the aid of a mortgage in May 1968. It was largely uncultivated and the only livestock consisted of a few pigs, calves, and chickens. Incidentally, pig keeping hardly commended itself to Arthur's father, since the pig is considered unclean by good Moslems. For finance Arthur depended on his sewing machine with which he used to produce trousers for London's East End tailors. Nevertheless, Arthur Hosein, who possessed delusions of grandeur, fancied himself as the local squire and spent freely in the neighbouring bars. He even tried, without success, to join the local hunt. At his trial he gave his occupation as "fashion designer". He was known in the neighbourhood as "King Hosein".

Both brothers were charged with murder, kidnapping, blackmail, and sending threatening letters. Their victims were an attractive, 56-year-old Australian married woman named Muriel Frieda McKay and her husband Alick. One reason, the principal one, why the trial had already received such extensive press coverage was that Alick McKay was the Deputy Chairman of the *News of the World*, which

"ALICK, DARLING" . . . the wife of Alick McKay was snatched from her home, and never seen again. Mr. McKay was Deputy Chairman of the biggest-selling newspaper in Britain.

has the largest circulation of any English newspaper. The *News of the World* had recently been bought by another Australian, the young millionaire Rupert Murdoch.

The story which the stern and tight-lipped Attorney-General Sir Peter Rawlinson, who led the prosecution, recounted to the jury of nine men and three women was an extraordinary one. The Hosein brothers, he said, had devised "a brutal and ruthless scheme to kidnap a wife and by menaces to extort from her husband a vast sum of money."

Chauffeured Rolls

Arthur Hosein had noticed a luxurious chauffeur-driven Rolls Royce driving round London. He took a note of the registration number ULO 18F and determined to trace its owner. This he was able to do at County Hall, the headquarters of the Greater London Council where particulars of all motor vehicles in the metropolitan area are filed. At his brother's prompting, Nizamodeen made the inquiry in person, giving a false name in the application form he filled out. The reason for his inquiry, he told the counter clerk, was that the Rolls had sustained minor damage in a collision with his own vehicle and he was anxious to get into touch with its owner. As a result he learned that the car belonged to the *News of the World* and was allotted to the chairman for his use.

The brothers then proceeded to follow the Rolls one evening from the *News of the World* offices off Fleet Street to the prosperous London suburb of Wimbledon, where it deposited its occupant, whom they took to be Rupert Murdoch, at the door of a fine Georgian-style house in Arthur Road, No. 20, known as St. Mary House. However, the man in the Rolls was not Rupert Murdoch. Rupert Murdoch had left England with his wife a short time before on a business trip to Australia and lent the car to the deputy-chairman, who was in charge of the paper during his absence. The man in the Rolls was Alick McKay, and he owned St. Mary House.

Gagged and trussed

During the late afternoon of Monday, December 29, 1969, the Hosein brothers used some pretext to get into the McKay house, since Muriel McKay always left the door on the safety chain. Having overpowered her, they took her away with them. "It was obvious," said the Attorney-General, "that they thought they were abducting Mrs. Rupert Murdoch, but she was safe and at home in Australia."

When Alick McKay returned an hour or so later, he found several articles which the intruders had left behind. They were some sheets of a newspaper, a roll of twine, a piece of sticking plaster tape, and a billhook. This latter is an implement resembling a small axe, which is used by farmers for hedging and ditching work. The telephone was on the floor, but had not been ripped away from the wall. Muriel McKay's reading glasses, hand-bag, wallet, keys, and cheque book were lying scattered about the stairs. Some short time before, the house had been burgled, and Alick McKay now thought that the burglars had returned and used some of the twine to tie up his wife before abducting her.

The picture which Sir Peter Rawlinson presented to the jury was a horrifying one. "Can you imagine the horror of a woman, one minute beside the fire waiting for her husband to return, and minutes later — gagged and trussed — then driven away in the darkness?"

Five hours later the phone rang in St. Mary House. Alick McKay heard a voice at the other end of the line identifying himself with "Mafia Group Three from America," or M3 for short. "We tried to get Rupert Murdoch's wife," said the caller. "We could not get her so we took yours instead. Have one million pounds by Wednesday night or we will kill her!"

During the next few weeks there were 18 calls from the kidnappers, most of which were taken by Alick McKay's son Ian — who moved into the house in order to spare his father, who was suffering from a serious heart condition, since the excitement of continuing to speak to the kidnappers on the telephone might prove fatal.

"Frankly we want to know if she is alive and well," said Ian McKay in response to one call. "We have the money. But why should we give you the money if we do not know if she is alive?"

"I have told you what she is wearing," M3 replied. "What do you want me to do? Take her clothes off and send them to you? If you do not cooperate you will get her dead on your doorstep."

A request by Ian McKay to speak to his mother, or have her voice taped as proof of her continued existence, was ignored. Three letters had been received from her, Sir Peter went on, two addressed to her husband and one to her daughter Dianne. ("Alick darling, I am blindfolded and cold. Only blankets. Please do something to get me home.") But when Ian McKay continued to press for proof that she was still alive, he was told that she would not be allowed to write again.

Never murdered

"It's because you have not got her," Ian shouted over the telephone to M3. "You have got a corpse. You are trying to trick us. How many other people have you kidnapped before?"

"We have never murdered anyone as yet," was the ominous reply, "but there will always be a first time."

A further letter, postmarked January 9, 1970, was addressed to the editor of the *News of the World*. Written in block letters on a single sheet of white lined paper,

the message, which bore no signature, asked the editor to inform Mr. Alick McKay that they had his wife, that he would get some proof, that they wanted a million pounds, and that if Mr. McKay failed to cooperate his wife "would be disposed off" [SIC]. In fact some pieces of the dress, coat, and shoes, she was wearing at the time were later sent to the unfortunate husband.

Meanwhile, a sheet of paper similar to that on which the *News of the World* letter was written had been found by the police in Nizamodeen's bedroom at Rooks Farm. The sheet had been torn from an exercise book and exactly matched the letter. In addition, there were two ransom notes which a handwriting expert stated were in Arthur Hosein's disguised handwriting, and one of these notes had impressions of Arthur's thumb and one of his fingers. Apart from this, a palm print found on the newspaper lying on the floor of St. Mary House on the night of the kidnapping was positively identified as being that of Arthur Hosein.

In this instance the English police were up against a completely novel kind of crime. In no case since that of King Richard the Lion Heart in the twelfth century had the kidnapped person been held to ransom.

It was otherwise in America and the European continent where the F.B.I. and the police authorities have learned from

"I APPEAL" . . . Mr. McKay pleaded with the kidnappers for news of his wife, at a Press conference. With him, daughter Diane. Son Ian (above) rallied the family during the search.

experience to put the safety of the kidnapped person first, and the capture of the abductors second, and do not usually take action against the kidnappers until after the ransom money has been paid and the victim released. This procedure has as a rule worked well in practice, although there have been exceptions, of which the case of the Lindbergh baby in 1932 is the best known. But in America and the continent the kidnapping is normally the work of professionals who leave notes plainly stating their ransom requirements at the time the victim is taken away.

The amateurish Hosein brothers left no such message behind at St. Mary House, and with hoaxers frequently calling up the house as a result of the newspaper publicity, the police were hampered in their investigations through being unable to say whether Muriel McKay had, in fact, been abducted at all. Indeed, there was a suggestion that she had gone off to Australia on her own.

Enormous publicity

Furthermore, for the first two weeks in January 1970 no word was heard from the kidnappers, who were no doubt alarmed by the enormous publicity which Muriel McKay's disappearance had attracted. Then, on January 14, the telephone calls from M3 were resumed. Six days later Alick McKay received a letter containing directions for his son Ian to go to a certain telephone call box outside London on the Cambridge Road on the evening of February 1, where he would get a call at 10 p.m. telling him where to proceed with the money. This was followed by a second letter on January 26 repeating the directions, and enclosing a letter from Muriel McKay with the pieces of her clothing. In this letter M3 threatened that she would be "executed" if her son failed to keep "our business date without any error".

The date was kept—by Detective Sergeant Street who posed as Ian McKay. He took the call and was told to proceed to another telephone box on the road and wait for another call. The second call duly came through at 10.45, and "Ian" was told to look on the floor where he would find a used packet of Piccadilly cigarettes with further instructions. A note inside the packet ordered "Ian" to travel to a place called High Cross, beyond which he would see a road junction. At the side of the road there was a bank marked by some paper flowers, and this was the point where he was to leave the suitcase with the ransom money.

The Detective Sergeant did as he was instructed, while another police officer kept watch. But no one came to collect the suitcase, although the paper flowers were there. The result was that the police

eventually collected it themselves and took it back to Wimbledon.

Next day Ian McKay had a call from M3 accusing him of doublecrossing the kidnappers by going to the police, since they had seen a police car in the High Cross area the previous night. Later the same day M3 called again, this time saying he would do no more business with Ian McKay, but must deal with his father—who was instructed to pack the money into two smaller suitcases on February 6, and follow a similar call box procedure. This eventually led the police to Bishop's Stortford in Essex, where the suitcases were to be placed near a hedge by the side of a road leading into the town.

Here the kidnappers' luck ran out. A security officer, who had nothing to do with the investigation, happened to be driving past with his wife, and his suspicions were aroused by the sight of the two suitcases at the side of the road. He went to a call box and telephoned the local police, after which he returned and kept watch over the two cases. Meanwhile the Hosein brothers had been cruising round in Arthur's Volvo car, and noticing several police in the area, they thought it too risky to stop and pick up the suitcases. Thereupon they drove off—but not before the police had noted the Volvo's registration number. The number was checked; it was found to belong to Arthur Hosein, and it led the police to Rooks Farm.

No trace of Muriel McKay was found at the farm, but there were various articles there which connected the brothers with the abduction. These included paper flowers, which corresponded with those left at High Cross. It appeared that

THE MOST thorough and prolonged searches . . . whether Mrs. McKay died on the farm, and how she met her death, remains a mystery.

Nizamodeen's girl friend, Liley Mohammed, who worked as a hospital nurse, had shown Arthur's sister Hafiza how to make them—a process Liley had learned from a patient in the hospital. All this amounted to enough to incriminate the brothers as the kidnappers, and they were consequently arrested.

The first prosecution witness was Alick McKay, who looked very pale and shaky. He described the last time he saw his wife, which was the morning of her disappearance. "She was a very bright person."

Alick McKay was followed by a string of other witnesses who confirmed every point in the Attorney-General's story. Everyone who had spoken to M3 on the telephone—the operator who connected the first call, the editor of the *News of the World,* and various members of the McKay family—all testified.

Then the fingerprint and handwriting experts identified the prints and writing on the various articles exhibited in court as belonging either to Arthur or Nizamodeen Hosein. Finally, a neighbouring farmer in Hertfordshire swore that he had missed his billhook after visiting Rooks Farm in October 1969. When shown the billhook which had been found in the McKay house, he waved it from the witness box and exclaimed: "That's my bill. I defy anyone to say it's not!"

Both brothers gave evidence in their own defence, and denied all knowledge of the charges. But each tried to put the blame on the other for any suspicious happening or circumstance on which he was questioned.

Questioned about the billhook, Arthur said he could not recognize it and he thought the farmer had made up the story about it. However, he did admit, on being pressed, that he had borrowed a billhook to cut up a calf which had been brought to the farm. From time to time Arthur burst out into wild accusations against the police, who he said had frequently beaten him up after his arrest.

Nizamodeen, on the other hand, said he had been "scared stiff" of his brother.

He admitted going to County Hall and making inquiries about the Rolls, of which Arthur, he said, had supplied him with the registration number. It was Arthur, too, who told him to give the counter clerk a false name and address. His brother did not say why he wanted this information, Nizamodeen added, and he "did not give it another thought".

In his summing up of the evidence, the judge (Mr. Justice Sebag Shaw) mentioned every relevant point. "Each one perhaps is small in itself," he told the jury, "but from them it may be that an edifice is slowly erected by one tiny brick after another tiny brick."

It was clear that the jury thought so too. After an absence of just over four hours, they returned a verdict of guilty on all counts, but they recommended Nizamodeen to leniency.

Denounced judge

Asked by the judge whether they had anything to say before sentence was passed, Nizamodeen remained silent. But Arthur burst into a hysterical denunciation of the judge for his partiality. In

passing sentence, the judge addressed grave words to the men in the dock: "The kidnapping and detention of Mrs. McKay was cold-blooded and abominable. She was snatched from the security and comfort of her home and so long as she remained alive she was reduced to terrified despair.

"The crime will shock and revolt any right-minded citizen and the punishment must be sanguine so that law-abiding citizens will be safe in their homes. There cannot have been a worse case of blackmail. You put Mrs. McKay's family on the rack for weeks and months in an attempt to extort money from them by monstrous demands."

Both brothers were then sentenced to life imprisonment for murder. On the

other charges, Arthur got 25 years and Nizamodeen 15 years for kidnapping, and both got 14 years and 10 years respectively for blackmail and sending threatening letters—all the sentences to run concurrently.

Among the spectators in the crowded court was old Shaffi Hosein, who had come over from Trinidad for the trial. "I still cannot believe my boys would have done this," he said with a stupefied look. "I am sure they are not guilty."

However, it is abundantly clear that both brothers were convicted on overwhelming circumstantial evidence. Yet there is one puzzling factor about the case. Muriel McKay's body was never found. Not the slightest trace of her was discovered at the farm, or in the large surrounding area, in spite of the most thorough and prolonged searches.

There was a gruesome story current at the time that after they killed her the brothers cut up her body into pieces which they then fed to the pigs on the farm. But this is entirely unsupported by the evidence. Had it been so, some bones must have remained, but nothing of this kind was ever forthcoming. Nor was anything in the way of bones found in the large stove and chimney in the farm house, where it was likewise suggested that she had been cremated.

On the other hand, she may have died

from exposure during the bitterly cold weather at the time of her kidnapping, and her death may have been accelerated by lack of the drugs which she had been taking under medical prescription. It is possible too that she may never have been at the farm at all, but held in some hide-out, perhaps in nearby Epping Forest, and after her death her body was weighted and dumped in a river or the sea.

Reprisals danger

Exactly how Muriel McKay met her death remains a mystery. How long it will remain so depends largely on Nizamodeen Hosein, who may conceivably be persuaded to solve it in return for an early parole by the prison authorities. Asked by Elsa Hosein, when she visited him in prison whether there was a third party in the case, Nizamodeen replied enigmatically:

"Arthur says that we must never talk about that, because if we do the children will be in great danger. There would be reprisals."

THE MEN WHO WALK ALONE: A lost wife, a shattered life . . . Alick McKay (centre), pictured leaving court. Parted, prisoners . . . the brothers Nizamodeen (left) and Arthur Hosein (right). Was there another person involved in the puzzling case of Mrs. McKay? The brothers remained enigmatic . . .

THE LADYKILLERS

LADYKILLER CHRISTIE . . .
Victims like 26-year-old Miss Hectorina MacLennan (above) were boarded up in a hidden cupboard. Gradually, the stripping of the house revealed more bodies (top).

One alarming theory about the Ladykillers is that they murder to make their presence felt. There are many cases to support this, few more spectacular than that of the haunting necrophiliac Reginald Christie, the notorious killer of Rillington Place. Christie was a weakling and a hypochondriac. He may have killed as many as seven women and a baby. Some of the bodies were found in a cupboard by a tenant at the house where Christie had lived. By then, another (presumably innocent) resident of the same house had been hanged for two of the murders.

THE three doctors called in to pronounce upon Henri Désiré Landru's mental condition were agreed upon one thing: the man, despite the ten women he was said to have murdered, was not mad. The first medical expert, Dr. Vallon, faced the crowded court at the lady-killer's trial and stated:

"I already had to examine the accused in 1904, when he was being charged with obtaining money by false pretences. I found him then in a state bordering on the psychopathic, but he was not mad. Perhaps he was on the borderline, but not beyond it. I find now that Landru is perfectly lucid, perfectly conscious of what he is doing. He is quick and alert in his mind. He is easy and facile in repartee. In short, he must be considered responsible for the acts of which he is accused."

The second doctor, Roques de Fursac, added: "There is no trace of obsession. In examining Landru's personality, we have found him to be normal in every way." While Dr. Roubinovich said: "We were struck by his subtlety and presence of mind. His psychology is what might be called that of the 'transportee'. Transportation is always before his eyes as a nightmare which threatens him . . . The transportee has to live, and his past means that he cannot be choosy about the means he employs to keep himself alive. He will use any means to avoid being caught and sentenced afresh, to avoid transportation. Landru was in this position in 1914."

Lack of feeling

Landru—whose criminal and sexual career had been under police surveillance for some twenty years—was jubilant when he heard this. "The crimes of which I am accused could only be explained by the most pronounced insanity," he asserted. "The doctors say I am sane—therefore I am innocent."

Said to be "completely lacking in moral responsibility", Landru displayed an ambivalent attitude towards women, whom he courted like any other men and later killed with a brutal lack of feeling that branded him as a monster without humanity or heart.

If murderers derived their interest, like butterflies, from their rarity value, then Landru would belong to the rarest and strangest of species, the lady-killer. A surprising statement, perhaps, if you consider that over fifty per cent of all murder victims are women. But this is because the commonest type of murder is the family quarrel, in which the husband kills his

THE BRIDES IN THE BATH murderer, George Smith, with four of his wives. The lucky ones were deserted. The alternative was drowning in the bath.

MURDER CASTLE: He built a house riddled with secret passages . . . and killed 27 women. H. H. Holmes was one of America's most remarkable murderers.

wife in a fit of rage or jealousy. Much lower on the list—but still providing a high proportion of the crime figures—is the sex murder. The sex killer has the mentality of a hungry fox; women are chickens, who are protected from him by a screen of social conventions; like a fox, he waits for his opportunity to slip under the wire and help himself.

Landru, however, was not a sex killer in this sense. On the contrary, he belongs to the very small group of killers who chose to make a poor living (Landru "earned" about £100 [$250] a victim) by the destruction of gullible women. He was possessed by a strange, morbid compulsion—the same compulsion we can see in the case of the French "werewolf", Martin Dumollard, of George Joseph Smith, the British Brides in the Bath murderer, of H. H. Holmes, the American mass-killer, of the wife poisoner George Chapman, of the Hungarian Bluebeard Bela Kiss—perhaps even in the case of Jack the Ripper himself.

Killer of children

In order to understand the nature of this compulsion the question must be asked: Why are these lady-killers called "Bluebeards"? The original Bluebeard, the 15th-century Marshal of France, Gilles de Rais, who fought beside Joan of Arc, was not a killer of women, but of children. Noted because of his glossy blue-black beard, he was a sexual pervert, and also thought he could use the children's blood in the making of gold. But it was the French writer of fairy stories, Charles Perrault, who created the popular version of Bluebeard the lady-killer in the late seventeenth century. One of his more macabre stories tells how a young girl, Fatima, marries the rich landowner Bluebeard, and one day looks into a secret

room—to find there the bodies of his previous wives. Although Perrault wrote the tale from the Gallic viewpoint, many countries have similar legends of wife-killers—Cornwall has a story of a giant called Bolster who killed his wives each year by throwing rocks at them. The folk-imagination understands these dark male compulsions to destroy women—and also the woman's half-frightened, half-fascinated attitude towards it, which in some cases leads her to invite assault and violence upon herself.

A modern crime

The strange thing is that all the known cases of real-life Bluebeards are fairly modern. Of the hundreds of criminal cases contained in such compilations as *Lives of the Most Remarkable Criminals* (1735), *The Newgate Calendar* (1774), and even Camden Pelham's *Chronicles of Crime* published as late as 1886, there are no "lady-killers". Highwaymen, pirates, cut-throats, housebreakers galore; but no lady-killers. Why should this be? If folk-legend had been obsessed by Bluebeards for centuries, why, up until then, should there have been no real-life Bluebeards?

The work of the psychologist Abraham Maslow suggests a fascinating explanation which, if correct, throws an entirely new light on this question, and on the history of crime. Maslow's basic theory, first published in 1942, is known as "the hierarchy of needs" or values. It was intended as a counterblast to Dr. Sigmund Freud's theory that man's basic needs are sexual—not to mention Karl Marx's theory that his basic needs are economic, and Alfred Adler's theory that the basic human urge is the Will to Power.

Maslow pointed out that if a man is starving he has *no* other strong urge except the urge to eat, and he cannot imagine any higher bliss than having large and regular meals. But as soon as he achieves regular meals, he begins to brood on security—the need for a roof over his head. If he achieves this, he now begins to think about sex—not just rape, but a mate to settle down with. And when a man has got a home, a good job, and a happy family, what is the next thing he wants? Respect and admiration, to be accepted socially, to be liked—and if possible envied—by his neighbours. This is the stage at which men join rotary clubs, and wives form coffee groups and worry about keeping up with the Joneses. At this stage, the urge for *self-esteem* becomes paramount, and this explains the penchant of some killers—Heath is a classic example—for dressing-up as heroes and officers.

Once all these needs are satisfied, what then? According to Maslow, the highest level of all can emerge: the creative urge

—what, in more old-fashioned days, we would have called his "spiritual drives". But this is not restricted to the emotional and egotistical need to write symphonies, compose plays in blank verse, or build cathedrals. Anybody who wants to do a job *well,* just for the sheer pleasure of it, is expressing the creative urge. From this it can be seen that Maslow's hierarchy of needs is a kind of ladder. If you are stuck on the bottom rung, then Marx's materialistic theories will strike you as true. If you are stuck on the next rung, it will be clear that the psychoanalyst Freud was right when he said there is nothing more important than sex. On the next rung, the Austrian analyst Adler's Will to Power—and self-esteem—will seem the profoundest truth about human nature. All are partly right; none is wholly right.

Food and territory

Maslow's theory is borne out by the history of crime. In primitive societies, food and "territory" are the most important things, and if a man commits a murder, it is likely to be for one of these two reasons or drives. Until a hundred years ago, for instance, most people in Europe and America were living at mere subsistence level. These were the conditions under which Burke and Hare, the two Edinburgh body-snatchers, committed their murders in 1828, and it is not surprising that they killed human beings for the sake of the few pounds paid by Dr. Knox of the medical school for the corpses. *This* is basically the reason that *The Newgate Calendar* is so full of footpads and burglars and highwaymen. And why there are so few rapists. Society was still stuck on the bottom rung of Maslow's ladder.

The Victorian age rolled on; the tide of prosperity spread slowly across Europe. Most of the famous British Victorian murders were still for gain; but the age of middle-class murder had arrived, bringing in the domestic dramas of such killers as Constance Kent who butchered her four-year-old half-brother, mass-poisoner William Palmer, wife-poisoner Dr. Edward Pritchard, Madeleine Smith, the Scottish girl who disposed of an unwanted and awkward lover. Then, in 1888, the savage and apparently motiveless murders of five London East End prostitutes, by the unknown killer nicknamed Jack the Ripper, signalled the beginning of a new age—the age of sex crime. Society, by virtue of its progress and growth, had reached the next rung of Maslow's ladder. By the 1940s, sex crime, once the rarest of all reasons for murder, had become commonplace. It still is; but already, the next age has begun—the age of what could be called "the self-esteem murder". Why did the London gangster-brothers Ronnie and Reggie Kray commit murders in

front of a crowd of witnesses? The answer sounds astonishing: to *impress* the London underworld. The element of pride, of self-esteem, becomes increasingly common among murderers, whatever the motive appears to be. Multiple sex killer John Reginald Halliday Christie loved exerting his authority as an English war reserve constable; Heath posed as "Group Captain Rupert Brooke"; Arthur Hosein—kidnapper of Mrs. McKay, wife of an executive of the London *Sun*—set himself up as a "gentleman farmer"; Charles Manson saw himself as leader of a world revolution. Typical of this new trend in murder is the statement of 18-year-old Robert Smith, who made five women and two children lie on the floor of an Arizona beauty parlour and shot them all in the back of the head: "I wanted to get known—to get myself a name," he stated afterwards.

There is one major consolation in all this. If society can get past the stage of the self-esteem killer, the murder rate should drop steeply. The next rung up the ladder is the purely creative stage, and creativity and murder are usually incompatible. Whether that stage will ever be reached in our overcrowded world is a matter for speculation; but if Maslow's theory is correct, there is ground for hope.

Masked inadequacies

As for Landru—the prototype and most quoted example of the 20th-century lady-killer—a brief examination of his adult sexual career reveals that he is a typical self-esteem killer. His Paris childhood certainly provides no hint of his subsequent "anti-women" activities. He was a sunny, good-natured child, liked by everyone, and adored by his parents (as his name—Désiré—hints). His father was an ordinary workman—a stoker. When Landru left school, he went to work in an architect's office—and his old friends immediately noticed the change. He became "stuck up", and he lost no opportunity to mention that he was a white collar office worker. He had achieved middle-class status—which, in the French provincial society of the 1890s, meant considerably more than it would today. For the rest of his life, Landru played this part of the member of the professional classes: he posed as lawyer, doctor, engineer, businessman, accountant—anything that boosted his ego, masked his inadequacies, and made him feel "talented" and a "gentleman".

Unfortunately for Landru and his future victims, society had no special place for the intelligent but mercurial young man. In the army—where he did military service—his record was excellent. Then he returned to civilian life, married the cousin he had got pregnant, and faced the

task of making a career for himself and providing security for his family. But the prospect of a lifetime in an office bored him, and he was too unstable to stay in any one job for long. Attempts to launch his own businesses invariably failed. His natural charm and alertness suggested petty fraud and false pretences as a means of tiding his wife and four children over bleak periods. And it was with the enthusiasm of someone who has finally found his niche that he turned to crime—a more exciting, more "creative", way of living than office work. Experience showed him that elderly widows were particularly gullible, and eager to give him the keys to their hearts and deposit boxes. Being a confidence trickster—especially such a well-loved and successful one—appealed to his vanity, to his intelligence, even to his artistic impulse (for, as Thomas Mann, the German Nobel Prize-winner pointed out in his novel *Felix Krull—Confidence Man*, the confidence trickster has a touch of the artist about him). Inevitably there were periods in gaol; and when, in 1912 (when Landru was 43) his father committed suicide, overwhelmed by his son's disgrace, the con-man entered a new phase of his career. He determined to throw all scruples to the wind and make an audacious career of murder.

It is a curious fact that—with one borderline exception—the life-styles of all the best known lady-killers resemble Landru's in certain basic respects.

Johann Hoch, born in Strasbourg in 1860, was intended for the ministry, but left Germany—for undisclosed reasons—and went to the United States. There he advertised in German language papers for widows without children, "object, matrimony". This technique was very like Landru's. He represented himself as a wealthy businessman or a man with a respectable position in a commercial company. He married the woman—if necessary—parted her from her money, and decamped. Unlike Landru, he appeared to prefer poison when it came to despatching his brides. He was married some thirteen times—unlucky number as far as his "wives" were concerned—and poisoned six of his brides. He was executed in Chicago in 1906.

Carefree scale

H. H. Holmes, perhaps the most remarkable American criminal of the 19th-century was also born in 1860, the son of a postmaster. Determined to rise in the world, he studied medicine, then became a swindler. His first known murder was of a store-owner, a Mrs. Holden, in Chicago. Holmes duly became owner of the store. He then built a house, riddled with secret passages, and proceeded to murder women on a large and carefree

PHOTOGRAPHS A.P.

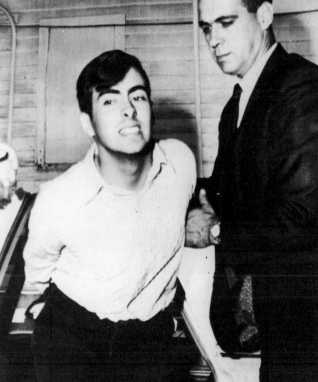

TO MAKE A NAME for himself, Robert Smith, aged 18, made five women and two children lie down, like spokes in a wheel, on the floor of an Arizona beauty parlour. Then he shot them all twice, in the back of the head. He was a typical case of the "self-esteem" murderer. "I wanted to get known," he said.

FATAL FAME . . . the cost of Robert Smith's bid for attention: Clockwise: Toddler Debra Sellers, Glenda Carter, Mary Olsen, Bonita Sue Harris, who was seriously wounded, Carol Farmer, and the Sellers baby, Tamara Lynn. Mrs Sellers, who was killed, is below. Centre: Robert Smith arrives in court.

scale. The motive was not sexual, for most of the girls had been his mistress for some time before they "vanished". At least eight women disappeared after entering his "murder castle", and he later schemed with a man named Pitezel to swindle an insurance company. In the end —as often happened with Holmes' friends—Pitezel and three of his children were killed. Mrs. Pitezel was also on the murder list, but Holmes was arrested before he could eliminate her. In all, he confessed to 27 murders.

George Chapman—actually a Pole called Klosovski—was executed in 1903, having been found guilty of poisoning three wives. Chapman's English was poor, and the early part of his life was spent abroad, so altogether less is known about him than about other notable lady-killers.

Son of a carpenter, he spent much of his life trying to "better himself", setting up in various businesses, including those of barber and publican. (He was in White-chapel in London's East End at the time of the Ripper murders, and has been suspected of being the Ripper.) There is no evidence that he was ever involved in swindling and the motive for the poisonings has variously been put down to sexual lust, craving for security and money, and sadism.

George Joseph Smith, the infamous "Brides in the Bath" murderer was a Londoner, born in 1872. He was in and out of reformatories and gaols from the age of nine. After a two year sentence for receiving stolen goods, he embarked on the career of a swindler of widows and unmarried females. He married and

authorities had been notified of his death in action during the First World War. Later stories, however, told of him enlisting in the French Foreign Legion under the name of Hofmann, and of being spotted by a New York Homicide Squad detective emerging from the subway station in Times Square.

One other thing that the lady-killers —the men who mask their loathing of women with love—have in common is the so-called "hypnotic power" which they have wielded over their victims. This again can be explained by the way in which they carefully chose as their "wives" women who wanted—needed—to be subjected to the power of a "superior" man. These eager and willing victims —the "murderees"—cannot wait to meet a man who is going to mistreat them, both physically and emotionally, and then strip them of their pride, their dignity, their money and their possessions. Without such women—who seem to draw their killers towards them—the Landrus and

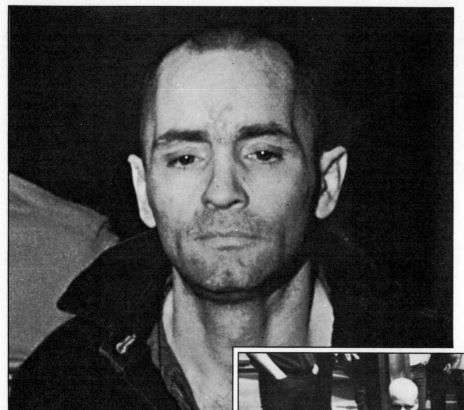

U.P.I.

A.P.

LEADER of a world revolution? Charles Manson wasn't short on self-esteem. He had a "happy family", and impressed them by instigating a rampage of murder.

deserted an unspecified number of women before deciding to drown Bessie Munday in 1912. When his third "wife" drowned in her bath, a newspaper report aroused the suspicions of a relative of a previous victim. Protesting his innocence to the end Smith was executed in 1915.

Frederick Deeming, born in England about 1853, was a confidence swindler who specialised in cheating jewellers by pretending to be the manager of a diamond mine. For reasons of gain, he also posed as a millionaire, and as "Sir Wilfred Lawson" and "Lord Dunn". He was a braggart and a remarkably inventive liar. In 1891, he murdered his wife and four children, and buried the bodies under the floor in a rented house. He then went to Australia with a new wife, who was soon murdered and buried under another floor. Posing as Baron Swanston, he had persuaded another girl, an heiress, to marry him when the discovery of his

second wife's body led to his arrest. Three houses in which he had previously lived in South Africa also proved to have girls buried under the floors. He declared that the ghost of his dead mother urged him to murder women. Despite this "defence", he was executed in 1892.

Bela Kiss, an amateur astrologer and Hungary's most spectacular lady-killer, claimed a total of at least twenty-four victims. When he joined the army in 1916, the new tenant of his house opened seven petrol drums and found them to contain bodies of women preserved in alcohol. Kiss proved to be well known in the red light district of Budapest—a man of immense physical strength and boundless sexual appetite. He had advertized for ladies to share his rural seclusion in Cinkota; the ladies vanished, and their valuables provided Kiss with more funds for excursions to the city brothels. By the time his victims were discovered, the

other Bluebeards would have no one to abuse, take advantage of and fleece. Their "hypnotism"—George Joseph Smith was reputed to have "eyes that could make a girl do anything"—would go for nothing simply because there would be no one on whom they could successfully practice. Every Landru has to have a Madame Cuchet—his first widow victim—and but for her, and those like her, he would be no more than another eccentric possessed with "strange" ideas about the sexes and the roles played by men and women in the marriage game.

Lady-killers are to be abhorred, and their victims pitied. But compulsion can be a two-way process: the compulsion to kill and to be killed. Lock up the lady-killers by all means, but also educate their "wives", teach them to beware of men like Smith, men like Landru, who are too smooth, too polite, too charming—and, underneath it all, too deadly.

Rodney Shackell

AN OFFICER
AND A GENTLEMAN...

A tall, handsome young Air Force hero, home from the war . . . to women his easy charm was utterly fatal. Neville Heath was more than a fraud . . . he was a suave sex-maniac, one of the most violently depraved men the world has known. In a few summer days, he haunted England's genteel South coast.

POLICE GAZETTE

PUBLISHED BY AUTHORITY.

NEW SERIES.　　　TUESDAY, JUNE 25, 1946.　　　No. 147, Vol. XXXIII.

Manuscript for publication should be addressed "THE COMMISSIONER OF POLICE, NEW SCOTLAND YARD. S.W.1." with "C.R.O. (P.G.)" in top left corner.

HAROLD SCOTT
The Commissioner of Police of the Metropolis.

Special Notice

MURDER

M.P. (FH).—It is desired to trace the after-described for interview respecting the death of MARGERY GARDNER, during the night of 20th-21st inst.—NEVILLE GEORGE CLEVELY HEATH, alias ARMSTRONG, BLYTH, DENVERS and GRAHAM, C.R.O. No. 28142-37, b. 1917, 5ft. 11½in., c. fresh, e. blue, believed small fair moustache, h. and eyebrows fair, square face, broad forehead and nose, firm chin, good teeth, military gait ; dress, lt. grey d.b. suit with pin stripe, dk. brown trilby, brown suede shoes, cream shirt with collar attached or fawn and white check sports jacket and grey flannel trousers. Nat. Reg. No. CNP/2147191.

Has recent conviction for posing as Lt.-Col. of South African Air Force. A pilot and believed to possess an " A " licence, has stated his intention of going abroad and may endeavour to secure passage on ship or plane as passenger or pilot. May stay at hotels accompanied by woman.

Enquiries are also requested to trace the owner of gent's white handkerchief with brown check border, bearing " L. Kearns " in black ink on hem and stitched with large " K " in blue cotton in centre.

LUNCHTIME had come and gone, yet there was still no sign of life from Room No. 4 at the Pembridge Court Hotel in Notting Hill, London. The maid responsible for the room, eager to get on with her cleaning and tidying, was understandably irritated. She peeped through the keyhole. The room was in darkness and there was nothing to be seen. She knocked at the door again. Still there was no answer.

Perhaps she should inform someone. She sought out Mrs. Alice Wyatt, who helped her father-in-law to run the 19-bedroomed hotel, and explained the situation. Mrs. Wyatt looked at the clock. It was 2 p.m. She thought it was time to investigate. She let herself into the bedroom with her pass key and drew back the curtains. In one of the single beds, the sheets and blankets pulled up around her neck, lay a young, dark-haired woman. It was hardly necessary to move the bedclothes to establish that she was dead. The red bloodstains all over the second bed told their own story.

The police arrived within minutes. Beneath the bedclothes they found a badly mutilated body. The dead woman's nipples had been practically bitten off. There were 17 weals, apparently made by the plaited thong of a whip with a metal tip, across her back, chest, stomach, and face. Her ankles were bound together with a handkerchief and she had bled from the vagina. It was clear that her face had been washed, but there were still traces of blood on her cheeks and in her nostrils. The blood on the second bed suggested that she had been killed there and her body moved after death — while interlacing markings on the pillowcase pointed to a bloodstained whip having lain there.

Female companion

The victim's body was removed to Hammersmith Mortuary where Dr. Keith Simpson, the pathologist, carried out a post-mortem. He found the woman had died from suffocation, probably caused by a gag or by having her face pressed into a pillow.

Meantime, the police had started the hunt for the killer. The trail did not prove difficult to follow. The woman's body was found on Friday, June 21, 1946. Room No. 4 had been let the previous Sunday to a man with a female companion (not the dead woman), who had signed the register "Mr. and Mrs. N. G. C. Heath", giving an address in Hampshire.

"FIANCÉE" Yvonne Symonds (right): "Yvonne, there's been a nasty murder in London . . . in the room where we stayed last weekend." Police soon pinpointed Heath, but the use of his photograph (left) placed them in a fatal dilemma.

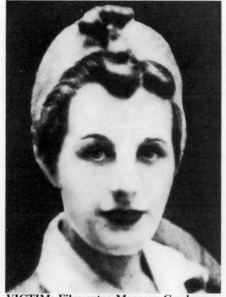

VICTIM: Film extra Margery Gardner liked the "bohemian" life. At the Panama Club, she drank and danced her way to a dreadful death with debonair Heath.

Within hours, Superintendent Thomas Barratt, who was in charge of the case, had established that Mr. N. G. C. Heath was Neville George Clevely Heath, a handsome, 29-year-old former officer, six feet tall and the possessor of a criminal record, although not for violence. The police had also uncovered the identity of the dead woman. She was 32-year-old Mrs. Margery Gardner, occasionally a film extra, separated from her husband and fond of the gay, bohemian life.

On the night before the killing, she drank and danced with Heath at the Panama Club in South Kensington. Around midnight they left the club together, hailed a cruising taxicab and directed it to the Pembridge Court Hotel. Harry Harter, the cabdriver, remembered the journey well. "I picked them up in

the Old Brompton Road and put them down about 50 yards from the Pembridge Court Hotel," he told detectives. "The man asked me how much the fare was. I said it was 1s. 9d. and he gave me 2s. 2d. Then they walked towards the hotel. He put his arm round the woman's waist and I saw them enter the hotel gate."

The police were well pleased with their progress. It was beginning to look as if an arrest was merely a matter of days. It was decided to release Heath's name and description to the newspapers as a man who, in the cautious legal phrase, the police would like "to assist them with their inquiries". At this point, however, the police faced a dilemma. They had collected four photographs of Heath from his home in Merton Hall Road, Wimbledon. Should these photographs be published along with Heath's name and description. It seemed on the one hand that identification would prove a critical issue in Heath's trial if, as expected, he proved to be the murderer, and widespread publication of his likeness might easily prejudice the chances of a conviction. If, on the other hand, Heath's suave and easy charm masked a sex maniac, he might easily kill again unless he were captured quickly. In the end the decision was taken not to release the photographs. As a result, another woman was to die.

Name and description

While his name and description was being flashed to police stations and newspapers all over the country, Heath was in the Sussex seaside resort of Worthing. He had travelled down to the South Coast on the day Margery Gardner's mutilated body was found, and booked in under his own name at the Ocean Hotel. The purpose of his visit was to look up yet another of the many women in his life,

A RAKE'S PROGRESS...THAT ENDED IN MULTIPLE MURDER

Police pieced together details of Heath's extraordinary career of crime and service in the armed forces, during which, in the course of ten years, he managed to get himself commissioned and dishonourably discharged on three occasions. In outline, his dossier reads:

February 1936. Obtained short-service commission in R.A.F.

August 1937. Court-martialled for being absent without leave for nearly five months. Other charges included escaping while under arrest and "borrowing" a non-commissioned officer's car without permission. Sentenced to be cashiered. Commuted subsequently to dismissal.

November 1937. Placed on probation on charges of fraudulently obtaining credit at a Nottingham hotel and attempting to obtain a car by false pretences. Eight other offences, including posing as "Lord Dudley", taken into account.

July 1938. Sentenced to three years' Borstal treatment for housebreaking and stealing jewellery worth £51 from a friend, and for obtaining clothing worth £27 by means of a forged bankers' order. Ten other offences taken into account.

September 1939. Released from Hollesley Bay Colony because of the outbreak of the war.

October 1939. Enlisted in Royal Army Service Corps.

March 1940. Commissioned and posted to the Middle East.

July 1941. Placed under arrest after a dispute with a brigadier. Went absent without leave. Court-martialled for these offences and for obtaining a second pay-book by making a false statement; making a false statement to his commanding officer, enabling him to be absent from his unit; and on five charges relating to dishonoured cheques. Sentenced to be cashiered.

November 1941. Absconded from the troopship that was bringing him to England when it docked at Durban in South Africa. Went to Johannesburg where he passed himself off as a Captain Selway, M.C., of the Argyll and Sutherland Highlanders.

December 1941. Enlisted in South African Air Force under the name of Armstrong. Commissioned.

May 1944. Seconded to Royal Air Force. Shot down on the Dutch-German border while piloting a Mitchell bomber.

August 1945. Court-martialled and dismissed the service in South Africa on six charges, three of conduct prejudicial to good order and military discipline and three of wearing military decorations without authority.

February 1946. Arrived back in Britain.

April 1946. Fined at Wimbledon Magistrates' Court in South London for wearing a military uniform and decorations to which he was not entitled.

Yvonne Symonds, whom he had met at a dance in Chelsea the previous Saturday. After the dance he took her to the Panama Club. "Let's find a hotel and sleep together," Heath suggested. His new companion refused.

Heath spent the whole of the next day with her. He was at his most debonair and charming. Yvonne Symonds found him fascinating. When he proposed, she gladly accepted—although she had known him for only a few hours. Once again Heath suggested: "Let's spend the night together." This time she agreed, and she was the "Mrs. N. G. C. Heath" who had occupied Room No. 4 at the Pembridge Court Hotel the previous Sunday night. Heath phoned her several times in the course of the week. Now, down in Worthing, he phoned again and arranged to take her out to lunch on the Saturday.

Utmost courtliness

By then the news of Margery Gardner's killing was out, and, in the course of the meal, Heath suddenly said: "Yvonne, there's been a nasty murder in London. Have you read about it in the papers?" Miss Symonds said she hadn't. "I'll tell you all about it later," Heath promised. He returned to the subject that night when he took her to dine and dance at the Blue Peter Club in Angmering. "That murder I mentioned," he said. "It took place in the room we stayed in last weekend. I knew the girl. She was with some man who had nowhere to stay so I gave him the key to the room and went and slept somewhere else. The police—an Inspector (it should have been Superintendent) Barratt—got on to me and took me round to the room. I saw the body. It was a pretty gruesome sight."

Miss Symonds did not doubt Heath's story for a moment. This, after all, was the man who had swept her off her feet, who, in their brief time together, had always treated her with the utmost courtliness and consideration. How had the girl died? "A poker was stuck up her," replied Heath bluntly. "I think that's what killed her—although Inspector Barratt seems to believe she might have been suffocated."

Miss Symonds was horrified. "What sort of person could commit a brutal crime like that?" she asked.

"A sex maniac, I suppose," shrugged Heath.

He took her home safely at the end of the evening and chastely kissed her goodnight. She was to speak to him only once again. That was the following morning after she and her parents had read Sunday newspaper accounts of the murder and a renewed appeal by the police—the first one had been published on the Saturday—for Heath to come forward. Miss Symonds immediately rang

HEATH'S ROOM

BUILDER'S LADDER HERE

"A LITTLE DECEPTION": After savagely murdering Doreen Marshall, Heath returned to his hotel room by way of a fire escape and a ladder.

her fiancé at his hotel.

"My parents are very worried about the story in the papers," she told him.

Heath remained the cool man-of-the-world. "I thought they would be," he said laconically. Then he added: "I've got a car and I'm driving back to London to sort things out. I'll probably give you a ring this evening." But he did not ring. Nor did he return to London. Instead he caught a train to Bournemouth where he booked into the Tollard Royal Hotel, using the improbable name of Group-Captain Rupert Brooke—Brooke being the brilliant young English poet who died in Greece in the First World War.

Ur til now, Heath had acted in a careless, almost reckless, manner for a killer who, presumably, did not want to be caught. Margery Gardner had been found in a room rented to him, and, in describing the murder to Yvonne Symonds, he had revealed an intimate knowledge of the crime. His claim that "Inspector" Barratt had taken him to the scene was quite untrue and would not withstand investigation if Miss Symonds talked. Before leaving Worthing, Heath therefore took his first positive step to try to point the

finger of suspicion away from him. He wrote to "Chief Inspector" Barratt. The letter arrived on the police officer's desk at New Scotland Yard on the Monday morning. It read:

"Sir, I feel it to be my duty to inform you of certain facts in connection with the death of Mrs. Gardner at Notting Hill Gate. I booked in at the hotel last Sunday, but not with Mrs. Gardner, whom I met for the first time during the week. I had drinks with her on Friday evening, and whilst I was with her she met an acquaintance with whom she was obliged to sleep. The reasons, as I understand them, were mainly financial.

Invidious position

"It was then that Mrs. Gardner asked if she could use my hotel room until two o'clock and intimated that, if I returned after that, I might spend the remainder of the night with her. I gave her my keys and told her to leave the hotel door open. It must have been almost 3 a.m. when I returned to the hotel and found her in the condition of which you are aware. I realised I was in an invidious position, and rather than notify the police I packed my belongings and left.

"Since then I have been in several minds whether to come forward or not, but in view of the circumstances I have been afraid to. I can give you a descrip-

tion of the man. He was aged approximately 30, dark hair (black), with a small moustache. Height about 5ft. 9ins., slim build. His name was Jack and I gathered that he was a friend of Mrs. Gardner's of some long standing.

"The personal column of the *Daily Telegraph* will find me, but at the moment I have assumed another name. I should like to come forward and help, but I cannot face the music of a fraud charge which will obviously be preferred against me if I should do so. I have the instrument with which Mrs. Gardner was beaten and am forwarding this to you today. You will find my fingerprints on it, but you should also find others as well. N. G. C. Heath."

The parcel containing the instrument never arrived, and for the next 13 days—from Sunday, June 23, until Saturday, July 6—Heath lived what was apparently the life of a carefree holidaymaker in Bournemouth. The guests, and the staff, at the Tollard Royal Hotel found him pleasant and amusing company. His entire wardrobe seemed to consist of grey flannel trousers and a mustard-coloured sports jacket, and during most of his stay he appeared to have no cash, putting all his drinks on the bill, but nobody was particularly concerned. The man they knew as Group-Captain Rupert Brooke was obviously an officer and a gentleman.

It was also established that, while in South Africa, Heath was married in 1942 and had a son. His wife had divorced him in October 1945, on the grounds of desertion.

Within a couple of days of Heath's arrival in Bournemouth, every police force in the country, including the local one, had a copy of his photograph as a wanted man. The decision not to release pictures to the newspapers was adhered to, however, even as the days passed, producing nothing but the inevitable crop of frustrating false leads as to Heath's whereabouts. With each 24 hours that passed, death came a day nearer to 21-year-old Doreen Marshall.

Doreen Marshall was a pert and pretty ex-Wren (the Women's Royal Naval Service), the daughter of a Pinner, Middlesex, company director. After being demobilized she suffered a severe attack of influenza, and her father decided that a few days by the sea would help to put her on her feet again. He packed her off to Bournemouth where she booked in at the Norfolk Hotel.

It is not exactly clear how her path crossed with Heath's. His own account, written later, said: "On Wednesday, July 3, during the morning, I was seated on the promenade on Westcliff when I saw two young ladies walking along the front. One of these two was a casual acquaintance whom I had met at a dance at the Pavilion during the latter half of the preceding week (her Christian name was Peggy but I was unaware of her surname). Although I was not formally introduced to the other I gathered that her name was "Doo" or something similar. The girl Peggy left after about half-an-hour and I walked along the front with the other girl whom I now know to be Miss Marshall. I invited her to have tea with me in the afternoon and she accepted.

Smilingly agreed

In the course of tea at the Tollard Royal Hotel that afternoon, Heath asked: "Would you care to join me for dinner tonight?" Miss Marshall smilingly agreed. After dinner they sat in the hotel lounge until shortly after midnight. Other guests noted that Heath seemed to be slightly drunk and, as the evening wore on, his companion appeared unhappy. At one point she begged one of the men present to order her a taxi. Soon afterwards, Heath cancelled it and said: "My guest has decided to walk home." He left the hotel with Miss Marshall about 12.15 a.m.

"I'll be back in about half-an-hour," he told the porter.

"A quarter-of-an-hour," snapped Miss Marshall.

Nobody saw her alive again. As for Heath, it was never established at what time he returned to the hotel. He regained his room by climbing a ladder and getting in through a window. It was, he explained later, "a little deception" on his friend the night porter. The mystified porter confessed subsequently that at 4.30 a.m. he had peeped into Heath's bedroom to see if he was there. The guest was fast asleep.

Thursday passed apparently normally. So did most of Friday. Then the manager of the Tollard Royal Hotel, Ivor Relf, received a phone call from the manager of the Norfolk Hotel. "One of our guests appears to be missing," he said, "and we believe she dined at your place on Wednesday." He added that the missing guest, Miss Marshall, had come from Pinner, outside London.

Suave demeanour

Heath, in the meantime, showed no signs of agitation or excitement. The only changes in him—both significant, it was to turn out—was that he now seemed to have money in his pockets and had taken to wearing a silk scarf to hide a couple of scratches on his neck. There was nothing else about the demeanour of Group-Captain Rupert Brooke to arouse suspicion, and it was not until the Saturday morning that Mr. Relf got around to mentioning the phone call from the Norfolk Hotel.

Heath, playing it as coolly as ever, laughed off the notion that the missing woman might have been his dinner guest. "I believe she came from Pinner," said Mr. Relf. "I have known that lady for a long while, and she certainly doesn't come from Pinner," replied Heath airily.

But he was now to take a step as extraordinary as his decision to write to Superintendent Barratt. He telephoned the police and asked if they had a photograph of the missing woman. The officer in charge of the case was out and Heath said he would ring again later. He phoned for a second time at 3.30 and, on hearing that the police did have a photograph of Miss Marshall, offered to come round a couple of hours later to have a look at it and see if he could be of any help.

He can hardly have suspected it, but the step he took through the door of the police station was to be his last as a free man. Heath identified himself as Brooke, but he was almost immediately recognized from the photographs circulated to police stations throughout the country as the man wanted for questioning about the death of Margery Gardner. Heath still insisted that he was Brooke. At 9.45

VICTIM: "Miss Marshall did not wish me to accompany her." Not far from the beach, police with bloodhounds searched for the body of Doreen Marshall in wooded Branksome Chine.

p.m., however, Detective-Inspector George Gates told him: "I am satisfied that you are Neville George Clevely Heath and I am going to detain you pending the arrival of officers of the Metropolitan Police."

"Oh, all right," murmured Heath, not, it seemed, particularly concerned.

Now the evidence began to pile up on all sides. Heath, who had gone to the police station without a coat, apparently believing that he would not be there long, asked if his sports jacket could be brought from the hotel. In a pocket the police found a cloakroom ticket issued at Bournemouth West station on the Sunday Heath arrived in the town. The ticket led the police to a suitcase which, on being opened, was found to contain a blood-stained scarf and a leather riding-whip with a plaited thong. The tip had worn away, exposing the metal underneath.

Artificial pearl

Detectives also found in the sports jacket the return half of a London-Bournemouth rail ticket, subsequently proved to have been the one issued to Miss Marshall, and an artificial pearl. In a drawer in Heath's hotel room was a soiled, blood-stained handkerchief, tightly knotted, with human hairs adhering to it. It was established also that, in the previous 36 hours, Heath had pawned a ring belonging to Miss Marshall for £5 and a fob watch for £3. But where was Miss Marshall herself?

A statement written by Heath after he was detained at Bournemouth hinted that she had probably left the town. After

SPECTATORS, attracted by one of the most horrifying murder stories the world has known, gather to see Heath at his trial in London's famous Old Bailey court.

walking out of the hotel in the early hours of Thursday morning, it continued, they had "sat on a seat near the hotel overlooking the sea. We must have talked for at least an hour, probably longer, and then we walked down the slope towards the Pavilion. Miss Marshall did not wish me to accompany her but I insisted on doing so—at least some of the way. I left her at the Pier and watched her cross the road and enter the gardens. Before leaving her I asked her if she would come round the following day, but she said she would be busy for the next few days, but would telephone me on Sunday if she could manage it. I have not seen her to speak to since then although I thought I saw her entering Bobby's Ltd., on Thursday morning."

The body of Doreen Marshall was discovered in Branksome Chine on the Monday, two days later. It was the circling flies that led a passer-by, who had heard about a missing woman, to her. Her body

had been dragged into some rhododendron bushes. She was naked except for her left shoe, but she was covered with her own clothing—underwear, a black frock and a yellow swagger coat—and some boughs of fir trees. Twenty-seven artificial pearls, which came from her broken necklace and matched the one found in Heath's pocket, lay nearby. Her powder compact and stockings were some distance away and her empty handbag was found at the bottom of the chine.

Like Margery Gardner, she had been savagely mutilated. Her throat had been cut, causing her death. In places the wound was three-quarters-of-an-inch deep. Before that, her hands had been pinioned, but there were cuts on them suggesting that she had tried to fight off an assailant with a knife.

Question of sanity

Heath was charged with both murders. but his trial, which opened at the Central Criminal Court on September 24, dealt only with the murder of Margery Gardner. The horrifying details of Doreen Marshall's death came out in evidence, however. It was quickly clear that the real question was not whether Heath had killed the two women but whether he was sane. The defence did not bother to put him into the witness-box. They pinned all their hopes for cheating the gallows on insanity, and the debate about whether Heath was or was not in his right senses proved the only interesting part of the short, three-day trial.

At the end, however, the jury took only 59 minutes to find him guilty. He was sentenced on September 26 and executed on October 26. To the very last he remained the debonair playboy, completely in control of himself, ordering a grey, pinstriped suit, grey socks, grey shirt and polka-dot blue tie for his trial, asking for his diaries and address books to be destroyed once the verdict was known: "I have caused enough trouble in this world already without causing more."

He refused to see any members of his family, but the day before he hanged he wrote two letters to his mother. The first said: "My only regret at leaving the world is that I have been so damned unworthy of you both." In the second he wrote: "I shall probably stay up reading tonight because I'd like to see the dawn again. So much in my memory is associated with the dawn—early morning patrols and coming home from nightclubs. Well, it wasn't really a bad life while it lasted . . . Please don't mourn my going—I should hate it —and don't wear black."

It was said that his last wish to the governor of the prison was for a whisky. Then, on reflection, he added: "In the circumstances, you might make that a double!"

He loved 283 women . . . and killed ten of them. In a country famed for its lovers, he was the most famous. His name was Henri Landru, but they called him . . .

BLUEBEARD.

THROUGHOUT the morning of December 7, 1921, a curious crowd of spectators gathered outside the Court of Assize in the Palais de Justice at Versailles. The entrance was guarded by police and troops, who turned away almost everyone who tried to gain admission to the small and shabby courtroom, since there was only accommodation for a handful of people inside apart from the court officials and lawyers concerned with the trial. It was a case which had already attracted worldwide interest, since the accused man was said to have had relations of one sort or another with no less than 283 women and to have murdered ten of them, having previously seduced them and persuaded them to hand over their money and property to him for safekeeping or investment.

Enormous indictment

Punctually at one o'clock in the afternoon President Gilbert in red robes and gold-braided hat took his place on the bench accompanied by two assessors. The uniformed soldiers on duty in their steel helmets presented arms smartly and the usher rang his bell calling everyone in court to order. Immediately below the judicial bench was a table containing the grim exhibits in the case, pieces of charred clothing and human bones. At a sign from the President, a little door at the side of the courtroom opened and the prisoner appeared, escorted by three gendarmes, two of whom stood on either side of him and one behind as he stepped into the appointed place in court which served as a dock. A tall red-bearded figure, he looked a rather weary old man, although in truth he was only 52. His complexion wore the familiar prison pallor, since he had been in custody for more than two years.

The President's first duty was to establish the prisoner's identity. "Your name is Landru?" he asked the man on whom every eye in court was firmly fixed. "Henri Désiré, son of Alexandre Julien and Henriette Floré Landru? You were born in Paris on 12 April 1869, and your last residence was 76 Rue de Rochechouart?"

"Yes," Landru quietly replied.

The Clerk of the Court thereupon rose to his feet and proceeded to read the indictment, a document of enormous length, which it took the Clerk three hours to do and which occupied the greater part of the first day of the trial. It was an extraordinary story of forgery, swindling, seduction and multiple murder. For the most part Landru listened to this appalling account with an air of apparent unconcern, his bearded face bent forward between his shoulders. Only once did he look up and scowl in the course of the lengthy recitation of his misdeeds. That

was when the Clerk uttered the phrase, "exploitation of women". An audible titter ran round the courtroom at the mention of the 283 women with whom Landru was stated to have had "relations".

Landru's usual technique was the familiar one of the matrimonial advertisement. A typical example of this "come into my parlour" technique appeared in *Le Journal,* a Paris morning newspaper, on May 11, 1915:

> Widower with two children, aged forty-three, with comfortable income, affectionate, serious, and moving in good society, desires to meet widow with a view to matrimony.

Among the women who replied to this advertisement was a 44-year-old widow named Madame Anna Collomb, who gave full particulars of her family and fortune, discreetly giving her age as 29. In due course she received a letter from a Monsieur Cuchet, who described himself as a director of a factory in Montmartre. At the meeting which followed Cuchet told Anna Collomb that he was a war refugee, an engineer from Rocroi, who had left everything before the advancing Germans and had come to Paris to build up his business afresh.

He added that he had a car, a little apartment in town and a modest house, the Villa Ermitage, at Gambais, near the forest of Rambouillet, not far from Paris. He now wished to marry and settle down, he said. The result was that Madame Collomb found Monsieur Cuchet most attractive and loved him "because he is a real gentleman and says such beautiful things to me".

Wife and children

After a while, however, Landru's ardour for the lady began to cool. The truth was that he had several other affairs on hand since there had been many replies to his advertisement and he could not spare all the time that the infatuated Anna Collomb demanded. However, they eventually came together again, she gave up her own apartment and went to live with her lover in his flat in the Rue Chateaudun, while she gave him her furniture to put into store. She also visited the villa at Gambais where Landru was known as Monsieur Fremyet.

Elsewhere and with other women he had different aliases: Petit, Dupont, Diard and Guillet. He had another villa at Vernouillet on the river Seine near Paris. He also had a second apartment in Paris, 76 Rue de Rochechouart, not to mention a wife and four children who lived at Clichy, where he ran a garage.

SURROUNDED BY WOMEN right to the end . . . Henri 'Bluebeard' Landru, some of his victims, and the garden at Gambais, where their bodies were burned . . .

MME. COLOMB

MME. LABORDE LINE

MME. BUISSON.

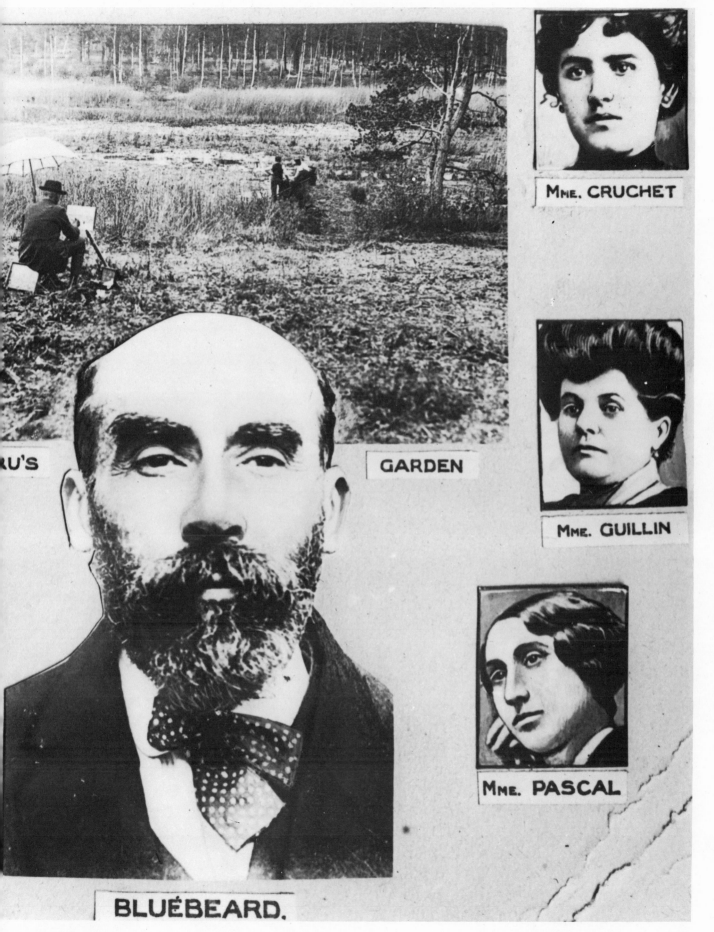

RU'S

GARDEN

Mme. CRUCHET

Mme. GUILLIN

Mme. PASCAL

BLUÉBEARD.

On Christmas Eve 1916, the court was told, Mme. Collomb invited her sister Mme. Pelat to Gambais to meet her lover. M. Fremyet ingratiated himself by saying that he would soon regularise their position by marrying his mistress, after which they would be moving to Nice. That was the last Mme. Pelat saw of her sister and M. Fremyet. After writing to both of them at Gambais and receiving no reply, she addressed a letter to the local Mayor, asking him if he could tell her where M. Fremyet was and how to get into touch with him.

It so happened that not long before this the Mayor had received a similar request from a certain Mlle. Lacoste about her sister Mme. Celestine Buisson, who also visited the villa in Gambais and had disappeared. On making inquiries the Mayor learned that the Villa Ermitage was occupied by a M. Dupont, of whom there was likewise no trace. The Mayor suggested that Mlle. Lacoste and Mme. Pelat should get into touch with one another. In due course they met and compared notes. Both women had seen the occupier of the villa and they agreed

that Cuchet-Fremyet and Dupont were singularly alike. Meanwhile the police were investigating another disappearance, that of a genuine Mme. Cuchet. It appeared that Jeanne Cuchet and her son André had gone to live with a certain M. Diard in his house at Vernouillet in December 1914 and had not been seen or heard of since. After making further inquiries, the police were satisfied that Cuchet, Fremyet, Dupont and Diard were one and the same person. On April 10, 1919, a warrant was issued for the arrest of the individual whose identity corresponded with any of these aliases.

Unmistakable figure

Next day, the court was told, Mlle. Lacoste happened to be walking along the Rue de Rivoli when she suddenly saw the unmistakable figure of the man she recognized as M. Dupont. He had a smartly-dressed young woman on his arm and Mlle. Lacoste saw them enter a shop. She followed them inside where she heard the man order a white china dinner service to be sent to his apartment. After the two had left the shop Mlle. Lacoste continued

"THE WOMEN never reproached me . . . perhaps some of them will turn up for the trial." The only people who turned up for Bluebeard's trial were a string of witnesses testifying that the missing women had last been seen with him. As the accused man gave evidence, the judge had to suppress laughter in court. When Bluebeard finally faced the guillotine, his humour could only be described as deadpan.

to follow them but eventually lost them in the crowd. She thereupon went to the nearest police station and reported her suspicions. On following up this clue, the police learned that the dinner service had been ordered by M. Lucien Guillet, an engineer, of 76 Rue de Rochechouart.

The following morning Landru was arrested in his apartment and told he would be charged with murder. He protested that he was Lucien Guillet, born at Rocroi, in 1874, and seemed shocked that he should be accused of a capital crime. He was then searched and the police discovered a black loose-leaved note-book in his pocket which he made an unsuccessful attempt to dispose of by throwing it out of the window.

Meticulous account

The note-book revealed that Landru kept a meticulous account of his daily expenses. For instance, on the day he invited Anna Collomb to Gambais, he had recorded one return ticket and one single ticket to the local station, similarly with Celestine Buisson. The note-book also showed that the replies to his matrimonial advertisements had been carefully classified and information had been filed about their fortunes, children, relations and so on. The names were briefly marked under the following heads:

1. To be answered *poste restante*.
2. Without money.
3. Without furniture.
4. No reply.
5. To be answered to initials *poste restante*.
6. Possible fortune.
7. To be further investigated.

The first police searches of the Villa Ermitage and the house at Vernouillet revealed nothing of importance, but later a stove was discovered in which Landru was alleged to have burnt the bodies of his victims after he had cut them up.

Afterwards 295 bone fragments of human bodies were discovered. These were believed to belong to three corpses; there was also a miscellaneous collection of women's clothing, buttons, and trinkets of various kinds.

Besides the Mesdames Buisson, Collomb and Cuchet and the latter's 18-year-old son, seven more women whom Landru knew were stated to have disappeared without trace. Their names were given to the court as Mme. Thérèse Laborde-Line, widow, aged 47, and a native of Buenos Aires, whom Landru called 'Brésil'; Mme. Desirée Guillin, a widow, aged 59, formerly a governess, who had inherited 22,000 francs which Landru drew out of her bank account with a forged signature, having also sold her furniture; Andreé Babelay, a servant girl, aged 19, whom Landru met in the Metro; Mme. Louise Jaume, a married woman, aged 38, who was separated from her husband, and whose money and furniture Landru appropriated after he had taken her to Gambais; Mme. Anne-Marie Pascal, a divorceé, aged 33, and a struggling dressmaker of easy morals, whose furniture and personal belongings were found in Landru's garage; and Mme. Marie-Thérèse Marchadier, a prostitute turned brothel-keeper, who gave up her establishment and went with Landru to Gambais, after parting with her furniture.

All the names with accompanying particulars appeared in the sinister black note-book which Landru had tried to hide from the police when he was arrested.

On the second day of the trial, President Gilbert examined the prisoner on his past record. "You have received seven sentences for fraud, Landru," he remarked. "Your parents were honest and decent folk. Your father was for a long time a fireman in the Vulcain Ironworks. Your mother worked at home as a dressmaker. After her death, your father who had retired to the Dordogne, came to Paris to see you but found you were in prison. He was so upset by your conduct that in 1912 he committed suicide in the Bois de Boulogne."

As the prisoner did not dispute these facts, the judge went on: "You were a clever boy at school and earned high praise from your teachers. On leaving school you were admitted as a subdeacon to a religious establishment?"

"Only for a short time," Landru added.

"Perhaps it was there," said the judge, "that you learned that unctuous manner which has been one of your chief methods of seduction, and which has helped you to capture the trust and affections of so many woman."

President Gilbert paused, but the prisoner remained silent. "Then," continued the judge, "you took up more profane occupations. Not far from you there lived your cousin Mme Remy, who had a young daughter."

"She had two," Landru interrupted.

"Very well. One of them became your mistress, and you had a daughter born in 1891. Two years later you regularized the position, married her and acknowledged the child. In all you had four children?" Landru nodded his agreement.

"You had a lot of different jobs," said the judge. "Clerk in an architect's office,

TRIAL BY PRESIDENT

PROCEDURE in French criminal trials differs from that in other national courts in several important respects. For one thing, the presiding judge, who sits with two legally qualified assessors and is called the President, takes a much more prominent part in the proceedings than, say, his British counterpart, whose function broadly speaking is limited to seeing that the rules of evidence and the rights of the accused are observed, to summing up the evidence to the jury, and in the event of the jury returning a verdict of guilty to passing sentence.

On the other hand, the President of a French assize court has the full record of the case in front of him which he has read, and he interrogates the prisoner on every detail of the charges during the proceedings. The basis of his interrogation is the dossier which has been compiled by the pre-trial investigating magistrate known as the *juge d'instruction*; this is usually the result of prolonged questioning by this official while the prisoner is in custody.

In French courts the whole of the prisoner's past criminal record forms an essential part of the indictment and is read out at the beginning of the trial. This also contrasts with British courts, where a witness of fact is only permitted to testify to matters of which he has direct and personal knowledge, but in France hearsay evidence is admissible—i.e. witnesses may repeat what they have been told by others.

Finally, in France the President of the Court must consult with the two assessors and take into account their views on the punishment due.

agent, toy salesman and so on. In fact you had no definite, stable occupation."

"Which proves how inadequate were the inquiries which were made about me," Landru again broke in. "The police are often inefficient."

"Yet," said the judge, "when the magistrate confronted you with this information you had nothing to say?"

Flattered conceit

The prisoner threw up his hands as if amazed at such official stupidity. "It was not my business to guide the police," he exclaimed. "Have they not been accusing me for the past three years of deeds which the women who disappeared never for one moment reproached me with?"

These words produced some laughter among the onlookers in court which the judge suppressed by calling for silence. "It is you," he emphasised his words by pointing a finger at the prisoner, "it is you who have made it impossible for these women to complain. That is as clear as anything."

Asked to explain to the jury why the names of so many women were in his note-book, at first he was evasive. Finally when pressed by the judge, he said: *"Eh bien! Voila!* It is the list of a business man, who entered the names of his clients with whom he did business." He had bought these women's furniture from them to help them during the war, he explained, intending to sell it back to them when the German armies had been driven out of France.

"Why then recruit your clients by means of matrimonial advertisements?" the judge asked.

"Just a little business ruse, very innocent," Landru replied. "It flattered their conceit," The prisoner let his gaze wander in the direction of the jury, as if to say what a clever answer he had given. But they did not look at all convinced. Then he turned again to the judge and said: "You say that some of these women have not been found. Perhaps they will turn up during the trial." However, none of them did so.

During the succeeding days a string of relatives of the ten women who had vanished came forward to testify to the occasions when they had last seen the women in question, usually in Landru's company. Others testified having seen dense smoke coming out of the chimneys of the houses which Landru had occupied at Gambais and Vernouillet, accompanied by a most offensive stench. Indeed one of the neighbours complained about it to the police at Vernouillet. This was at a critical stage of the First World War, and though the police did call at the house they eventually dropped the matter as they had more serious matters to think about at that time than malodorous smoke from a domestic chimney—particularly when Landru assured them that he had only been burning some refuse. There were also stories of portions of putrified human flesh being recovered from a lake near Gambais by fishermen.

One witness who attracted particular attention was the pretty young woman who had been with Landru when he went shopping in the Rue de Rivola, and as events fortunately turned out for her was "the one that got away". She gave her name as Fernande Segret, her age as 29,

"BE BRAVE? But I *am* brave," replied Bluebeard, refusing confession or Mass, rum or cigarettes. The execution was to be a public one, in the square outside . . .

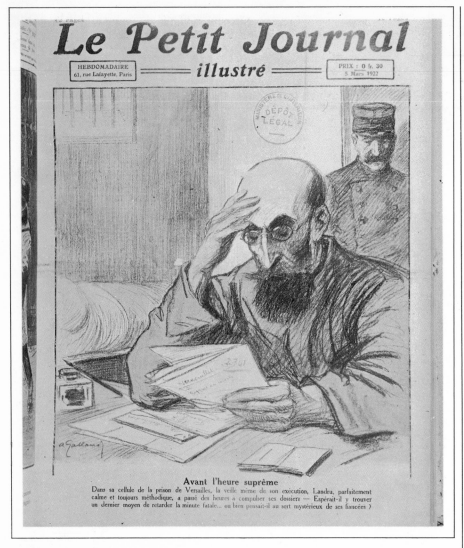

Le Petit Journal

illustré

HEBDOMADAIRE
61, rue Lafayette, Paris

PRIX : 0 fr. 30
5 Mars 1922

Avant l'heure suprême
Dans sa cellule de la prison de Versailles, la veille même de son exécution, Landru, parfaitement calme et toujours méthodique, a passé des heures à compulser ses dossiers — Espérait-il y trouver un dernier moyen de retarder la minute fatale... ou bien pensait-il au sort mystérieux de ses fiancées ?

THE FINAL HOURS: Did Bluebeard hope for a last-minute stay of execution? Cool as ever, he achieved the celebrity of a star at his trial.

and her occupation as "lyric artist". She described how she had become engaged to Landru whom she knew as Roger Guillet, how her mother had described him as an imposter and an adventurer, and how despite this warning she had insisted on going to live with him as his mistress. She was deeply in love with him, she said, and wished to marry him.

Rather disappointed

"I went to Gambais seven or eight times," said the love hungry Fernande Segret. "The villa was not what you would call well furnished. In one room there were some guns and cartridges which he knew well how to use."

"Do you know what means your fiancé had?" the judge asked her. "How did you live?"

"Landru told me his garage brought in a good deal, enough for our needs. I went there one day, and was rather disappoint-

ed, as there was only one apprentice working in the place, for he had told me he had a considerable business there."

Asked if they ever had any quarrels, pretty Mademoiselle Segret replied that they had two she remembered in particular. One was when a letter came for him addressed in another name. The other was when she began to look through some of his papers in their flat in the Rue de Rochechouart and he flew into a great rage. "I promised not to do it again," she added, "but I showed my astonishment since all my correspondence was read by him."

There was "a delicate point" he wished to clear up, said the judge to this witness. She had told the examining magistrate that in her sexual relations with the accused she had found him extremely passionate but at the same time quite normal.

"Is that right?"

"Oh, yes!" replied Mademoiselle Segret. "Very normal." What President Gilbert was trying to ascertain was whether Landru was a sadist and pervert. Apparently he was not, though the medical evidence pointed to his being a

dangerous psychopath, though well aware of what he was doing.

In his speech to the court, the chief prosecutor declared: "I demand the extreme punishment — death for Landru, the murderer of Vernouillet and Gambais. He is entirely responsible for his deeds. The doctors have certified this, and the ability which he has shown here is proof of his sanity. He had no pity on his victims. Why then should you have pity on him?"

It took the jury an hour and a half to find Landru guilty on all charges except two. Only in respect of those of defrauding the domestic servant Andreé Babelay of her property (she had virtually none) was he acquitted.

Mercy recommendation

Prompted by Landru's defence counsel, the jury surprisingly added a recommendation to mercy, calling upon the President of the Republic to reprieve the condemned man. However, the judge sentenced him to death by the guillotine, to be carried out publicly in front of the prison where he was confined.

"Be brave!" one of the officials said when they came to fetch him, as was customary, between five and six o'clock in the morning. "I *am* brave," replied Landru. Asked if he would make his confession to the priest and hear Mass, he exclaimed, "Never on your life!" "Anyhow," he added, "I cannot think of keeping these gentlemen waiting." He also refused the usual offer of a glass of rum and a cigarette.

As he was led out into the prison yard, he shivered a little in the cold early morning air, since he was wearing thin trousers and an open-necked shirt. Then the prison gates were flung open and for a minute or two he faced a cordon of troops holding back the spectators who had gathered in front of the guillotine which had been erected in the square outside the prison.

In a matter of seconds the executioner and his assistant strapped him face downwards on the platform of the guillotine.

Curious tailpiece

The Landru story has a curious tailpiece. More than sixty years later a film entitled *Landru*, scripted by the best-selling novelist Françoise Sagan, was made and publicly shown. Fernande Segret, whom everyone thought was dead as she had not been heard of for years — in fact she had been working as a governess in the Lebanon — suddenly turned up and sued the film company for 200,000 francs damages. She got 10,000. She then retired to an old people's home in Normandy where she eventually drowned herself, saying she was tired of people pointing to her as "the woman in the Landru case".

TRAPPED...BY THOSE TELL-TALE TRACES

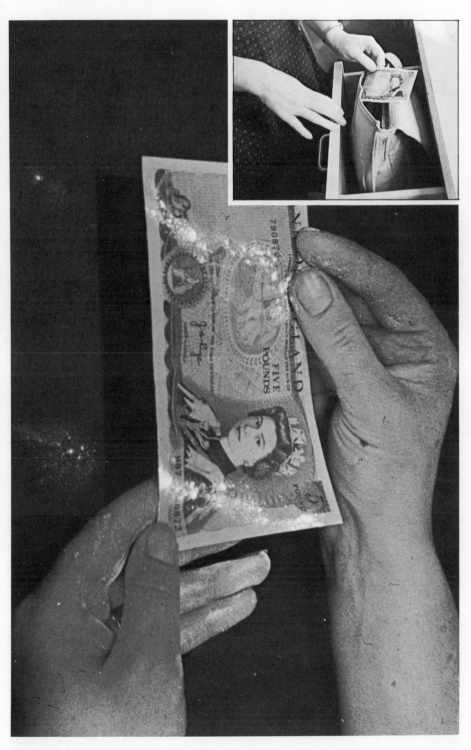

IT WAS a saying of the French criminologist Professor Edmond Locard, one of the greatest forensic scientists of the twentieth century, that "Everything a man does leaves traces". But when a man tries to alter those traces deliberately, he is in trouble.

Documents are so much the basis of modern life that they are obviously often involved in crimes. Documentary evidence does not mean forgery alone; the document examiner covers, both figuratively and literally, a large amount of territory.

Paper, the root of most of his work, is, to be briefly technical, an aqueous deposit of any vegetable fibre in sheet form. The name, as most people know, comes from the Latin *papyrus,* which in the hands of the early Egyptians, its first known users, comprised the pith of a sedge-like plant which was sliced into layers and beaten or pressed into sheets.

But, as so often happens, the Chinese were ahead of everybody and nearly 2000 years ago were using paper made by hand, fashioned by processes used all over the world until not long ago—though paper, as such, did not appear in Europe until about the eleventh century. In Britain paper first came from a paper mill erected around 1490; its products in fact were used for an edition of Chaucer's *Canterbury Tales.*

The forger, in his efforts to defeat science, has tried his hand at artificially aging paper. For example, the general discoloration due to age is a process of oxidation, which is easily confirmed by the expert examiner. The faker tries to imitate this, using liquids like coffee or tea, woodfire smoke, extract of tobacco, and even permanganate of potash to achieve that vital faint brown effect.

Age is also attempted by pressing a false document into folds and rubbing these folds along a carpet or an old wall to simulate an ancient fold; the micro-

TAINTED MONEY: Thefts have been taking place regularly, so banknotes are marked with a powder which is invisible until exposed to ultra-violet light.

scope will pick out in seconds the rubbing or dirt grains along a bogus fold.

Watermarks, another weapon of forgers, began in Italy about the thirteenth century. They are made when paper is a wet pulp. A dandy roll, a woven wire gauze-covered skeleton roll, has the watermark device soldered on to it. The impression of the roll on the wet pulp causes a thinning of fibres which, when the paper is finished, is the familiar watermark.

A faker's trick is to process finished paper by imprinting with his own dandy roll, using some sort of oily substance as a watermark; this looks genuine to the casual eye. But test it with a damp cloth or a petrol soaked paintbrush and the watermark will vanish.

One of the problems which bedevil

document, brilliantly forged, as it turned out. It was supposed to be 400 years old. The false writing was almost foolproof; the forger had found some old paper of the right age; the ink used was genuine carbon ink which goes back, according to the great Egyptologist, Professor Flinders Petrie, to Egypt 5000 years ago.

The expert working on this document saw hours of investigation ahead to produce evidence that would stand up in court about something he only "felt" was wrong. Then, through his microscope ocular, he saw something incredible. Embedded in the ink of a letter was an almost invisible particle that looked metallic. Elaborate examination showed that there were minute particles embedded in that ink—aluminium.

This modern metal was the giveaway,

the examiner of documents is what experts call "sample". A document cannot always be cut, marked, or touched with reagents—chemicals which act in certain ways on materials. Suppose it is desired to find out if a paper contains linen and cotton, important in dating it. It can be touched with something called zinc-chlor-iodine. The marked spot will turn wine red, unthinkable on a perhaps valuable document.

Then the microscope steps in. Dates of paper origins are generally well authenticated and if an old type of paper is examined, say, one made from rags, the linen or cotton fibres in it show distinctive features which are absolutely different from modern wood pulp papers. But—and here is the exception—many high grade modern papers are still made from linen or cotton.

There was the case of a questioned

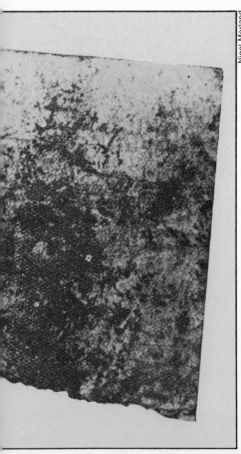

for the police were later able to show that the forger's brother, working in the same room during the actual writing, was filing an aluminium casing. Aluminium dust, floating invisible in air, settled in that carefully processed carbon ink writing until the microscope found the answer.

Inks, next to paper, are usually the expert's friend. When a letter is written in ordinary ink, and not blotted, it seems natural to the naked eye. A simple hand-lens, or magnifying glass, will reveal clues. The writer paused for a second to think of a word and then hyphenated it. The lens shows the faintest difference in ink shading, or perhaps the pen is lifted in the middle of a letter and then it carries on; the lens shows that, too.

Ink itself will "talk". One notable forensic chemist in the 1920's, claimed that ink in ancient times was made from soot taken from cooking vessels, which accounts for its almost indefinite life. Iron gall ink (a mixture of ferrous sulphate with an infusion of nuts, galls and gum) came in about the first century of the Christian era. The Romans generally used an iron compound ink, the one, for example, used in the *Codex Sinaiticus,* which dates from the fourth century A.D.

So the dating goes on—iron gall ink had logwood put into it in the middle of the eighteenth century to improve its colour. A hundred years later they were using logwood with potassium chromate, and no iron, for writing purposes. All this and more means reasonably accurate dating.

The first modern ink, aniline dye ink, came in a blue form in 1861, a fairly impermanent writing fluid. This was followed by a famous advertisement for blue-black ink which showed a large blot, dark in the centre and light at the edges. Indeed it was incorrect, for in practice the reverse order would have been the case.

In current years that well-known enemy of all who love good handwriting, the ball point pen, contains a so-called "solid" ink which is, in fact, a thick suspension of dye in a drying oil. Its stable companion, the fibre-tipped pen is one that, unluckily, does present problems in forensic document examination.

Traces of metal, usually iron, can be found when ordinary pen marks have been erased or bleached out. Ultraviolet light will reveal these interferences. Pencils or ball point pens often leave no residue which can be picked up after erasure, but embossing occurs in the paper used; fibres are disturbed in the paper as well, and these will answer to the expert.

The fibre-tipped pen, as it is usually called, is so light in its effect that it leaves behind no clue after erasure—other than disturbed sizing on the paper. But where additions or amendments have been made on a fibre-pen written whole, then all is reasonably well—close examination soon reveals the differences in ink quality, shading and such.

The copying pencil, the one which leaves mauve marks on the tongue when it is accidentally licked, can be a godsend to the document examiner. In the Southampton garage murder in England in 1930 a man named Messiter was found killed; there were no apparent clues until a sharp-eyed detective picked up a dirty little scrap of paper. The back was a lodging house receipt, the front also seemed to bear words—but they were invisible under tread marks, dirt, and oil.

Words bleached out

A simple method worked this time. The paper was very delicately "washed" in benzene and there, under the dirt, was the name "F. Thomas" written in copying pencil. A letter was found in the victim's files bearing this name, later proved to be an alias of a man named Podmore. It was not long before evidence was found to support a charge of murder. Podmore was duly convicted, the scrap of paper becoming vital court evidence.

Erasures have been mentioned and these continually arise in document examination. Erasures are, simply, the removal of words, bleaching out before substitution; such partial interference with documents being a not uncommon crime.

A first test is to hold the suspect document on an angle before a good light. The eye, or a hand-lens, often reveals interference—chemical erasures tend to "stand out", particularly those on paper with a high finish.

Suppose a word has been bleached out and another put in its place. The original word can generally be read by using ultraviolet light with the correct

A SCRAP OF EVIDENCE solved the murder of Vivian Messiter (left). He was killed in a garage (far left and above), and there seemed to be no clues until a sharp-eyed detective picked up a dirty scrap of paper (top). A "washing" in benzene removed the dirt, oil and tread-marks to reveal a name (ringed) which was to prove vital. This name also appeared in mail filed by the victim, and thus led police to suspect a man named Podmore (right). From this lead, conclusive evidence was built up.

A BANK FIRE "destroyed" these cheques . . . but they were identifiable after being photographed by infra-red light on specially-sensitized film.

plate and filter. This method shows up the original disturbed fibres of the paper, assuming an ordinary pen has been used, and a "shadow" of the word is revealed.

One of the most delicate and adroit recovery methods is one used by the late Paul Kirk, a leading American documentary expert. To recover erasures, obliterations, or indented ("ghost") writing he used plastic casts, a process so exacting and so difficult that an ordinary man would not have patience to try it. Kirk, however, achieved some excellent results.

Burning a document is not always a successful evasion. One man in a crime burned a vital cheque in a grate, and broke up the ashes with a poker. Experts worked for hours, spraying the fragments with diluted lacquer until they were strong enough to be touched.

Then the bits—they were no more— were reassembled until they were almost complete. Strong oblique light showed up the inked writing, which had carbonized, and the case was solved. The point of these examples is that the expert is a trained man who never neglects anything, no matter how trivial or even silly it may seem, and who possesses

patience so limitless that it appears unearthly.

Another facet of document examination is graphology. This is a suspect word, for it suggests people who profess to read character from handwriting. To some extent this may be possible, but it is seldom taken seriously.

Once, at a court hearing, the writer of a letter was designated by a "graphologist" (*not* a handwriting expert) as "French, middle-class, and young". When the man in question was called as a witness he turned out to be the English son of an Armenian father, educated in the United States and well over 50 at the time of the hearing.

But handwriting can turn out to be dangerous when the expert deals with it. Writing, after all, is the conditioned reflex of a person using a writing instrument, and to disguise one's natural *self* in such circumstances is extremely difficult.

For example, in 1970 a great controversy raged when a British journal, *The Criminologist,* published an article which indicated that the Duke of Clarence, Queen Victoria's grandson and until his death, heir to the English throne, might have been "Jack the Ripper"— the sex murderer who terrorized London's East End in the autumn of 1888.

The journal itself later put an end to all this excitement by asking Professor

C. L. Wilson, an important document examiner in government service, to study the handwriting of the Duke and the handwritings ascribed to the "Ripper".

Professor Wilson wrote: "To sum up, on the basis of the handwriting, all the evidence is against identification of Jack the Ripper with the Duke of Clarence."

Nor is the typewriter proof against the expert. The wear, the defects, the individualities of each machine all "talk" to the expert, who, given a sample, can produce all sorts of vital facts. The hand-lens, the microscope, and measuring devices play their part in studying wear, defects, accidentals (dirt, damaged letters, and so on).

The slant of the characters, angles, alignment, and footing are important— footing being that a letter may strike heavier on its right, its left, or its bottom.

Every typewriter is peculiar to itself, after a little use. Similarity in all details in two machines may be ignored (the chance of complete similarity of two machines is estimated to be one in 3,000,000,000,000).

Last comes forgery, and in this field, free writing is one of the most skilful forms. It means the forger practises endlessly from the subject's handwritten models until it can be copied without an original. In time and place it can be successful, but it does not stand up when the expert examines the *corpus delicti* (which does not mean corpse but "the sum or aggregate of the ingredients which make a given fact a breach of given law").

Counterfeit chaos

Banknotes, postage stamps, and insurance stamps are fair game for forgers. But the false banknote is often marked by indifferent or incomplete work—these poor examples the forger usually passes in crowded shops or presses on busy, overworked cashiers.

Forgery on a massive scale is not always successful. During World War II the Hitler government produced numerous £5 banknotes as a weapon against Britain—intending that the counterfeit money would find its way to England and cause chaos in the businesses and banks.

The full technical resources of German experts were used, and with what result? Ultraviolet light showed that the ink was different. There was a fault visible to the naked eye just above the B in the *Bank of England* watermark; the watermark also had three lines too many on one sample, and two lines lacking in the second.

A forged note and a real one were given to an ordinary bank cashier, who was blindfolded. He indicated the forgery immediately—it did not "feel" right.

THE GANGSTERS

Since Sodom and Gomorrah, it has been cities that have bred gangsterism. It was violence with Asian roots, in Hong Kong, that first infected the United States, but the Sicilian brand of gun law finally prevailed. And the organized crime that was spawned by Prohibition lives on today.

AP/The Bettmann Archive

ON the evening of July 22, 1934, people began to emerge from the Marbro Cinema, on Chicago's West Side. The plain clothes police who were standing around the entrance were tense with anxiety. They were hoping to arrest John Dillinger, America's Public Enemy Number One; they knew he'd gone into the cinema with a brothel madame—who had tipped them off—and another woman. What scared them was that some of the women and children in the crowd might get shot if Dillinger went for his gun. They had reason to worry; last time the Federal agents cornered Dillinger, in a Wisconsin farmhouse, they got so nervous they opened fire on a car full of innocent people, and killed several; Dillinger escaped.

Now, as Melvin Purvis and his agents waited outside the movie theatre, a police car suddenly drew up. The cinema cashier had noticed the plain clothes cops, assumed they were planning to stage a robbery, and rang the local police station. A Federal agent rushed up to the car, showed his identification, and ordered the police to move on fast. A few minutes later, John Dillinger walked out of the cinema with the two women, one of them wearing a bright red dress, so the police could identify her. To Purvis's relief, Dillinger pushed clear of the crowd, and started along an empty stretch of pavement. Purvis yelled: "Stick 'em up, John, you're surrounded." Dillinger went for his gun; dozens of shots sounded, and he crumpled to the pavement.

Most criminologists agree that the

DOOM DAY: An infamous date in the calendar of gangsterism was St. Valentine's Day, 1929 . . . when the notorious massacre took place. Two notorious figures were Bugs Moran (top left) and Al Capone (top right).

death of Dillinger was the end of an era. Capone had been in jail since 1932; prohibition had been repealed in 1933. There were still a few notorious gangsters at large—for example, "Creepy" Karpis and Ma Barker's gang—but never again would the hunt for a gangster produce the nationwide excitement provoked by Dillinger.

It was the notorious Volstead Act—better known as Prohibition—that plunged the United States into its greatest period of lawlessness, starting on January 16, 1920. The puritans and bigots who persuaded the United States Senate to ban all alcoholic drinks thought they were inaugurating "an era of clear thinking and clean living"; in fact, they were giving organized crime a stranglehold on the U.S.

The Irish and Italian gangs of New York City and Chicago seized their chance to move into the big time. It was the era of Dion O'Banion, Johnny Torrio, Al Capone, Joe Masseria, Salvatore Maranzano, Vito Genovese. On February 14, 1929, five Capone gangsters, disguised as policemen, walked into the garage owned by an Irish gangster, Bugs Moran, lined seven men up against the wall, and mowed them down with sub-machine gun fire.

The "St. Valentine's Day Massacre" shocked the world; suddenly, the U.S. wanted to be rid of its gangsters. A tough but intelligent Sicilian named Charles Luciano—known as "Lucky"—organized the killing of many of the old-style gangsters. He then called a meeting of the survivors, and warned them that the public was sick of gang warfare. In future, he said, there would be a policy of co-operation. Their common enemy was the law; their common prey was the public. A few of the older mobsters—such as Dutch Schultz—preferred to carry on in the old way. After Schultz had eliminated his chief rival, Legs Diamond, he himself was shot down as he sat in a restaurant in Newark, New Jersey, in October 1935. After that, America was more securely than ever in the grip of the mobsters—but the average American knew nothing about it.

Murder incorporated

Quietly and efficiently, Luciano organized "Murder Incorporated", a pool of professional killers who committed murder only when the gang bosses decided someone was stepping out of line. Instead of booze, this new syndicate—sometimes known as the Mafia, sometimes as "Cosa Nostra" ("Our Thing")—dealt in narcotics, gambling, prostitution, extortion, labour racketeering, and anything else that made money.

The general public became intrigued by its existence in November 1957, when the New York State Police stumbled on a business conference of more than 60 top racketeers near the village of Apalachin. All at once, "Murder Incorporated" was world news. There was a national scandal, and a special commission to investigate crime, headed by Senator Kefauver, produced amazing revelations of mass corruption. A top member of the Mafia, Joe Valachi, decided to talk, in exchange for police protection. Some of the more notorious gangsters, including Luciano, were deported. A book about the Mafia,

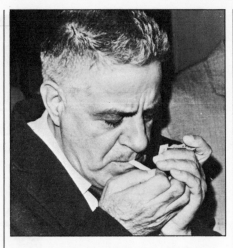

JOE VALACHI, the Mafioso who decided to talk . . . in exchange for police protection. His testimony revealed the workings and methods of the Mafia.

written in 1959, ends with a chapter entitled: "Twilight of the Villains?" The years since then have shown that the answer is: Definitely not.

Soon after the immense success of Mario Puzo's Cosa Nostra novel *The Godfather* in 1971, there were further outbreaks of gang warfare in New York City. Gangleader Joe Colombo was shot and critically wounded at a rally in Central Park; the rival gangster responsible for this shooting, Joe Gallo, was himself murdered as he celebrated his birthday in April 1972; in between these shootings there were a dozen other Mafia executions. Nor, forty years after the death of John Dillinger, America is still firmly in the hands of its "mobs". Capone and Luciano have been replaced by the mild-looking Carlo Gambino; but there is always a "Godfather" ready to step into the shoes of his predecessor.

Will this ever change? An unprejudiced look at history suggests that the answer is: Probably not. If prostitution is the world's oldest profession, then gangsterism is probably the second oldest. Moreover, scientific investigation suggests that this is more than just plain wickedness; it is a deep-rooted animal instinct. An instinct that is activated and intensified by conditions of overcrowding —not only in present-day communities and cities, but in the living areas of long ago.

This gives an interesting insight into the beginnings of crime—and of gangs. It is known that most of man's earliest cities, some of which sprang up 5000 years B.C., contained overcrowded slums. This may sound strange; after all, the world of those days had a tiny population. So why didn't the people spread themselves out more? The answer is simple. Men built cities for mutual protection; they preferred to be huddled

together. Moreover, these cities were often in river valleys where there was a limited amount of space to expand. The result was inevitable—crime on a large scale. To people from quiet country villages, the wickedness of the cities must have seemed terrifying—as is instanced in the Bible, with its stories of Sodom and Gomorrah, and those godless cities of Mesopotamia that were destroyed by the Flood (which actually took place about 4000 B.C.). The City, therefore, literally created crime—at least, large-scale crime. And, unfortunately, the pestilence soon overflowed into the surrounding countryside; travellers were robbed and murdered; small villages were overrun by robber bands who killed the men, raped the women, and burned the houses.

It can thus be said with some confidence, that the first gangsters appeared soon after the first cities. But at this point, an important distinction must be made. There are two distinct kinds of gangster which, for convenience, can be labelled the bandit and the "true gangster". Bandit obviously means the same as gangster (since a gang is a band); but their motivations are different. To put it simply, the gangster tends to be crueller and, more vicious than the bandit. The bandit lives in rural areas; he has space. He may have taken to crime for a variety of reasons; but one of these is *not* overcrowding. He prefers to be a member of a band because being a loner in wide open spaces is a demoralizing business. (Criminal loners often commit far more atrocious crimes than "bandits", because boredom and solitude make them lose their sense of identity.)

Emotional damage

Apart from his criminal activities, the bandit may be a normal human being with normal human emotions. On the other hand, the man who becomes a gangster because of the pressures of an overcrowded slum, has often suffered permanent emotional damage. To begin with, as already noted, overcrowding produces bad mothers and brutal fathers. The true gangster is the product of the slum, and he sees the world as a place to be plundered—if he can get away with it.

The city of Hong Kong offers some gruesome examples of this dating from recent years. Trapped between the sea and steep hills, Hong Kong is one of the most overcrowded cities in the world, and its murder rate has always been high. After World War II, the population quickly rocketed from half a million to more than two and a half million. Consequently, there was a terrifying wave of gang murders—murders so atrocious that the police speak of them as the work of "horror cults".

In 1958, there were more than 900

JOE VALACHI talked about "Cosa Nostra" . . . "This thing of Ours", but the architects of organized crime in the United States were more popularly known as The Mafia. Either way, an Italian expression or a Sicilian one, there was no doubt of the organization's racial origins. That was one reason why "Dutch" Schultz had to die at dinner (left). His death was at the hands of Sicilian "Lucky" Luciano (below), perhaps the biggest ever of the Mafia's bosses. Luciano was eventually caught and imprisoned, then deported after serving a 10-year sentence. Ironically, the action of the American authorities enabled him to die peacefully. He had a heart attack at Naples airport, while waiting for a friend from the United States. His funeral (bottom picture) was magnificently ornate . . .

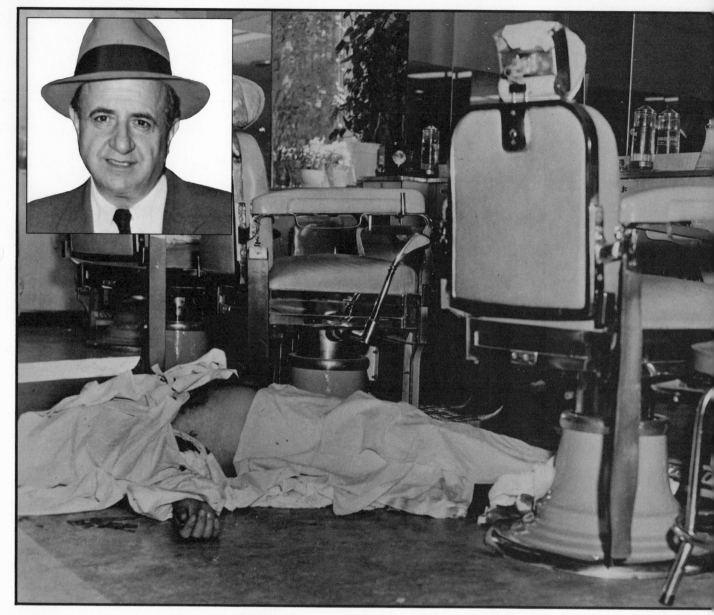

murders—five times the American murder rate, and 150 times the English. These "horror cults" are, in fact, Chinese "tongs", or "Triad Societies". (The earliest tongs were called "Three Harmonies Societies".) Like their American counterpart, the Mafia, they operate prostitution, drugs rackets, protection, and extortion. But their methods of ensuring obedience depend upon terrorism.

For example, in 1958, a rich merchant named Ko Sun Wei, together with four of his family, was horribly murdered in his house in Kowloon. The victims were staked out, with their arms and legs spreadeagled. Three women—the merchant's two daughters and his daughter-in-law—were raped repeatedly, then tortured to death with knives. One woman was still alive when the police arrived, but was unable to speak—her tongue had been cut out.

These were only five among 350 mur- ders that took place in Hong Kong in September 1958. Sergeant Arthur Ogilvie, of the Hong Kong Police, who gives these figures, also mentions that during the riots of 1956, Triad Societies took the opportunity to pillage more than $25,000,000 worth of goods. With a figure of this size involved, it can be seen that crime in modern Hong Kong is an even bigger business than it was in the Chicago of the 1920's. The interesting point here is the verification of observations about overcrowding. It produces true gangsters—men who are adepts in cruelty and violence, because they are unable to experience ordinary human emotions.

Bearing in mind this important distinction, it can be seen that many of the famous criminals and gang leaders of the past 200 years have been bandits rather than gangsters. For example, Australia's most famous criminal, Ned Kelly, was definitely a bandit. Kelly, the son of an Irish farmer and former convict, became Australia's public enemy Number One when he killed three constables at Stringybark Creek in 1877.

From then on, he lived the traditional life of the bandit on the run, moving around the countryside with his gang— which included his brother Dan—and robbing banks. He made himself head and body armour, weighing 97 lb., and was wearing it when the police finally ambushed his gang in Glenrowan. He was only 24 when he was executed in 1880. Asked why he had decided to confront the police at Glenrowan, Kelly made a reply that was to be echoed by many American gangsters of the Bonny and Clyde era: "A man gets tired of being hunted like a dog . . . I wanted to see the thing end."

The most significant feature about Kelly is that he was a man who thought he had

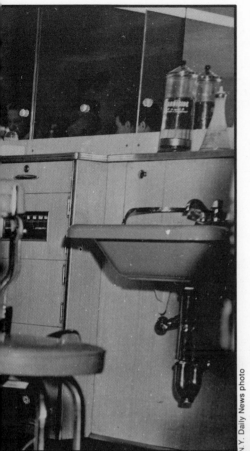

BIG SHOTS: The end came for senior Mafioso Albert Anastasia (inset left) as he sat in the barber's chair at a smart New York hotel. He had become too ambitious. The result: one of the world's most memorable news-pictures. The assassination habit dies hard. In 1971, Joe Colombo was shot in New York's Central Park. Soon afterwards, the rival responsible for the shooting, Joe Gallo (below) was killed while celebrating his birthday at a New York restaurant. Life may be cheap to the Mafia bosses, but death still brings tears . . . for Gallo's wife and daughter (bottom).

N.Y. Daily News photo

AP

a grievance against the law—and in this he resembles many of the famous "bandits", from Billy the Kid to John Dillinger. Whether the grievance is real or not is beside the point; but it starts the bandit off on the road that leads to the gallows, or the final bloody shoot-out with the police.

Most wanted man

The story of South Africa's most famous "gangster" may be taken as typifying the pattern. William Foster was born in 1886, and his family moved to Johannesburg in 1900. While still under 20, William decided to seek his fortune in German South West Africa. Plodding around in the desert one day, he met two companions who were driving a pack of donkeys. He joined them—and a few miles farther on, all three were arrested and charged with stealing the donkeys. The young men claimed they had found the donkeys wandering in the desert, and were driving them back to the nearest village. William lost his temper with the officious German magistrate. As a result of this, he was sentenced to a month in prison, while his companions were allowed to go free. The injustice of this infuriated him. When he came out of jail, he was aggressive and inclined to drink too much. A series of minor offences led to further prison sentences—and a thoroughly resentful William Foster was ready to become a "complete" criminal.

He fell in love, and wanted money to marry. His first major crime, therefore, was a well-planned robbery of a jeweller. He and two accomplices ran into bad luck and an efficient police force, and each received 12 years' hard labour. Foster's girlfriend Peggy married him while he was in jail, awaiting trial. Nine months later, Foster escaped. In a bank robbery a few months later, two clerks were killed, and Foster's career as a "hunted dog" began. Like Kelly, he had an amazing ability to shoot his way out of tight corners; and, as the deaths piled up, he became South Africa's most wanted man.

Committed suicide

Whenever possible, his wife—who now had a baby daughter—joined him. The tragic end came in September 1914, when Foster and two companions were cornered in a cave in the Kensington Ridge. One of the men committed suicide. Foster's parents, his sisters, and his wife Peggy were then sent for. They agreed to try and persuade him to give himself up, and bravely entered the cave. The parents and sisters came out, with Foster's baby daughter. Then three shots rang out. Peggy had decided to die with her husband.

In the United States, the gangster era began long before Prohibition. New York

Camera Press

GANG MURDER and organized crime . . .?
In Chinese Triad Societies, the flag is
for ceremonial purposes, the sword for
the ritualistic beheading . . . of a cockerel.

to practise gang assassination. In 1897, a rich Chinese gangster, Little Pete—owner of several gambling houses—was sitting in a barber's chair in San Francisco. He had made the mistake of sending his bodyguard out to find the result of a horse race. Two men who had been trailing him for months, awaiting their opportunity, came in and literally filled him full of lead. The killers were never caught. A similar scene was to be repeated half a century later when, in October 1957, Albert Anastasia, one of Murder Incorporated's assassins, was shot in a Manhattan hotel barber's shop.

Black Hand Gang

In the early years of the century, most of America's most formidable gangsters were Chinese. By comparison, the Irish were relatively amateurish and badly organized. But another racial group was slowly achieving ascendancy—the Italians. Fleeing from the poverty of their homeland—and from its chronic political troubles—they also had their tradition of secret societies. The word "Mafia" originally described a Sicilian outlaw who had taken to the hills, covered with low scrub (mafia), to hide from justice (either at the hands of the police, or of the family of someone he had killed).

The Mafia came to New Orleans—under the name of "the Black Hand")—in the 1880's. Almost without exception, mafiosi preyed upon their fellow citizens, who, in turn, were too terrified to appeal to the police of their adopted country. Similarly, the Irish gangsters tended to prey upon their fellow Irish, and the Chinese on the Chinese.

Escape from slums

As the century progressed, the Chinese slowly lost their reputation as gangsters—perhaps because many of them succeeded, through hard work and intelligence, in escaping from the slums—and the Irish, and their bitter rivals the Italians, took over. Then came the double-edged sword of Prohibition. Chicago's crime industry was run by men like the O'Donnell brothers, and the flamboyant Dion O'Banion, who was quoted as saying angrily: "To hell with them Sicilians!"

On November 10, 1924, four men walked into O'Banion's flower store, and unceremoniously gunned him down. The man who arranged the murder commented ironically: "O'Banion's head got away from under his hat." His name was Al Capone. The United States had entered its third and most lethal era of gangsterdom. It is still in the midst of it.

was America's first major city, and as early as 1790 it had slums that were as foul and miserable as any in the world. In the hundred or so rooms of the Old Brewery, human beings were packed like rats, and murders averaged one a night. When the district was demolished in 1852, the builders filled numerous sacks with human bones and remains. There were many tough and colourfully-named gangs: the Dead Rabbits, the Roach Guards, the Shirt Tails, the Plug Uglies (which referred to their huge plug or top hats). Then, during the 1840's, Tammany Hall politicians discovered that gangsters could be useful allies, threatening rivals and drumming up votes. And it was from this period that the real history of American gangsterdom began.

At the time, most of the gangsters were Irish—and, oddly enough, Chinese. The Chinese were accustomed to their "Triad Societies" at home. When they came to settle in America—mostly on the West Coast—they naturally formed themselves again into "tongs" for mutual protection.

The Chinese were also among the first

AL CAPONE

The flashily-dressed hood who became the prosperous and impeccably-tailored self-made businessman. He had a ready smile and a quick handshake . . . which often turned out to be fatal. For it took 500 gangland murders to make Capone the boss of Chicago . . . they called him Public Enemy Number One.

JOHNNY TORRIO, new boss of the Chicago underworld, was a man of vision. The response to the introduction of Prohibition in the United States had been like a gold rush. Small-time bootleggers were springing up everywhere. Torrio grasped that a fortune of millions of dollars awaited the first man to control this new get-rich-quick industry, and he decided he would be that man—not merely in Chicago but in the 932—square miles of neighbouring Cook County.

It would be a mammoth task, requiring both organizing genius and ruthlessness. He needed help, and in search of it he turned to the Five Points gang in New York City. Torrio, himself an ex-Five Pointer, had had his eye for some time on a 21-year-old Five Points lieutenant, good with guns as well as his fists, who had already twice been questioned by New York City police over murder cases. His name was Alphonse "Scarface" Capone, known to his friends as Al.

Straightforward offer

At the time, 39-year-old Torrio was netting $100,000 a year from gambling, vice, and other rackets. His offer to Capone was simple and straightforward. "Al," he said after outlining his plans, "you can have a quarter—$25,000 a year—of what I'm making now, plus half the profits out of bootlegging." "It's a deal," snapped Capone.

It was the first step up the ladder for the man who, within less than a decade, would earn himself the label Public Enemy Number One . . . who would be known as the wickedest, and one of the richest, men of his time . . . whose name would be synonymous in every corner of the globe with American gangsterism.

Miscellaneous rackets

By 1927, when Torrio's dream of a bootleg monopoly in Chicago and Cook County was a reality, it was estimated that he and Capone were pocketing $105 million a year between them. Sixty million came from beer and liquor, 25 million from gambling saloons and dogtracks, 10 million from dancehalls, roadhouses, and the sale of sex, and a further 10 million from miscellaneous rackets.

Making him rich wasn't the only change the years wrought in Capone—the product of poor Neapolitan parents and the slums of Brooklyn, New York. The loud-mouthed, flashily-dressed hoodlum brought to Chicago by Torrio in 1920 had disappeared. Capone was now impeccably tailored, with a rose in his buttonhole and a diamond solitaire—the badge of the Big Shot—in his tie pin.

He had two fortified headquarters and a home in Chicago, plus a magnificent estate on Palm Island off Miami Beach,

THE INCREDIBLE IRONY of Capone's downfall was the charge brought against him . . . failing to fill in tax forms. His impudent, but realistic, defence . . . that he didn't realize tax was payable on money earned by illegal means.
The man who taught him to be a gangster, Johnny Torrio, was jailed for the same offence (above), betrayed by Capone. Pupil Capone laughed at the Federal Grand Jury (right, top picture), but ended up in an undignified position, handcuffed to a lesser criminal (right, bottom picture). It was a wry exit for Chicago's Caesar of Crime . . . though he lived well in jail, and was released after eight years to return to his luxurious Palm Island Estate.

Florida. He had learned the usefulness of the ready smile and the quick handshake.

Capone's life style was, in part, very much that of the prosperous self-made businessman. That, indeed, was how he saw himself—a tough, but honest man of affairs. And if bootlegging, his chief business, happened to be against the law, well, it was legitimate in human terms.

"They call Al Capone a bootlegger," he used to complain. "Yes, it's bootleg while it's on the trucks, but when your host at the club, in the locker room, or on the Gold Coast hands it to you on a silver tray, it's hospitality. What's Al Capone done then? He's supplied a legitimate demand. Some call it boot-

The Bettmann Archive

AP

legging. Some call it racketeering. I call it a business. They say I violate the prohibition law. Who doesn't?"

He conveniently overlooked the murders it took to put him on the top of the heap and keep him there, and the corruption of politicians, judges, and police which ensured the law did not interfere with his activities. In 1929, after he called a conference in Atlantic City, at which the major gangs carved up the United States between them, it was said of him admiringly that—like J. P. Morgan, the financial wizard of Wall Street—he was "the first man to exert national influence over his trade".

In fact, Capone was a fat, syphilitic killer, whose sordid empire was founded on the Thomson sub-machine gun, the revolver, the sawn-off shotgun, and the bomb. It took 500 gangland murders to establish him as the boss of Chicago, and rival gangs offered rewards as high as $50,000 for anyone foolhardy enough to take on the task of rubbing him out.

This, too, was reflected in his life style. By day he travelled in a steel limousine which weighed seven tons and cost him $20,000. It was equipped with bullet-proof glass and a special combination lock so that his enemies couldn't break in and plant a bomb under him. Once inside, he was safe from buckshot, shrapnel, or machine gun bullets. Nevertheless, a scout car always preceded his "personal tank", and a gang of handpicked sharp-shooters followed it in a second car.

When he went to the opera, one of his favourite relaxations, he was accompanied by a bodyguard of 18, bigger even than the President's. The trouble-shooters were scattered strategically around the theatre, watching the audience instead of the show. If Capone decided to step outside for a cigarette between acts, they would rise as one man to follow and surround him.

At the peak of his career, in the latter part of the 1920's, Capone had 700 of the toughest hoodlums in America under his command, 30 per cent of them paroled convicts, 20 per cent aliens. It was as vicious a gang as has ever been assembled outside a penitentiary.

In the early days, however, Capone did his own killing at Torrio's behest. One of his victims was Joe Howard, a small-time crook who made the tactical mistake of hijacking two loads of Torrio booze in one night. The next evening, about six o'clock, Howard was having a quiet drink in the bar where he usually hung out, when the door opened and two men walked in.

"Hello, Al," he said, sticking out his hand. Capone fired six shots into him and Howard slumped to the floor dead—his smile of welcome still on his face. The police put out a general arrest order for Capone, but by the time they found him all of the eyewitnesses had suffered an attack of lost memory. It was a common ailment in Chicago in the 1920's. Two months later a jury found that Howard had been killed by "one or more persons unknown". The case against Capone, like all the cases except his last two, had been effectively blocked.

By 1924, he had established himself in control of the respectable Chicago suburb of Cicero. By a combination of sluggings, kidnappings, shootings, and intimidation, he had done what the politicians demanded—delivered the vote. Now, in return, he had his own mayor, his own town clerk, and his own town attorney.

Nothing and no one could touch him. Gambling was illegal, but he ran what was reputed to be the biggest roulette game in the country, with as much as $150,000 riding on a single turn of the wheel. Capone also had 161 bars, open night and day. In adjoining Stickney were the brothels, the form of vice in which Torrio specialized. Some of the houses offered a choice from as many as 60 prostitutes of different colour, skills and nationalities.

By this time he and Torrio were each pocketing $100,000 a week. But they were still a long way from controlling the whole of Chicago. The two major impediments to their ambitions were Dion O'Banion —Torrio's only serious contender to become boss of the underworld—and the six Genna brothers from Sicily, who controlled the Unione Sicilione, the chief source of alcohol.

O'Banion was ostensibly a florist, but he always carried three guns and could shoot with either hand. He had an Irish face with a perpetual grin and fathomless blue eyes. Although he had never been brought to trial, he was credited in gangland with 25 killings. His territory was the 42nd and 43rd wards—comprising the Gold Coast, where the houses and apartments of the city's richest and most fashionable residents look out over Lake Michigan.

With the coming of prohibition, the Gennas had had the bright idea of importing poor Sicilian families, setting them up in tenements with a still, and paying the man of the house $15 a day—a fortune by "old world" standards—to smoke his pipe and keep the still stoked up.

Flowers for funeral

Alky-cooking, as it was known, had grown into a $10 million-a-year industry, supplying the basic ingredient for synthetic bourbon, rye, Scotch, brandy, rum, and gin—and controlling the sale of sugar to the affiliated Italian districts of Melrose Park, Cicero, and Chicago Heights.

On 4 November, 1924, O'Banion was in his florist's store awaiting a visit from some friends of Mike Merlo, president of the Unione Sicilione, who had just died a natural death. One former henchman had already been in to place a $750 order for flowers for the funeral.

O'Banion was in the back room, just saying to William Crutchfield, a Negro porter, "Better brush up the leaves on the floor, Bill," when he heard some more customers enter. There were three of them. "Hello, boys. You from Mike Merlo's?" he asked, going forward to meet them. In his left hand, he had his florist's shears. He held out his right.

"Yes," replied the man in the centre, grasping the extended hand. Five shots rang out in quick succession, followed a few seconds later by a sixth, the clincher. The last bullet was fired into O'Banion's left cheek as he lay sprawled among his flowers. The gun was held so close that his skin was burned black with powder.

Police inquiries were met by the inevitable Mafia wall of silence, imported like the alky-cookers from Sicily. Torrio, Capone, and the Gennas were then questioned. "The day before he was killed I gave him an order for $10,000 worth of flowers," stated Torrio. "Our boys wanted to send some floral pieces to Mike Merlo's house and we all chipped in and gave the business to Dion." The coroner,

unable to surmount the wall, finally wrote the killing off.

The era of the lavish big-time gangster's funeral began with the burial of O'Banion. He was laid to rest in a $10,000 coffin, shipped out to Chicago from the East in a special express freight car. A woman columnist described it as "equipped with solid silver and bronze double walls, inner sealed, and airtight, with heavy plate glass above and a couch of white satin below, with tufted cushion extra for his left hand to rest on; at the corners, solid silver posts, carved in wonderful designs."

Another recorded the scene at the undertaker's where O'Banion's corpse was exhibited for three days. "Silver angels stood at the head and feet," she wrote, "with their heads bowed in the light of ten candles that burned in solid

golden candlesticks they held in their hands. Beneath the casket, on the marble slab that supports its glory, is the inscription, 'Suffer little children to come unto me.' And over it all the perfume of flowers."

Mounted police cleared the streets on the day of the funeral—at which there were 26 truckloads of flowers, valued at $50,000. They included a heart of American beauty roses standing eight feet high; a blanket of roses, orchids and lilies, measuring seven feet by ten, sent to cover the grave at Mount Carmel; and a basket of roses labelled simply, "From Al."

Capone and Torrio solemnly attended the funeral. Their show of piety, however, did not fool anyone. The coroner might be forced not to put a name on the assassins, but the O'Banion gang had no doubts about where the responsibility lay. Three of its gunmen, Drucci, Moran, and Weiss, sought out Capone's automobile—an ordinary sedan at that time —and raked it from front to back with machine guns and sawn-off shotguns.

MRS. CAPONE avoided photographers . . . here she ducks cameramen outside Alcatraz. Top: Capone's $20,000 steel "armoured car", with gun-turret.

AP

QUICK ON THE DRAW . . . one of Capone's bodyguards has his gun ready as a popcorn seller accidentally brushes his arm. No chances are taken when Capone makes a rare public appearance at a baseball game, especially when a small disruption is created by the arrival of star Gabby Hartnett to sign for young Al Capone junior.

Capone missed death by minutes. He wasn't in the vehicle, having just stepped into a restaurant in the course of an inspection of his liquor empire.

Torrio, who had left town to give things a chance to cool off, was trailed to Hot Springs, Arkansas, New Orleans, the Bahamas, Cuba, Palm Beach, and finally back to his Chicago home — where he was shot down by two gunmen in full view of his wife, with whom he had been shopping. He survived the attack after 16 days in hospital.

Moran, one of the three men involved in the attempted assassination of Capone, was identified as the man with the revolver in the shooting of Torrio. Neither Torrio nor Capone would help the police, however. They remained true to the Mafia tradition of silence, and put the two attacks down to "unfinished business".

Although they had survived, their experiences had given both men a healthy respect for the opposition. His narrow

escape persuaded Capone that $20,000 for a steel limousine would be a worthwhile investment. For his part, Torrio was so badly scared that, when jailed for nine months shortly afterwards on a charge of operating a brewery, he had the three windows of his cell equipped with steel screens and hired three extra deputy sheriffs for sentry duty.

Uncharacteristically, no reprisals followed the attacks on Capone and Torrio for well over a year. The reason was that Capone had more important matters on his mind. With Mike Merlo dead, there was the question of who would now control the vital Unione Siciliène with its vast network of stills. Capone was eager to put in his own candidate as president, Antonio Lombardo, partner in a firm of commission brokers and cheese merchants.

The six Genna brothers, however, had other ideas. They installed the toughest of them, Angelo, in the post. Throughout the latter part of 1924, and much of 1925, Capone was preoccupied with the task of "persuading" them that they had made the wrong decision.

Angelo was the first to die. On May 25, 1925, he was assassinated in his own automobile by a volley of slugs from sawn-off shotguns. Mike Genna was next, killed by a policeman in a shoot-out while — without knowing it — he was being taken for a ride by Capone's two star gunmen,

Scalise and Anselmi. That was on June 13. Less than a month later, on July 8, Antonio, brains of the Gennas, got his in yet another "handshake murder", when he kept an appointment with "a friend".

The remaining three Gennas acknowledged that they had received an offer they could not refuse. They fled to their home town of Marsala in Sicily, leaving Capone to instal the man of his choice as boss of the Unione Siciliène.

But peace still did not come to Chicago's gangland. The O'Banions made yet another attempt to remove Capone from the scene — an attempt which demonstrated clearly in what contempt the mobs held the forces of law and order. In broad daylight, eight carloads of gunmen made an assault on the mobster's Cicero headquarters, firing a thousand shots into it from machine guns and the familiar sawn-off shotguns in a matter of seconds.

Generous gesture

Once again Capone escaped and, in the kind of generous gesture for which he was well known, paid $10,000 out of his own pocket to save the sight of a woman accidentally injured in the eye during the incident. This time, however, he was not prepared to file the matter away under "unfinished business".

Leadership of the O'Banion gang had

119

World Wide Photos

AP

AP

A HOOD'S HAVEN . . . Palm Island, near Miami, Florida. In his heyday, Capone would entertain 100 guests for a weekend. After eight years in jail, the sweeping solitude of his sea-lapped, palm-fronded isolation was a solace to him in his pursuit of more leisurely pastimes. But the sins of his youth caught up with him, as the syphilis of long ago rotted his brain. In his final madness, friends would gather for a game of cards . . . always letting Capone win. When one forgot himself and won by mistake, Capone cried: "Get the boys . . . I want this wise guy taken care of!" On his death, he was surreptitiously buried . . . in Chicago. His tomb at Mount Olivet was an imposing affair . . . a dynasty had ended.

AP

been taken over by Earl "Little Hymie" Weiss, the only man in the world Capone was said to be afraid of. Weiss was a Pole, unemotional and coldly ferocious, who had brought a new sophistication to gang murders. It was his killer's brain that had originated the ceremony of taking a victim for a ride, using a stolen car and carrying out the "execution" in another county, or even another state. It made the crime virtually impossible to solve.

The removal of Little Hymie, three weeks to a day after the Cicero attack, is looked back on as the most scientific killing in the history of the gang wars of the 1920's. Little Hymie's headquarters was above the flower store of the late Dion O'Banion. A few days after the Cicero raid, a young man using the name of Oscar Lundin took a second-floor room in the boarding house next door. The window gave a clear shot at the pavement outside O'Banion's store. Meantime, a young woman had taken a room in another nearby boarding house which overlooked the rear exit from the florist's.

The new tenants were not then seen again. Instead, three gunmen moved into each room. They had to wait ten days for a clear shot at Weiss, unimpeded by pedestrians. Then, as he stepped from his car, the guns roared and he collapsed on the sidewalk with ten bullets in his body. He died without regaining consciousness.

One of his companions, a beer pedlar named Patrick Murray, stopped seven bullets and was dead before he hit the sidewalk. The other three — W. W. O'Brien, a criminal attorney; Benjamin Jacobs, a politician and O'Brien's investigator; and Sam Peller, Weiss's chauffeur — were seriously injured but survived.

But they told no tales. They hadn't seen a thing, couldn't identify the killers, didn't know what it was all about. Capone, informed of the death of his hated foe, commented: "I'm sorry, but I didn't have anything to do with it. I telephoned the detective bureau to say I would come in if they wanted me, but they said they didn't. I knew I would be blamed for it, but why should I kill Weiss?" So another coroner's inquest was stymied.

For a time after that, Chicago was comparatively quiet and murder-free. With the main opposition out of the way, Capone got together with what rivals remained and agreed, "We're a bunch of saps to be killing each other." The truce did not last long, however. Three strangers, found dead with a nickel clutched in one hand, turned out to be out-of-town hoodlums. They had come to Chicago because someone had put a price of $50,000 on Capone's head.

Who was that someone? Once again the finger pointed at the O'Banion's and, in particular, George "Bugs" Moran. Moran, who had taken part in the attempts on the lives of Torrio and Capone four years earlier, now led the O'Banions. Settling that old score led to the legendary St. Valentine's Day massacre in which seven members of the Moran mob were gunned down in a garage as they prepared to set out on an expedition to hi-jack some of Capone's rum.

Moran himself escaped, having spotted a telltale sedan with drawn curtains just before he arrived at the garage. But he was left a leader without a gang. Capone was at last without a serious rival.

Throughout the years when Capone's killers roamed the streets, butchering their rivals, shooting up and beating up saloon keepers who showed a reluctance to buy Capone beer and liquor, they had

121

virtually a free hand. With votes and money, Capone bought politicians, judges, and policemen. If necessary, he bribed juries. And, if anything went wrong, there was always a friendly governor to grant an early parole.

Capone outlasted four chiefs of police, two municipal administrations, three U.S. district attorneys, and a regiment of Federal prohibition agents. He survived innumerable crime drives, grand jury investigations, reform crusades, clean-up election campaigns, police shake-up, and Congressional inquiries and debates.

Now he was sitting pretty. In Chicago he had 10,000 speakeasies buying six barrels of beer a week at $55 a barrel, a total of $3,500,000 a week. They also bought two cases of liquor a week at $90, a total of $1,800,000 a week. Beer cost about $4 a barrel to make, liquor about $20 a case. With vice, gambling and other rackets he was pulling in about $6,500,000 a week.

Then he slipped up for the first time. He was arrested while leaving a cinema in Philadelphia and jailed for a year for having a gun. In prison, he made plenty of friends, including Dr. Herbert M. Goddard, of the Pennsylvania State Board of Prison Inspectors, who removed his tonsils and operated on his nose.

"I can't believe all they say of him," the doctor later declared. "In my seven years' experience I have never seen a prisoner so kind, cheery, and accommodating. He does his work as a file clerk faithfully and with a high degree of intelligence. He has been an ideal prisoner. I cannot estimate the money he has given away.

"Of course, we cannot inquire where he gets it. He admits he's in the rackets. But you can't tell me he's all bad after I have seen him many times a week for ten months, and seen him with his wife and his boy and his mother."

Capone lived well in jail. His cell had a $500 radio, a pair of easy chairs, a table, tufted rugs, and other hotel comforts. He was finally allowed to leave it after ten months, his sentence commuted for good behaviour, but he returned to a changing, hostile world.

The newspapers, which had once made

THE ODD MIX of comfort and starkness which Capone grew accustomed to in jail seemed to be echoed as he whiled away the twilight of his life . . . his violence spent.

him something of a folk hero, were now bent on destroying him. President Hoover had been jolted into starting a personal campaign against him, and a picked band of agents from the Justice Department set out to smash his booze empire by physical force, raiding and wrecking 30 of his breweries and seizing 50 of his heavy trucks in one year. Finally, it was the taxmen who got him, with the aid of informers.

Found guilty of three years' tax evasion and of failing to file tax forms for another two years, Capone—who could think of no defence except that he didn't think he had to pay tax on money made from illegal operations—was fined $50,000 with $30,000 costs and sentenced to 11 years in a federal penitentiary.

He was released after eight years and retired to live quietly at the Palm Island, Florida, estate, where, in his heyday, he often entertained as many as a hundred guests for the weekend. He died in January 1947, aged 52 and a raving lunatic, his brain eaten up by paresis from an early case of syphilis. One of the most remarkable facts about him is that he died in bed, instead of being gunned down in a Chicago gutter.

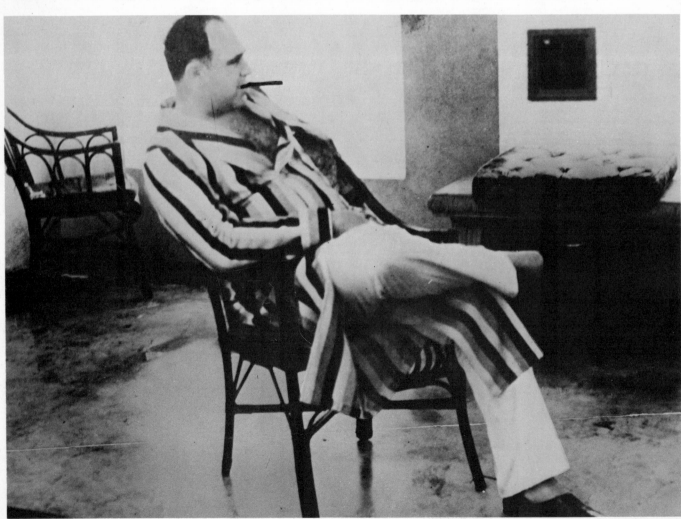

THE DEADLY DELINQUENTS

THIS WAS NO WEST SIDE STORY... IT WAS THE THEATRE OF CRUELTY

It had all the vivid romance that the teen-age gangs of New York could muster . . . with their names like the Dragons and the Jesters. But slum life could get too colourful among the Puerto Ricans and Irish Whites around 152nd Street. During a stifling summer in the late 1950's, the Dragons went looking for trouble. It was a swimming pool that caused blood to flow . . . and the night had a dramatically tragic finale.

Antony Cobb

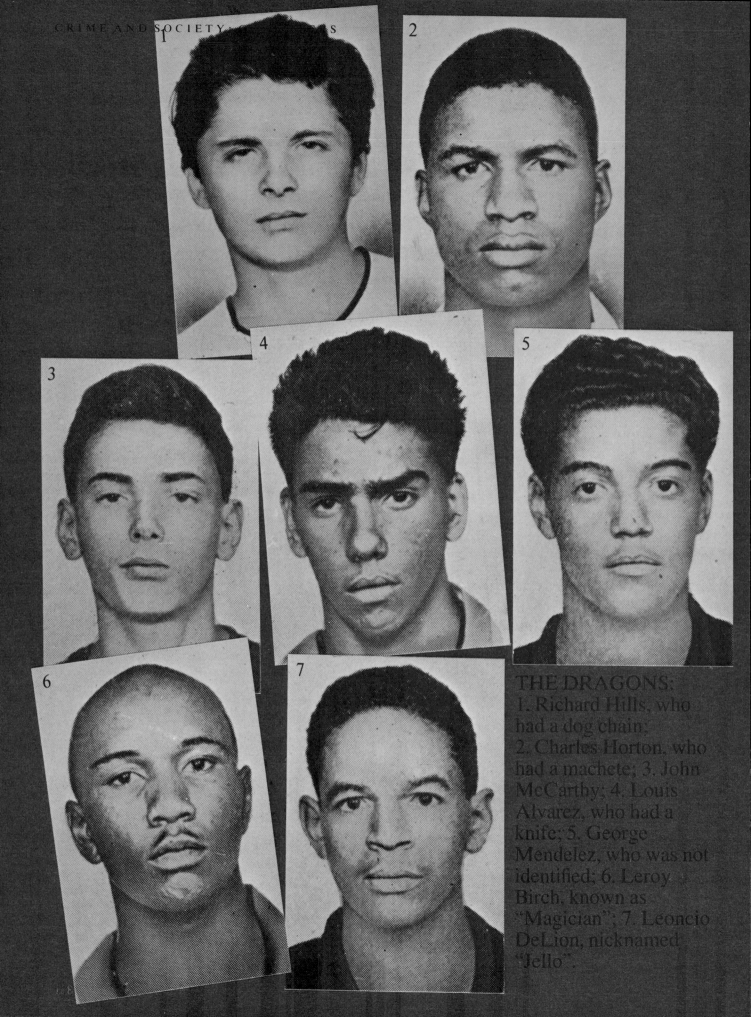

THE DRAGONS:
1. Richard Hills, who had a dog chain;
2. Charles Horton, who had a machete; 3. John McCarthy; 4. Louis Alvarez, who had a knife; 5. George Mendelez, who was not identified; 6. Leroy Birch, known as "Magician"; 7. Leoncio DeLion, nicknamed "Jello".

THE trial, which began on the morning of Monday, January 13, 1958, in the Court of General Sessions on the 11th floor of the Criminal Courts Building in Center Street, New York City, aroused immense interest from coast to coast of the United States. It was a high spot in juvenile delinquency in America's overcrowded cities, and it served to focus public attention upon a major problem of community living—what to do about teen-age kids who roam the streets in gangs, get into fights with rival gangs, and terrorize the neighbourhood generally.

In London there were the Mods and Rockers. In New York there were the Egyptian Dragons and the Jesters. At this trial seven Egyptian Dragons were arraigned before Judge Irwin Davidson on a charge of murdering a boy named Michael Farmer.

Two of the youths were white, John McCarthy, aged 15, and Richard Hills, aged 16. The other five were Negroes or dark-skinned boys of Spanish-American descent. Leoncio DeLeon, for instance, nicknamed Jello, was a Negro from the Dominican Republic, while George Melendez, incidentally the best-looking of the group, was a Puerto Rican—both were 17-year-olds. The most powerfully built was Leroy Birch (18), a Negro of five foot ten in height who was known as "Magician".

The remaining two defendants were 18-year-olds—Charles Horton, a Negro, and Louis Alvarez, the most sinister looking of all, whose face was lined and pockmarked with pimples and boils. The two white boys and Melendez seemed frightened and were less tough-featured than their companions. From their general appearance in court, it was obvious that all seven came from poor families.

Meaningful glance

Robert R. Reynolds, the New York District Attorney, presented the case for the prosecution in a terse and businesslike manner. The crime he described took place about 11 p.m. on the hot and stifling night of July 30, 1957, at Highbridge Park—a public recreation area that borders Amsterdam Avenue between 155th Street and Dyckman Street not far from Columbia University and which is the site of a fine municipal swimming pool.

According to the best estimates, about 18 boys were involved, all belonging to the Egyptian Dragons. It was the contention of this gang that their members were being prevented from using the facilities of the pool by a number of other gangs in the neighbourhood, mainly by the Jesters, who consisted for the most part of white American-Irish boys.

Earlier in the evening the Egyptian Dragons had gathered at the corner of 152nd Street and Broadway and made

VICTIM: Mrs. Farmer lost her son. He fought polio as a child . . . but never recovered from the beating handed out by the Dragons. Whether he was a member of the rival Jesters gang was never established. His father was angered by what he felt was the court's leniency.

their way in twos and threes to Highbridge Park where they lay in wait for members of any rival gang which might appear. Two youngsters did so in the persons of Roger McShane, a slender 16-year-old, and Michael Farmer, a small boy who was a year younger. The Dragons assumed they were Jesters, although it was never established that either of them belonged to this gang. Farmer had been afflicted as a child with infantile paralysis. The newspapers covering the case invariably referred to him as the "polio victim" or the "polio boy", although he had made a satisfactory recovery from the disease.

"The defendants and their associates descended upon Farmer," said the District Attorney with a meaningful glance at the youths in the dock, "and wilfully feloniously and with malice aforethought, hit him with fists and feet, a dog chain, a garrison belt, a club, a metal pipe, and stabbed him with a knife and a machete. These acts were going on simultaneously with each other. In the meantime McShane ran about 240 feet from the swimming pool steps towards Amsterdam Avenue until he too was stopped and assaulted."

Both were left lying on the ground as the gang scattered. Farmer, discovered by Patrolman John T. Collich of the 34th Precinct, died a few minutes after he arrived at the local hospital. McShane, fearfully battered, took three months to recover from his injuries. He was the prosecution's key witness.

First to take the stand after formal police evidence had been given was the murdered boy's father, Raymond Farmer, a New York City fireman.

"Do you have a son, Michael?" the District Attorney asked him.

"I *did*," the witness replied after a pause.

"Was there anything wrong with Michael's foot?"

Before Raymond Farmer could answer, one of the defence lawyers, James Murray, who appeared for McCarthy, the youngest of the accused, was on his feet, objecting that the question was immaterial and irrelevant. The objection was sustained.

The District Attorney tried again. "Did you ever observe Michael walk?" Again Murray objected.

Dreadful crime

The D.A. had two good reasons for asking these questions. First, he wanted to bring out the newspapers' characterization of Michael Farmer as a polio victim, which would make the jury regard the gang's crime as more dreadful than it would appear if it had been committed against an unhandicapped boy. Secondly, he wanted to show that Farmer could not run very well, and he did not wish the jury to draw the inference that Farmer had chosen to stand and fight, while McShane had run away. However, the judge sustained Murray a second time.

Raymond Farmer was followed on the stand by Roger McShane, who recounted how he and Michael had been walking along the promenade alongside the swimming pool when they were set upon by the Dragons.

"How many boys were there in the group that stepped out from behind the bushes?" Reynolds demanded.

"A large group."

"Well, give us your best guess."

Another defence counsel objected to a guess, but he only succeeded in heightening the suspense in court.

Lives menaced

After the witness said he thought there were about 15, the D.A. asked him whether he could point out any in court at that moment. "Yes, sir," was the reply.

McShane then stepped down from the witness chair and went across to the dock, where he pointed his finger at each boy with the exception of Melendez.

"There is one defendant you have not identified," said the D.A. "Are you able to say whether he was there or not?"

"No, sir."

McShane was being cross-examined when the court recessed for the weekend. During the recess, young Roger received a threatening letter, advising him to watch his step and telling him that "if them guys gets the chair, we'll kill you". As a result he was assigned police protection for the remainder of the trial. The lives of other witnesses and even the judge himself were similarly menaced.

Try as the defence lawyers did, none of them could make McShane admit that either he or the murdered boy had been members of the Jesters—although the youngster did say that he and Farmer were looking round for "our friends" on the night of the affray.

"Were you looking to collect a group?" asked the attorney who appeared for Hills.

"No, sir," McShane persisted.

Murray did particularly well for his client, McCarthy, since he got McShane to agree that he had never spoken to the accused teen-ager, although he had seen him on a previous occasion.

"You didn't see McCarthy do anything to Farmer, did you?"

"No, sir," was the reply.

The next witness was 14-year-old Ralph Lago, who in spite of his extreme youth was actually the leader, or "War Lord", of the Egyptian Dragons. He had been present on the fatal night, but because he was under 15 had to be dealt with by the Children's Court which sent him to a reformatory school. He had

subsequently agreed to testify for the prosecution. He described how he had gone uptown with Horton and Alvarez and another teen-ager who was not charged. Horton carried what Lago thought was a broom stick, and Alvarez a knife. "If I catch 'em," Alvarez had said, "I'm going to try to stab 'em."

Horrifying exhibit

The knife which Alvarez used was then produced. It was a vicious looking instrument made in Japan. The blade was razor sharp, so much so that when Reynolds picked it up to display it to the jury it accidentally cut his finger. Another equally horrifying exhibit which Lago identified was the dog chain. This the witness swore he had seen Hills carrying "with a weight on it" at the scene of the crime. The D.A. then wrapped a couple of hitches of the chain around his hand and let a length dangle down to show the jury that it could have the effect of a lethal weapon. Another such weapon, which formed an exhibit in the case, was "an object wrapped with the black handle sticking out", which Lado stated had been passed to him by Horton. It was a machete.

A further teen-age witness, too young to be tried in this court, was Patrick O'Kelly, who said he was a member of the Dragons. He, too, saw Horton hit Farmer, who was lying on his face with his right arm extended. Asked how and with what Horton had struck Farmer, O'Kelly stated that it was with the "object" that had been wrapped in paper. "I am not sure if it was with one hand or two," he added, "but he went up and down."

"You saw the object come down?"

"Yes."

"After you saw Horton hit Farmer with the object, where did you go?"

"I went around and I ran down the stairs."

Machete, chain

Like all the other prosecution witnesses, young O'Kelly was unshaken under cross-examination. He had no weapon when he went up the steps to the pool, he said, and nobody forced him to go. Horton's defence attorney failed to shake O'Kelly's statement that he had seen Horton strike the boy on the ground.

It was the same with Vincent Pardon, another 14-year-old, who related how Horton had told him to go to Hill's house in West 135th Street off Riverside drive. Pardon did so and was given "a thing wrapped in a bag" which turned out to be a machete. Hills himself, according to the witness, had a dog chain.

The D.A. then interrupted the parade of reformatory inmates to call Martin ("Marty") Sullivan, a tall youth, of

17, with a bland, insolent face, a weak chin, a protruding upper lip and shifty eyes. Sullivan had had nothing to do with the killing. A short time before he had been arrested on a charge of burglary, and while being held in the Brooklyn Prison for Youths he had met Leroy Birch in the "TV playroom", and while there he had a conversation with him.

According to Sullivan, he asked Birch, "You didn't mean to kill Farmer, did you?" To which Birch was said to have replied, "I told you the next time I came up we were going to kill somebody."

This testimony threw the court into an uproar, since it was the first time that premeditation had been alleged in the trial. Hill's attorney Irving Mendelson jumped to his feet and waving his hand in the direction of the jury, exclaimed: "The testimony is so inflammatory it is now impossible for the defendants to get a fair trial."

Torrent of blows

Judge Davidson replied that the testimony only applied to Birch and he would so instruct the jury. "You can tell them from now to domesday," Mendelson retorted angrily, "but how anyone can eliminate it from his mind is beyond human understanding." Nevertheless, the judge held fast to his ruling and the testimony stayed on the record.

At this point in the proceedings the D.A. called the medical evidence, after producing photostatic copies of the autopsy which had been performed on the body of Michael Farmer. The doctor's testimony indicated that Farmer had raised his hands to defend himself against the torrent of blows inflicted on him, since one incised wound appeared beneath the left armpit.

There were other stab wounds including one four inches deep which went through his back and penetrated his lungs. It was this wound which caused his death, the doctor said. The jury were plainly impressed by the doctor's matter-of-fact but none the less horrifying description.

Perhaps the most graphic description of the attack came from another of the prosecution witnesses, pale little Victor Carasquillo, who was visibly shaking throughout his testimony and spoke with a thick Puerto Rican accent. Horton, whom Carasquillo called "Big Man"—he was over six feet in height—was close to Farmer. "He picked up his hand and he had the blade (of the machete) and he hit him once and he put it back in the paper thing and he hit him again and ran."

Carasquillo added that he then came over next to Farmer and he saw "Jello" DeLeon hit the polio victim twice with his stick and the third time the stick broke.

"Can you tell us what part of the boy's

126

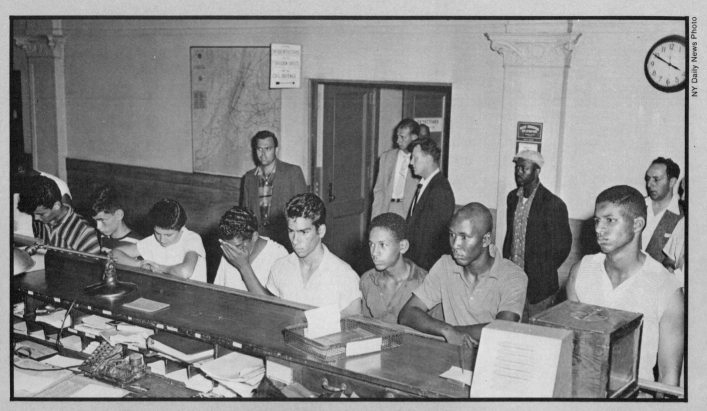

HOMICIDE is the charge . . . and a bunch of kids, aged from 15 to 18, are ordered to be held without bail for more than two weeks pending the hearing of their case. Sixteen-year-old Roger McShane, who came to court with his mother, was one of the gang's victims. Fearfully battered, he took three months to recover, but his friend Michael Farmer died within minutes of the attack. The spectre of brutal death stayed with McShane . . . he received a murder threat during a court recess, and was given police protection. He is pictured below under guard with Ralph Lago, a member of the murder gang who was dealt with in a children's court, and who later gave evidence against his associates. One of the main attackers was the smiling Louis Alvarez (bottom left).

body Jello hit with the stick?"

"The back."

"Across the back of the head and the back of the neck, right?"

Carasquillo nodded.

"Did Jello say anything to you?" the D.A. went on.

"He said 'Kick him!' I swung with my leg, but I didn't touch the boy." He was so scared, he continued that he "swung out" and missed. He then started running and did not stop until he got home.

An unexpected witness was a pretty 14-year-old girl, Mary Jean Rivera, who appeared neatly dressed in a grey cotton dress over a stiff petticoat, with a crimson cardigan and matching crimson knee socks. She turned out to be Louis Alvarez's girlfriend and she described how Alvarez gave her his knife, as also had another member of the gang named José Garcia. The newspapers called her the "knife moll".

"What did you do with the knives?" Reynolds asked her.

"I brought them home."

"What did you do with them at home?"

"I put them in my bureau," the child answered without a trace of emotion. "Then I took them out and looked at them. Then I put them in my bureau in a bag."

After Alvarez had been picked up by the police, he guided them to the girl's house where the police recovered the knives, and this was confirmed by Mary Jean. There must have been some in court like the judge who looked at Alvarez, pock-marked, sullen and greasy-haired, and wondered what this fragile child could have seen that attracted her to him.

The defence attorneys were faced with a difficult task, since it was impossible to deny that all their clients had been present when Farmer was killed. It was particularly difficult for Hill's attorney Irving Mendelson, since Hills was the defendant with the dog chain. However, he was able to convince the jury that Hills had a dog, and that he was in the habit of walking about with the un-attached chain. He was also able to show that Hill's actions were largely the result of fear that if he refused to cooperate with the other gang members he would be beaten up—which indeed he had been on one occasion.

PROSECUTION WITNESS . . .
Michael "Pee Wee" Ramos (ringed) was said to have been invited to the killing . . . and told to bring some guns. Shortly after the trial, he himself was killed in a gang shooting at a Bronx candy store. The killer, who fired a shotgun blast into his face, was Ramon Serra (inset). He nonchalantly admitted his guilt, according to police.

128

The case against Alvarez was particularly strong since he was shown to have boasted that he was "not chicken" and had blood on his knife after the attack. Indeed his attorney, seeing that there was a strong likelihood of his client going to the electric chair for murder in the first degree, tried to persuade the prosecution to accept a plea of manslaughter. But the D.A. refused.

The other tactics employed by the defence consisted of trying to show that the statements made by the defendants after their arrest were made under pressure and the result of rough treatment in the police station. In several instances the defendants had gone back on their statements and said they had lied to avoid being assaulted by the police.

As a rebuttal witness, the D.A. called another gang leader, Michael Ramos, known as Pee Wee, a sinister looking youth, with previous convictions for assault and burglary, who stated that Alvarez had telephoned him twice on the night of the killing asking him to come up to the swimming pool and bring some guns with him. But Pee Wee had his own troubles and did not show up. Shortly after the trial these troubles culminated in Pee Wee being shot to death by a member of a rival gang outside a Bronx candy store.

In his summing up to the jury. Judge Davidson explained the different kinds of homicide. Under United States' law, he said, murder in the first degree involved proof, beyond all reasonable doubt, of premeditation and deliberation and intent to kill. Murder in the second degree required proof of intent to kill, without proof of premeditation or deliberation.

Manslaughter in the first degree is homicide without design to effect death. It may be committed in the heat of passion, in a cruel or unusual manner or with a dangerous weapon, while manslaughter in the second degree is killing in the heat of passion but without the use of a dangerous weapon or other cruel or unusual means.

The judge made it clear that murder in the first degree could only apply to

CANDY STORE ARREST . . . in striped jacket, Ramon Serra is held by police. The scene of the murder is marked out in the blood of his victim.

those who went up to Highbridge Park with lethal weapons in their hands — namely Alvarez with his knife and Horton with his machete.

The jury deliberated for a total of nine hours and 35 minutes, this being divided by the court adjourning for the night. The verdict they eventually brought in found Horton and Alvarez guilty of murder in the second degree, while Birch and DeLeon were found to be guilty of manslaughter in the second degree. The remaining defendants, McCarthy, Hills and Melendez were acquitted.

"a farce"

The judge sentenced Horton and Alvarez to 20 years to life imprisonment, while DeLeon got 5 to 15 years and Birch $7\frac{1}{2}$ to 15 years. "I am not happy about sending them to jail," said Judge Davidson afterwards, "but under the law this is what I am compelled to do."

Asked to comment on the verdict, the murdered boy's father thought it had "made a farce of our society". He said: "It's a sign to juvenile delinquents that they can get away with murder — a green light for them to get away with anything."

THE MUTINY at Alcatraz—the fist-shaped island prison in San Francisco Bay—started shortly after lunch on Thursday, May 2, 1946. It was then that some prisoners in "C" Block overpowered a guard, took his keys from him, and released their fellow convicts. Within minutes, the men had opened the gun cage and armed themselves with rifles. They moved on to the isolation block—"D", where the prisoners considered "too dangerous to associate with others" were kept—and set free rapists, gangsters and murderers.

Only one man refused to join the riot as his cell door slid open. He was a tall, benign-looking person with a green eye-shade cap, metal-rimmed glasses and grey, close-cut hair. His name was Robert F. Stroud. He was 56 years old, and had been in solitary confinement—in one prison or another—since March 1916.

He stood transfixed in thought as the convicts raced past him, hellbent on violence and destruction. Then, his mind finally made up, he leant over the gallery rail and shouted: "Get back—all of you! Get back in your cells! There's going to be bloodshed!"

It seemed a futile thing to do. But there were many who stopped running, looked

IT WAS the world's most famous prison on Alcatraz island in San Francisco Bay. Its name: the Spanish word for pelican. Its most renowned resident: Robert Stroud, the Birdman of Alcatraz.

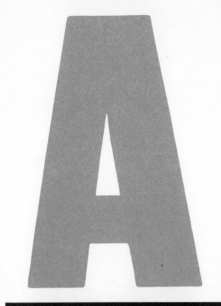

A
ALCATRAZ

up at convict No. 594, and sensibly returned to their cells. For Robert Stroud was no ordinary convict and his was no ordinary story. It began, his tale of crime, punishment and redemption, in January 1909 when he shot an Alaskan barman in a quarrel over a woman.

At the time Stroud was a labourer in a railroad gang. He was sentenced to twelve years' penal servitude at the maximum security prison at Leavenworth, Kansas. While in there he knifed a sadistic prison guard to death and was due to be hanged for the offence in April 1920.

His sentence was commuted by President Woodrow Wilson. After months of deep self-examination, Stroud realised that his hostility had been caused by his hatred of his father—a bad-tempered drunk who had betrayed and deserted Stroud's mother.

To start his rehabilitation he began to paint seasonal greeting cards for his mother to sell in the outside world. He found this pursuit relaxing and rewarding. But it wasn't until the summer day in 1920 when he stumbled upon a nest of abandoned sparrows in the exercise yard that he discovered what his vocation—and therapy—really was.

He took the baby birds to his cell and nursed them back to health with pieces of bread dipped in vegetable soup. As the sparrows' foster parent, he decided to read up on the birds and their habits in books taken from the prison library. Before long he had smuggled other birds

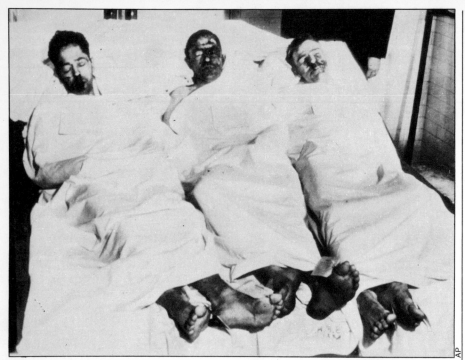

THREE MEN died in the Alcatraz mutiny. It all started when a prisoner forced the bars of his cell (arrowed). Only Birdman Stroud refused to join the riot. After sheltering a wounded prisoner Stroud helped to quell the violence.

inside and was feeding them on dead flies and scraps from his own meals. He built a cage for his sparrows and canaries from an old soap-box, using a nail and a broken razor-blade as tools. The sound of bird-song and the flutter of wings soon drew official attention to his activities, and, after some discussion, he was allowed to continue with his harmless "hobby".

But to Stroud his preoccupation with birds was more than just a pastime. With professional skill and patience he observed the canaries' breeding and sexual habits, and sought the causes of their various ailments. In 1925, he raised and sold (through his mother) 53 canaries for more than $200.

His study of bird pathology showed him that his charges improved both in health and spirits when he took them into the prison yard for sun. The grey-painted cell shared by him and his birds measured some 12 feet by six, and he found the shape soothing to their senses.

"I want to go on record," he wrote, "against that very popular and very stupid abomination, the round canary cage . . . Birds like corners for the same reasons that you like them; they give a sense of protection . . . it is so very real that a large proportion of humanity would go mad if compelled to live in round rooms."

On that basis Stroud then turned his cell into a bird hospital. He was allowed to purchase feeding dishes, roosts, cages,

pans, dissecting instruments, scalpels, chisels, hammers—and later was even given a microscope.

He discovered that he could cure septic fever in birds by feeding them an oxidizing salt called sodium perborate, and that fowl paralysis could be cleared up by minute quantities of the drug sulfanilamide. His experimental work led him to compile the material for his massive *Digest of Bird Diseases,* published in 1943, and containing many plates, hand-drawn by himself.

In this book—hailed as "the number one bird disease volume in the world" —he wrote: "Years of work, of study, of careful observation; the lives of literally thousands of birds, the disappointments and heartbreaks of hundreds of blasted hopes have gone into these pages; almost every line is spattered with sweat and blood . . . I have dedicated my book to the proposition that fewer birds shall

suffer and die because their diseases are not understood."

Gradually, as the years passed, Stroud became known outside of the prison walls. He spent an average of eighteen hours a day working on the dietary problems of birds and conducting controlled experiments into their diseases and germs. Using an ancient Remington, he wrote hundreds of letters to bird-lovers and scores of articles for bird magazines. "Write me your needs!" he implored in an advertisement. "Tell me your troubles! 1 can save you money! I can save your birds!"

In August 1936—six years before his transfer to Alcatraz—his work received top level recognition when he was visited in his cell by J. Edgar Hoover, Director of the F.B.I. The lawman bought one of Stroud's canaries for $10 and told the convict it was a gift for his mother in Washington. On hearing that, Stroud wrote to Mrs. Hoover saying:

"I have just had the pleasure of meeting your remarkable and illustrious son, and of selling him one of my fine white canaries. The bird . . . will be in tip-top condition at the time shipped. If for any reason he should not arrive in good condition, please . . . return it to me. I will then ship another bird at once."

It was this background and this kind of stature that made the stir-crazy cons listen to Stroud on that spring afternoon in 1946. For two days "D" Block was under siege as the authorities moved in two platoons of U.S. Marines armed with bazookas, machine-guns, hand-grenades and tear-gas bombs. Two Navy destroyers hove-to off the island—commonly known as "The Rock"—and pumped 2-inch shells at the mutineers.

After sheltering a wounded prisoner in his cell, and acting as spokesman with the prison guards, Stroud helped to quell the riot, which petered out at 7 a.m. on Saturday, May 6. Two of the rebel ringleaders were dead, and three others were later put on trial. Stroud sympathised with the rioters and described the isolation block as "a private purgatory where carefully chosen victims can slowly be driven mad."

Despite his valour and a poignant plea for pardon—"The writer," he said, "knows exactly as much about driving a car, or modern traffic regulations, as a Berkshire hog knows about the quantum theory. Unassisted, he would probably starve to death before he could get to the other side of Market Street"—he was not to know freedom again.

A sick and tired man, Stroud remained in captivity until his death on November 21, 1963. Eight months before that Alcatraz (its name in Spanish means "Pelican") closed down and later became a tourist attraction for visitors to San Francisco—who now share it with the birds.

EUGENE ARAM

The inhabitants of Knaresborough, a small town in the West Riding of Yorkshire in England, got little sleep on the night of February 7, 1745. Three of the communities best-known characters—shoemaker Daniel Clark, linen weaver William Houseman, and schoolmaster Eugene Aram—were out on a drinking bout that did not end until dawn. As the small hours went by, they called on the houses of friends and acquaintances, joking, teasing, causing trouble, demanding beer and wine. For the past nine years Aram had been noted for his unorthodox out-of-school activities, which included petty theft and the receiving of stolen goods. His pupils spoke of him as a "rigid disciplinarian", and his wife, Anna, and seven children knew just how severe, strait-laced, and bigotted he could be. With his cronies, however, Aram showed another side of his personality—that of a drunken profligate— and it was no surprise that he had teamed up with Clark, a "pock-marked, weedy, and stammering" man who rashly carried some £300 of his wife's dowry around with him.

Shortly before breakfast on February 7, as the townsfolk were getting up and about their business, Aram and Houseman lured the 23-year-old Clark to the banks of the Nidd river and there one of them—it was never established who—dealt the shoemaker a deadly blow on the back of the head with a pickaxe. They then doubled up the still warm body and dragged it to the nearby St. Robert's Cave, where they

EUGENE ARAM
convicted at York Afsizes Aug.ᵗ 3.ᵈ 1759. for the murder of Danˡ Clark of knaresborough in the county of York. His body was hung in Chains purfuant to his fentance in knaresborough foreſt. Executed fourteen Years after the murder. His own defence is very artful and ingenious, but yet before he fufferᵈ he confeſs'd the fact.

ARTFUL AND INGENIOUS Eugene Aram was a learned schoolteacher . . . and a drunken profligate. He and a friend murdered for money, then hid their victim's body (below).

buried it beneath some rocks. Now possessing the money to pay his numerous debts, Aram and his accomplice returned to the town and proceeded about their daily duties. The son of a gardener-poet, Aram had been born in Ramsgill, Yorkshire, in 1704, and was proud of the fact that he was self-educated. He was learned in Latin, Greek, Hebrew, and Celtic, and had originally tried to earn a living in London. There, however, he was struck by smallpox and he came back to Yorkshire to "drum knowledge" into the sons of tradesmen and farmers.

An unprepossessing man with a Roman nose, backward sloping forehead, and high skull, he was immediately suspected when Clark was found to have "disappeared". The murder victim had obtained various goods—rings, cambrics, velvets, and books—without paying for them, and his creditors posted a notice stating: "Whoever can give any account of the said goods (so as they may be had again) . . . shall receive fifteen pounds reward for the whole, or in proportion for any part thereof . . . and no questions ask'd." Disturbed by the reward, and the inquiries that were being made, Aram deserted his wife and family and fled to London, where he arrived on April 18, 1745, with money to spend. He courted a lady who was "living under the protection" of another man, lavished jewellery upon her, and generally led a "gay" if dissolute life.

He spent the next 12 years in the capital, teaching Latin and French (which he had also acquired), and in 1757 moved

Above: Mary Evans

Mary Evans

MUCH-ADMIRED at school (left and below left), Aram was a self-taught man of intelligence and wit. His pupils "wept brokenly" when he was arrested.

a little room of the great schoolroom". He refused to answer any of the questions put to him, and it was said that his pupils "wept brokenly" as he was escorted to a waiting chaise and taken at bone-bruising speed to Knaresborough. The people of the town turned out *en fête* to welcome him, and as he dismounted from the carriage he was confronted by his wife and children. He had not set eyes upon them for more than 13 years, but greeted them as if he had seen them only yesterday. "Well, and how do you do?" he said off-handedly, before being taken to York jail—where he spent a year preparing for his defence and studying such books as John Burton's *Monasticon Eboracense,* which dealt with the bones and relics of saints and hermits.

At his trial, held in August 1759, the prosecution was led by Fletcher Norton—known as "Sir Bull-Faced Double-Fee"—who felt he had more than enough evidence to have Aram found guilty and hanged. The scholar conducted his own defence and offered the court what was later described as a "literary masterpiece". "My lord," he said solemnly, "I concerted no schemes of fraud, projected no violence, injured no man's person or property. My days were honestly laborious, my nights intensely studious . . . Mankind is never corrupted at once—villainy is always progressive, and declines from right, step by step, till every regard of probity is lost, and every sense of moral obligations totally perishes . . .

"Now, my lord, having endeavoured to show that the whole of this process is altogether repugnant to every part of my life . . . that no rational inference can be drawn that a person is dead who suddenly disappears—that hermitages were the constant repositories of the bones of the recluse . . . that the revolution in religion or the fortune of war has mangled or buried the dead—the conclusion remains perhaps no less reasonably than impatiently wished for."

Despite Aram's contention that the bones in St. Robert's Cave were those of a religious martyr, the jury found him guilty as charged. Back in his cell, he tried to kill himself on the night before his execution by cutting his wrists. He was then dragged, "half-alive and half-dead", to Tyburn Field, outside the gates of York, where he was duly hanged. His corpse was kept in chains at Knaresborough, and his case inspired a novel, *Eugene Aram,* by Edward Bulwer-Lytton, author of *The Last Days of Pompeii,* and a narrative poem, *The Dream of Eugene Aram,* by Thomas Hood.

to King's Lyn in Norfolk, where he obtained a new mistress and a new job. He was paid £20 a year by the local grammar school to give Latin lessons, and was greatly admired by the gentry for his intelligence and wit. He was an early riser, and to the less sophisticated townsfolk he cut a somewhat sinister figure as he roamed the surrounding fields in a loose-flowing horseman's cloak and wide-brimmed hat. A year passed in this fashion and Knaresborough—and all that had happened there—was but an "insubstantial shadow" in Aram's mind. Then in June 1758, according to a Norfolk writer, "A man came out of Yorkshire with a stallion and casually recognised Aram in Lynn. The schoolmaster, being greeted cordially as a fellow-townsman, denied all knowledge of Knaresborough and of the stranger—to the latter's profound astonishment and enduring wrath."

Despite this incident, Aram—because of financial and emotional ties—remained in King's Lynn. It would have been better for him had he left the area, however, for a few months later a labourer hewing stones on the banks of the Nidd uncovered a skeleton which was taken to be that of the long-missing Clark. In fact the bones turned out to be those of another murder victim (probably a young Jew Aram was thought to have slain), and it was not until Houseman was arrested that the truth was known. He took the arresting officers to St. Robert's Cave and showed them where the remains of Daniel Clark were hidden. An inquest was arranged and, acting on information supplied by the horse dealer, two "stern-faced" men went to King's Lynn to apprehend Aram and bring him to trial.

The constables arrived at the town on August 19, 1758, and arrested Aram "in

SHORTLY BEFORE midnight on September 21, 1780, the British war sloop *Vulture*, slipped up the Hudson River taking Major John André to a secret meeting that could change the entire course of the War of Independence. It was moonless and windy as the sloop anchored on the west bank near Stony Point, and a boat set out from the shore. A few minutes later André — Adjutant General to Sir Henry Clinton, one of the British commanders — was rowed ashore by two farmers, their oars muffled in sheepskins.

As soon as he reached dry land, André was taken to a spot surrounded by fir trees. There he met General Benedict Arnold, the commander of the vital riverside post of West Point, the strategic site of the Hudson Valley. André wore a dark blue cloak over his scarlet uniform, and he and Benedict warmly clasped hands. Under the pennames of Anderson and Gustavus, the two officers had already exchanged letters in which Gustavus, or Benedict, had promised to surrender West Point if the money and the terms were right.

At the time 39-year-old Arnold was one of General George Washington's most respected and trusted officers. Born on January 14, 1741, in Norwich, Connecticut, he had been a rebellious boy, and at the age of 14 had run away from home to fight in the French and American

BENEDICT ARNOLD

TRAITOR: As a General in the American Army during the War of Independence, Benedict Arnold sold defence secrets to the British. A British Army Major hid them in his boots.

Indian War. After serving at Lakes George and Champlain he later deserted and made his own way back through the wilderness.

The army forgave him because of his youth, and in 1775, on the outbreak of the revolutionary war, he joined the colonial forces as a colonel. He accompanied an expedition of "Green Mountain Boys", or Vermonters, which under Ethan Allen captured Fort Ticonderoga, and later led a detachment of 1000 men through the wilds of Maine and on to Quebec, taking a major part in the unsuccessful siege of the city.

His leg was broken in the battle, but his courage gained him promotion to brigadier-general. The following year he superintended the building of a fleet on Lake Champlain which routed the British in October — the first engagement of the British and American fleets.

After this brilliant start to his military career, however, Arnold's fortunes seesawed. In 1777 — after being acquitted of charges of misconduct in Canada — he was bitterly disappointed when Congress appointed five new major generals, all younger than himself. He temporarily lost his commission after quarrelling with a senior officer, but in the second battle of Saratoga, on October 7, was severely wounded and had his horse shot from under him.

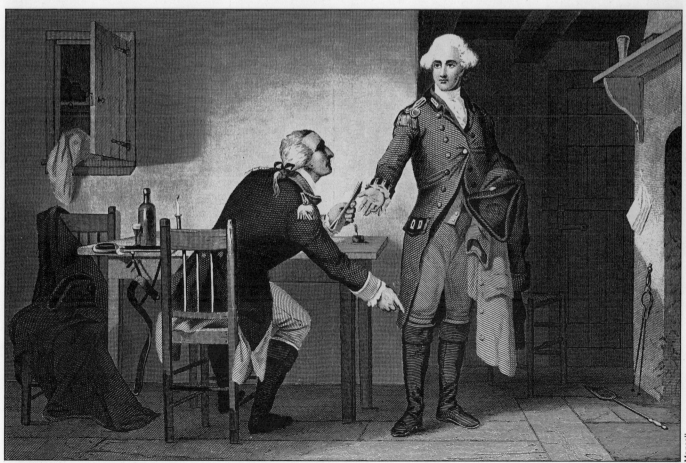

Mansell

Together with General Horatio Gates, he was credited for the capture of the invading army under General John Burgoyne, and 1778 Washington gave him command of the city of Philadelphia—where he married Peggy Shippen, a beautiful society girl.

Once again, however, Arnold's conduct was not that expected of someone in his position. He lived extravagantly and beyond his means, entertained on too lavish a scale, and developed pro-English sympathies. He soon fell foul of the state executive council, which brought eight charges against him—including that of using military personnel as personal servants.

The charges were presented to Congress in the spring of 1779, whereupon four of them were thrown out. Arnold demanded a speedy trial to deal with the remaining counts, but the court-martial was not convened until that December. During the delay, he brooded about the "wrongs and injustices" that had been done to him. Always a sensitive person, he was now motivated by an overriding sense of malice. He entered into secret correspondence with Sir Henry Clinton, and by the time his trial started he was already halfway to siding with the British.

He conducted his own defence with fire and eloquence and was acquitted of all "intended wrong". Arnold had expected an absolute acquittal, and was additionally incensed when General Washington reprimanded him in terms almost of praise. He smouldered with resentment, and it was Washington's kindly rebuke which decided his next move.

He asked to be given command of West Point (with a view to delivering it, and possibly Washington himself, to the British). He took up his new post in August 1780, and lost no time in arranging a meeting "hidden among the firs" with André. He then passed on details of the number of men and armaments in the area. In return he asked for a "substantial sum" of money, and the rank of brigadier general in the British Army.

The bargaining lasted until dawn, when André was told it was too light for him to be rowed back to the *Vulture*. He would have to remain ashore and conceal himself as best he could. Afraid that the major would be captured, Arnold persuaded him to take off his military jacket and put on a purple coat belonging to one of the oarsmen. This change of clothing —from military to civilian—turned André into a spy, and would mean his execution if caught.

Arnold, however, was too wrought up to consider such matters. He hastily scribbled a note and gave it to the British officer. It stated: "To Whom It May Concern. Permit Mr. John Anderson to pass to White Plains, or below, if he chooses; he being on public business by my direction. B. Arnold". The traitor also handed over plans of West Point's fortifications and methods of defence.

Arnold went home to have breakfast with his wife, and André set off downriver. Two days later, on Saturday, September 23, he was stopped by three irregulars, who stripped and searched him. The compromising documents were discovered and he was arrested as a spy. As word of this reached Arnold, he kissed Peggy and his sleeping baby goodbye, and fled to the British lines. When Washington learned of his defection he paled and cried: "Arnold has betrayed us! Whom can we trust now?"

A short while later André was brought before a Board of Officers and put on trial for his life. Accused of plotting against America, he stood rigidly to attention and replied: "As a man of honour I cannot deny the facts. I can only hope you will sympathetically consider the circumstances surrounding them, and appreciate that what I did was in keeping with military custom. My one crime was in not wearing my uniform when behind your lines."

Despite his defence, and the good impression he made upon the court, André was found guilty as charged and sentenced to be hanged. He then wrote a polite and courageous letter to General Washington, saying: "I do not object to the sentence, sir, as much as to the manner in which I must die. May I not be shot like a soldier, instead of hanged like a criminal?"

Washington was too hurt by Arnold's treachery to even reply, and on October 2, 1780, 29-year-old Major John André mounted the scaffold, fitted the rope around his neck, and calmly waited for the trapdoor to open. As a tribute to his bravery, a tablet bearing his name was later placed in London's Westminster Abbey.

As for Arnold, he was given his commission and received £6315—not the £20,000 he demanded from the British—as compensation for property losses. After leading attacks upon Richmond, Virginia (in which the city was burned) and New London, Connecticut, he went to England where he was reunited with his family. King George III consulted him upon American affairs, although many people in court and society circles scorned and avoided him.

Most of his remaining years were spent as a merchant in the West Indies, and he finally died in London in June 1801, a lonely, disappointed and embittered man. The newspapers gave little space to his demise, and the *Morning Post* stated: "Poor General Arnold has departed this world without notice; a sorry reflection this for . . . turncoats."

ESCAPE: Arnold fled, fought for the British and went to London as an advisor to George III. Major André was caught and hanged as a spy on the orders of George Washington.

ASSASSINATION

The sixth day of peace had been a long and tiring one for Abraham Lincoln, the newly re-elected President. He had spent the morning at a cabinet meeting in the White House, when he had insisted upon leniency for the defeated members of the Confederate army. After a working lunch he reviewed the case of a convicted Confederate spy and a young soldier who had deserted from the victorious Union side in the Civil War. He granted pardons to both the offenders, stating: "I think these boys can do us more good above ground than under."

By the time evening came, fog had replaced the bright spring sunshine, and 55-year-old Lincoln was feeling more like sleep than keeping any social engagements. His wife Mary, however, had arranged an outing to Washington's Ford Theater to see a "celebrated eccentric comedy", *Our American Cousin,* and was loathe to go without her hero husband. "All right, dear," said Lincoln resignedly. "I'll do it for your sake. But if I don't go down to history as the martyred President, I miss my guess."

He ate a hasty dinner and then, shortly after 8 p.m. on Good Friday, April 14, 1865, Lincoln and his party left the White House. As their coach passed along the bustling thoroughfares, youngsters ran by with handbills announcing that the performance at Ford's Theater on Tenth Street would be "honored by the presence of President Lincoln". At 8.25 coachman Charles Forbes pulled up outside the theatre, and Lincoln and his wife entered the building with their guests, Major Henry Rathbone and his fiancée, Miss Clara Harris. The play had already started, but the men and women in the dress circle stood to applaud as the President led the way down a side aisle and through a white door into the State Box.

On the stage itself the leading lady, Laura Keene, stopped in the middle of a line and clapped enthusiastically. The cheering lasted until Lincoln was settled in a rocking chair at the side of the flag-festooned box. Only then did people resume their seats and allow the entertainment to proceed.

Before long the President forgot his tiredness and became engrossed in the antics of the players, the wit of their words. With Mary seated at his right, and the major and his fiancée in front of him, Lincoln relaxed and smiled con-

JOHN WILKES BOOTH leapt on to the stage to escape (top), breaking his leg. He managed to get away on horseback, but was caught hiding in a barn (right).

tentedly. The house was filled with more than 1600 theatre-goers (some of whom had only come in order to see Lincoln), and no one paid any attention to the young man in the hard hat who walked purposefully along a corridor leading to the entrance to the box.

The man halted beside a servant sitting in the corridor and handed him a note. The servant read the note, nodded, and allowed the visitor to enter the vestibule of the box. It had turned ten o'clock, and the play was well into its third act as the stranger stood within a few feet of the unsuspecting President.

A few minutes earlier the man—a failed Shakespearian actor named John Wilkes Booth—had stated to acquaintances in a nearby bar, "When I leave the stage I will be the most famous man in America." Now, to make good his boast, he opened the door to the box, stepped quietly inside, and took a small pistol from his pocket. He raised the derringer and aimed it at the back of the President's head. As he did so Lincoln let loose of his wife's hand, whispered something to her, and leaned forward towards the stage.

The next moment Booth—who had supported the Confederate cause during the war—squeezed the trigger. The noise of the shot went unheard in most parts of the auditorium. But in the box itself it sounded as though someone had burst a balloon. Mrs. Lincoln and her guests swung round, noticed the blue smoke coiled in the air, and saw that the President had stopped rocking in his chair. The bullet had entered below his left ear and moved diagonally through his brain towards his right eye. His head hung down to his chest and his assassin stood triumphantly behind him.

"*Sic semper tyrannis!*" ("So it always is with tyrants!") Booth shouted. He then dropped his gun, took out a knife and stabbed Major Rathbone in the arm as the officer jumped up and began to grapple with him. Pushing the major aside Booth cried, "Revenge for the South!" Then he leaped from the parapet of the box down to the stage, 14 feet below. The spur of his right foot caught in one of the banners, and as the flag ripped Booth fell rigidly to the boards, breaking his left leg just above the instep.

Despite his injury he managed to evade the actors and hobbled into the wings and out through an exit door to where a saddled horse was waiting. He pulled himself up onto the animal, grabbed the reins, and galloped off into the moonlit night. A short while later he was run to earth in a barn in Virginia and shot after

PRESIDENT LINCOLN at the theatre. He was engrossed . . . stepping quietly into the box, the assassin raised his gun. "So it always is with tyrants!"

refusing to surrender.

Meanwhile Lincoln, who was still alive, was carried gently from the theatre and into the home of a tailor, William Petersen, at 453 Tenth Street. There he was taken to a small bedroom under the stairs and, because of his great height, was laid diagonally across the bed. Doctors who were called gave the wounded President stimulants to revive his failing heart, and an all-night watch was kept at his bedside. News of the shooting sped through Washington and the citizens grieved for the man who had united the country both in name and spirit.

During the long, grey, early morning hours Abraham Lincoln held doggedly onto life. Gradually, however, as time passed and dawn came wet and cloudy, he began to relinquish the struggle. His right eye was black from the pressure of the bullet behind it, his breathing became quick and shallow, and every now and then he frightened those around him with loud, agonizing moans. The end came at 7.22 on Saturday, April 15. Lincoln's chest heaved, subsided, and he did not move again. One of his doctors, Surgeon-General Barnes, placed two silver coins on the President's eyes.

The silence that followed was broken by Secretary of War, Edwin M. Stanton. "Now," he said softly, "he belongs to the ages."

THE senior F.B.I. man stood by the wall map in the briefing room and addressed the agents seated in rows before him. "This is the hideout here," he said, turning and drawing a pencil ring around Lake Weir in Florida. "It's a white building on the shores of the lake. We'll surround the place and hope that we can get them to surrender. If not, we'll blast them into the open—and we're going to take plenty of guns with us!" A few hours later the agents flew from Chicago to join more of their colleagues at Lake Weir. All roads leading to the two-story white cottage were blocked. By seven a.m. on January 16, 1935, it was impossible for anyone unauthorized to get into the area—or to leave it.

The F.B.I. men's quarry—and the reason they were armed with rifles and machine guns—was not just a gangster in the Dillinger or Baby Face Nelson mould. In fact, it was not a man at all they were after. Hiding in the cottage was a 63-year-old woman with greying hair and a short, dumpy figure. Some people whom she had met—especially

B
MA BARKER

bank managers and their assistants—had called her "a nice motherly-looking woman". But to J. Edgar Hoover, the Director of the F.B.I., she was "a mean, vicious beast of prey".

Together with her four sons—one of whom, Fred, was crouched in the cottage beside her—she had terrorized businessmen and bankers throughout the centre of the United States. The holdups planned by her, and carried out by her boys and their henchmen, had netted countless thousands of dollars for "Ma Barker and her Viper Brood", as the newspapers dubbed them. For 12 years she had queened it over the gangster underworld. Now she listened with contempt and impatience as Special Agent in Charge E. J. Connelley stepped forward and shouted: "Kate Barker—the house is surrounded!

THE WOMAN who mothered, and led, an army of criminals . . . she died with her son, but it took machine-guns and gas-bombs to end the reign of Ma Barker. To J. Edgar Hoover, she was a "mean, vicious beast of prey . . . a she-wolf".

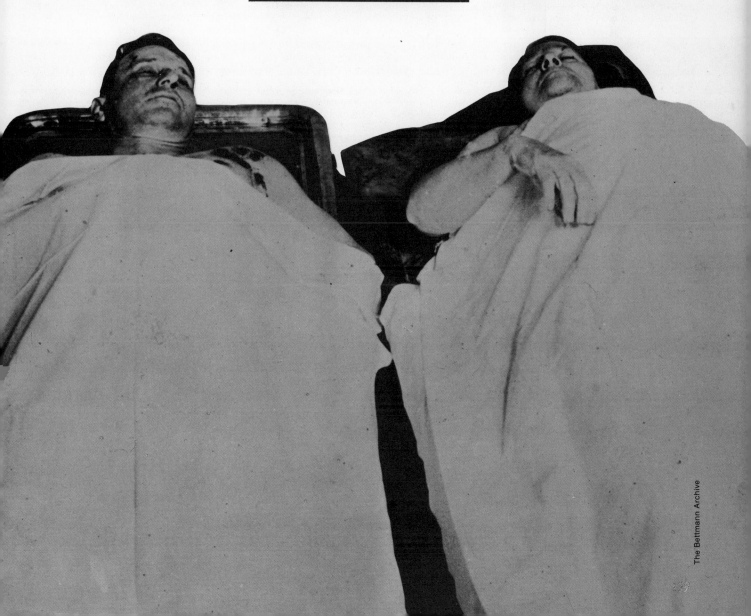

Come out one at a time with your hands raised and you won't be hurt."

Connelley then retreated and waited for an answer. He knew as much about Kate as she probably did herself, and had studied her criminal career and the life she had led before. Born Arizona Donnie Clark near Springfield, Missouri, in 1872, she grew up among the simple, God-fearing farmers of the Ozark Mountains. She was 20 when she married a farm labourer called George Barker, and was known as a good Presbyterian and a conscientious wife and mother to him and their fine boys—Herman, Lloyd, Dock, and baby Fred.

By the time they had moved first to Webb City, Missouri, and then to Tulsa, the four Barker boys had turned into teenage hooligans in trouble with their neighbours and the police. Their mother would hear nothing wrong said against them by merchants who complained of being "roughed up and robbed", and at least twice she argued with the authorities and kept them out of court. In 1915 she and her family were living in a two-roomed shack near the Santa Fé railroad, and it was there that she set up her first "cooling off" service.

Any ex-convict looking for shelter, or any crook on the run, had only to contact Ma Barker in Tulsa and she would give them food, a bed, and hours of advice. She told them how and why they had failed in their criminal endeavours, and gave special "tuition" to a quietly-behaved outlaw called Al Spencer. He listened to every tip, every tactic she gave him, and in 1923 repaid his debt by holding up the crack passenger train, the *Katy Limited,* and seizing more than $20,000 in Liberty bonds and cash.

From then on Ma agreed to plan and organize robberies and bank raids on a strict percentage basis. She would take no part in the coups herself, but would be the brains behind the big jobs. This was her life style throughout the 1920's, and by the end of the decade she was still in funds and still at liberty. However, this could not be said of her sons. Only Herman was not behind bars—and then he was gunned down by police after killing a traffic officer during a hold up in Newton, Kansas.

It was this final blow that turned Ma Barker from what Hoover called "an animal mother of the she-wolf type" into a "one-woman army against society". She spent years badgering parole boards until, in 1931, Freddie was at last released from Kansas State Penitentiary—

THE "BROOD" that robbed trains and raided banks were taught all they knew under the supervision of Ma Barker. She provided bed and board.

where he had been serving a five to ten year stretch for assault with intent to kill.

In her customary outfit of a drab, shapeless dress and floppy hat, Ma Barker looked no more than a fat middle-aged woman who was unable to get a man, money, or a home of her own. In fact, she had left George, her husband, lived with and abandoned a succession of lovers, and moved from rented house to rented house—always planning new robberies, and always one jump ahead of the police.

The Barker Gang, or the Holden-Keating Gang as it was also known, based itself in St. Paul, Minnesota, and made a point of concealing its sawed-off shotguns, automatic rifles and Thompson submachine guns in violin- and music-cases. Ma herself moved more into the foreground and even went as far as to visit a bank that was about to be robbed, talk with the manager about opening a "modest account with the money left me by my dear husband", and leave with every detail about the safes and security arrangements inprinted in her mind.

In the summer of 1932—after three leading members of the gang, Thomas Holden, Francis Keating, and Harvey Bailey, had been arrested while playing golf—Ma and Fred Barker went to earth at White Bear Lake, Minnesota. From

there they planned a $¼m. bank raid at Concordia, Kansas, and then went on the run again as Federal agents picked up their trail. The gang had now been reduced to four members—including Alvin Karpis, known by Hoover as "Public Rat Number One"—and, to Ma's disgust, their later activities concentrated upon kidnapping and not robbery.

It was after a second kidnapping job —that of Edward G. Bremer, president of the Commercial State Bank of Minneapolis—that Ma and Fred fled to Lake Weir and prepared to shoot it out with the ring of F.B.I. men. Her answer to agent Connelley's offer was to shout: "All right! Go ahead!" The next second a machine gun opened fire and Connelley scurried for cover. The battle that followed lasted for more than half an hour as the cottage was attacked by machine guns, rifles, and tear gas bombs.

At the end of that time there was silence. The agents closed in on the cottage, entered it, and discovered Fred and his mother lying dead in an upstairs room. Three bullets had entered Ma Barker's body, and her weapon, a .300 gas-operated automatic rifle, was still hot in her hands. She had lived for money and had died for it: in her pocketbook Connelley found more than $10,000 in crisp, large denomination bills.